Sujatha Fernandes

Who Can Stop the Drums?

URBAN SOCIAL
MOVEMENTS
IN CHÁVEZ'S
VENEZUELA

Duke University Press
Durham and London 2010

© 2010 Duke University Press

Printed in the United States of America
on acid-free paper ∞

Designed by Heather Hensley

Typeset in Warnock Pro by Keystone
Typesetting, Inc.

Library of Congress Cataloging-in-
Publication Data appear on the last
printed page of this book.

Chapter 5 was originally published
as "Urbanizing the San Juan Fiesta:
Civil Society and Cultural Identity in the
Barrios of Caracas," in *Ethnographies
of Neoliberalism*, edited by Carol
Greenhouse (Philadelphia: University
of Pennsylvania Press, 2009). Reprinted
by permission of the University of
Pennsylvania Press.

FOR AISHA
In memory of Yolanda Salas

Contents

List of Illustrations

Acknowledgments

This book would not have been possible without the generosity, humor, and patience of my friends in the Caracas barrios, and I owe them a great debt. Yajaira Hernandez and Johnny Moreno were my guides, my hosts, my good friends, and my rock through the various ups and downs of field research. Without them to come home to every night and share my stories over a meal of *arepas*, my experience in Caracas would not have been nearly as rewarding. Their friends, family, and neighbors who also extended hospitality to me included, among many others, Damarys, Amarilys, Zulay, Alexis, Ricardito, Palmiro, and Tito. I was also very lucky to have the friendship and guidance of the novelist and community journalist José Roberto Duque, "el embarcador," who introduced me to a large number of the people who would become my close collaborators in his native 23 de Enero and in La Vega.

I owe many thanks to the folks and organizations in each of the parishes where I worked. In 23 de Enero, I would like to acknowledge Gustavo Borges and Susana Rodriguez, as well as the *camaradas* of the Coordinadora Simón Bolívar, especially Juan Contreras and Guadalupe Rodriguez. In La Vega, there are Freddy Mendoza, Carmen Pérez, and all the *vecinos* from the Carretera Negra; Williams Ochoa and others from the Grupo Autoctono de la Vega; and Edgar "El Gordo" Pérez and those from the Grupo Caribes de Itagua. In San Agustín, there is Jesus "Totoño" Blanco and his group Tacusan. Antonio "Pelon" Marrero, and Carlos Palacios. The community radio folks also extended a great deal of help to me in my research, especially Carlos Carles, Rafael Fernandez, Madera, Carlos Lugo, and Fernando Pinto.

Although being immersed in the field often felt far from the halls of academe, I had some fruitful and engaging interactions with scholars and colleagues in Caracas that enriched my understanding of Venezuela. I owe a prime debt to the anthropologist Yolanda Salas, who, sadly, passed away at the end of 2007. Yolanda's decades of field research among the urban and rural poor were of great inspiration to me. We met regularly to discuss my research and to plan our collaborations, even toward the end when she was confined to her bed. But even in the most difficult moments, she would put on her lipstick and a brave smile, always positive and full of jokes.

The historian Alejandro Velasco was residing in el 23 while carrying out his doctoral research and we engaged in many dialogues that have proved central to my thinking on the issues. He read over several drafts of various chapters and provided insightful and critical feedback. Luis Duno provided important initial contacts in Caracas, and I am very grateful for his generosity, guidance, and solidarity. Jesus "Chucho" Garcia made available to me his archives at the Fundación Afro-America. I also learned a great deal from my interactions with Daisy Barreto and Miguel Angel Contreras.

The ideas in this book were not developed in isolation, and I have benefited from a series of interrelated discussions in conferences and seminars. My initial engagement with neoliberalism was sparked by the conference "Neoliberalism: Historical Perspectives and Critical Possibilities," which I organized together with Hairong Yan at Princeton University in October 2004. Related to this conference were a series of panels and then a workshop and edited volume that Carol Greenhouse organized at Princeton on politics, publics, and personhood at the limits of neoliberalism. The initial workshop also led to my participation in a panel at the American Anthropological Association (AAA) conference organized by Roger Rouse on the topic of neoliberal subjectivities, and that led to a Latin American Studies Association (LASA) panel and conference at the University of California, San Diego organized by Nancy Postero and Mark Goodale on post-neoliberalism. I have also been part of a series of discussions at LASA and through a list-serv and finally a volume edited by David Smilde on publics and civil society in Venezuela. My own thoughts have evolved through my participation in these various interdisciplinary gatherings, and I owe much to the organizers and other participants for the questions they have raised and the insights they offered.

In addition to these forums, I have also presented chapters from this work at the conference "Latin America's Informal Cities in Comparative Perspective," at Northwestern University; the conference "Latin American

Opposition to Neo-Liberalism" at the New School; a seminar, "The Popular Sectors and the State in Chávez's Venezuela," at Yale University; the conference "Changes in the Andes" at Brown University; and the public forum "Venezuela's Bolivarian Revolution at Home and Abroad" at Yale University. I have had the opportunity to discuss my work at the Race and Ethnicity Working Group in the Department of Sociology at UCLA; the Cotsen Seminar, Carl A. Fields Center, and the Program in Latin American Studies at Princeton University; as well as meetings of the American Sociological Association (ASA), American Political Science Association (APSA), and Western Political Science Association (WPSA). I have received invaluable feedback from all of these events, and I thank the organizers and participants.

This book has benefited greatly from the feedback and advice of various people. Nancy Postero reviewed the manuscript for Duke, and our ongoing dialogue over conference lunches, long distance phone calls, and email has been exciting and productive for my work. Nancy's imprint on my thinking and hence the book has been very strong. Likewise, Carol Greenhouse continues to be an important figure for my work and I appreciate her insights and guidance on various drafts. Steve Ellner also reviewed the manuscript for Duke, and was kind enough to answer my numerous questions over email. Greg Grandin and David Smilde were very helpful through the process of writing and publishing this book. They provided a sympathetic ear and sound advice when I ran into snags. The other people who read drafts of chapters and provided helpful suggestions were Priya Srinivasan, David Guss, and Naomi Schiller. I had the chance to workshop the book through a year-long informal writing group that included Amy Chazkel, Josie Saldaña, David Kazanjian, and Sarah Covington. The group taught me a lot about the process of writing and revising, and I am grateful to the participants for their detailed comments on my work. I would also like to thank two anonymous reviewers for Duke University Press, and my editor Miriam Angress, who guided the book to completion with speed and thoroughness.

Institutional support was necessary for the fieldwork, writing, and research that led up to this book. My fieldwork was carried out while I was a Wilson-Cotsen fellow at Princeton's Society of Fellows in the Liberal Arts. I received generous faculty research grants from the University Committee on Research in the Humanities and Social Sciences, and faculty summer research grants from the Program in Latin American Studies and the Center for Migration and Development at Princeton University. My three-year fellowship was a wonderful time for me to develop the project, and I thank Mary Harper and Cass Garner for their personal support, administrative work, and guidance that made my time at the Society so fruitful. I completed the writing and research as a member of the Department of Sociology at Queens College, City University of New York with faculty grants from the PSC-CUNY Research Foundation. My department chair Andy Beveridge was strongly supportive of my research and approved generous amounts of time away to complete the writing. My colleague Patricia Clough listened to my ideas and gave suggestions with her characteristic empathy, humor, and insightfulness. The final stages of the book took shape during my participation in a year-long seminar on place and politics, led by David Harvey and Peter Hitchcock at the Center for Place, Culture, and Politics at the CUNY Graduate Center.

I must thank the numerous research assistants and students who worked hard over many years on the project. At Princeton, I would like to acknowledge the work of graduate students Alberto Galindo, Cecilia Palmeiro, Jaime Kirzner-Roberts, Paola Cortes-Rocca, and Rebecca Wolpin. At the CUNY Graduate Center, I had the assistance of Salvatore Giametta and Amalia Leguizamon. In Venezuela, I was assisted by Amarilys Moreno, Victor Santos, and Sara Maneiro. The maps in the book were all designed by Karen Alyde Pren and redrawn by Bill Nelson. I also received a great deal of assistance with Adobe photoshop from Armin Moehrle and Nico Weckerle, who helped me to refine the maps. I received help with statistical data and political economy from Greg Wilpert from Venezuela Analysis and Mark Weisbrot and Luis Sandoval from the Center for Economic and Policy Research. Patricia Abdelnour, the cultural attaché from the Venezuelan Embassy in New York, also provided helpful information on cultural policy.

Finally, the ongoing support and encouragement from my family has been essential. I have followed my sister Deepa to Cuba, to New York, and ultimately to Venezuela, where it was her introductions and contacts that set me on the journey that became this book. My parents Joe and Sylvie Fernandes have provided moral support and love always, even from far across the ocean. My husband Mike Walsh was encouraging and supportive of my frequent trips to Venezuela, even as he faced some difficult times

alone, and he reminds me always of the things in life that are really important. This book is dedicated to our daughter Aisha Sinead, who was born
just as the book was being completed, with the wish that we are bringing
her into a world with a little more hope, a little more laughter, and a little
more justice than what has gone before.

Introduction

The Miraflores presidential palace in downtown Caracas has historically been the site of much political activity, from presidential victories to coups, impeachments, and protests. From 1998, Miraflores was occupied by President Hugo Chávez and a governing coalition of Bolivarian political parties, who carried out a radical program for redistribution and regional integration based on the vision of the early-nineteenth-century Republican leader Simón Bolívar. Next door to the Miraflores palace is Mirapollo, a fried chicken joint. Palmiro Avilan, a community organizer from the parish of Petare, carries out most of his political work here.

When I met Palmiro at Mirapollo, I had to elbow my way past noisy gatherings of swarthy men tearing through plates of greasy fries and roast chicken. The booth in the corner of Mirapollo is Palmiro's "office." Palmiro is in his fifties, short and broad shouldered, with a goatee and dark skin. He has three cell phones on the table which are constantly ringing and beeping with incoming text messages. Community activists come in and out of the booth. Over a cold *malta*, Palmiro tells me that he is a devotee of Maria Lionza, a popular cult based on various spirits of indigenous and black fighters from the past, such as Guaicaipuro, Negro Primero, and Maria Lionza herself.

"These spirits have the elements of blackness," said Palmiro, "a spirituality that's been gestating and has its roots in the *rochelas* [communities of escaped slaves] that formed for over two hundred and fifty years in the plains. It was in the plains that they created the liberation army of resistance to rescue five countries from Spanish imperialism. One of the first leaders was José Tomás Boves, who led a group of ragtag Indians and blacks against a Republican army that was in the hands of *mantuanos* [creole elites]."

In nationalist histories, Boves is an antihero who betrayed the cause of

Independence by launching a rebellion against the Bolívar-led Republican army in 1814. But he has been mythified in popular culture as a renegade caudillo who gave importance to marginalized Indians and blacks.[1] Palmiro sees himself as a modern-day Boves; he is leading an army of those who are being excluded from society.

Palmiro's deployment of Boves helps to frame a contemporary form of exclusion, based in geographies of marginality that were fortified over decades of economic crisis and consequent neoliberal policies of privatization, deregulation, and market-based growth. As economic inequalities increased, there was a growing segregation of urban space. Communal areas of city life such as cultural centers were taken over by malls and private interests. Urban barrio residents came to be seen as a threat to the property and security of the middle classes and were subject to greater policing. The spaces available for public life and deliberation were further reduced through media consolidation, a process that centralized the media in the hands of a small number of conglomerates.

Since Chávez was elected in 1998, he has embraced an anti-neoliberal and pro-poor agenda, in an attempt to reduce economic and spatial inequalities, create access to public spaces, and give voice to the black and mestizo majority. Highlighting his own mestizo features and dark complexion, Chávez has encouraged new forms of cultural identity based on blackness and indigeneity. Urban social movements elaborate these identities in fiestas and murals as they find themselves excluded from the ranks of a self-proclaimed, middle-class civil society. The Chávez government has sponsored local cultural and media collectives, passing legislation to authorize low-power radios as an alternative to media conglomerates. In his speeches and a new constitution, Chávez has encouraged barrio movements to occupy public spaces of the city. Chávez's election also created avenues for previously disenfranchised groups to participate in governance and decision making. The structures and discourses of exclusion have been contested in multiple arenas since Chávez has come to power. So why does the figure of Boves resonate so strongly for some in a Bolivarian Venezuela? What are the lines of conflict emerging as barrio-based movements demand inclusion in the state?

As urban movements engage with the political arena, they come up against the instrumental rationalities—both liberal and neoliberal—of state administrators. The economic policy of the Chávez government has been distinctly anti-neoliberal. Its restructuring of the oil industry has allowed the government to create protected areas of the economy such as social welfare which are not subject to market requirements. But the realities of Venezuela's continued participation in a global market economy are manifested in a neoliberal political rationality, present in areas such as culture and communications. By "political rationality," I refer to the calculus of cost and benefit that undergirds administrators' actions and decisions. Concerned with securing foreign investment, technocrats in state institutions apply market-based calculations in these fields. I argue that the disjunctures between state goals of fostering market competition and reducing poverty produce tensions that barrio-based movements experience in their interactions with the state and its intermediaries. Social movements counter the utilitarian logics of state and party officials with visions based in "lo cotidiano" (the everyday), cultural heritage, and historical memory. In this dimension, the figure of Boves—as a renegade figure who opposed Bolívar—also signals a response by barrio movements to the forms of exclusion they encounter in a new hybrid order.

An engagement with the lives and experiences of barrio residents reveals a reality of political life in the Chávez era mostly absent from the burgeoning literature on contemporary Venezuelan politics. State-centric and structuralist analysis has tended to dominate both among scholars sympathetic to Chávez and those who are critical. Some political scientists seek to understand the crisis of traditional politics and the electoral successes of Chávez as linked to the destabilizing effects of the 1980s debt crisis and neoliberal economic reforms across Latin America. According to Kenneth Roberts, the debt crisis weakened the traditional political parties and labor institutions at the base of nationalist development models, such as that associated with Import Substitution Industrialization (ISI). The crisis in mass representation left a void that was filled by populist leaders such as Chávez who fashioned new, unmediated relationships with the masses.[2] As Steve Ellner elaborates, unlike the brief reign of so-called neopopulist leaders in Latin America who embraced neoliberal policies, such as Brazil's Fernando Collor de Mello, Peru's Alberto Fujimori, and Argentina's Carlos Menem, Chávez has shown a deeper commitment to anti-neoliberal programs and has had a more enduring impact.[3] But at the same time, Ellner notes that all of these highly personalistic leaders emerged from a crisis of institutions under neoliberalism.

In contrast to this political economy approach, other political scientists have tended to focus in a circular way on the disfunctionality of traditional political parties as the cause of what they see as a breakdown of democracy.[4] They cite the inability of the traditional parties to cope with the economic crisis of the 1980s, and the changes brought about in the party system through decentralization and direct elections for governors and mayors, as crucial factors in the rise of nontraditional actors such as Chávez.[5] These political scientists claim that internal problems with the party system contributed to its weakening during a period of economic crisis. Some even consider that it is leftist groups,[6] populist strategies, and an increasingly powerful executive that have caused the disintegration of the two-party system, rather than the other way around. Others concentrate on the extraordinary personal charisma of Chávez, relying on psychosocial factors, such as people's "psychological need to believe in salvation" and "the personal appeal of a potential savior" or the suggestion by a former minister of trade and energy that "Chávez constantly caters to the emotional needs of a deeply demoralized nation."[7] These scholars explain Chávez's ongoing public support as due to his ability to politicize the masses, as well as his use of the substantial oil reserves of the country in order to fund social programs such as the missions.

These multiple approaches share a top-down perspective that reduces the present conjuncture to the consequences of a set of structural determinants or locates all agency in the figure of Chávez as the sole figure responsible for crafting policy, designing programs, and providing orientation to an otherwise incoherent mass. The descriptions of the urban poor as "susceptible," "ripe for mobilization," and "charisma-hungry"; the reduction of people to "voters" in most rational choice analyses; and the assumption of "unorganized mass constituencies" betray a concept of popular sectors as easily manipulated, depoliticized individuals.[8] Many rely on the erroneous assumption, expressed by Jennifer McCoy, that "the urban poor never successfully organized politically."[9] They do not account for the histories of urban social movements that have contested the existing order for over four decades, nor the ways in which these actors have continued to negotiate with and shape the political process.

On the other side, some left-wing and progressive supporters of the Chávez government have tended toward a celebration of the new spaces of participatory democracy that are emerging in contemporary Venezuela.[10] They do provide a useful counterpoint to state-centric perspectives by focusing on the units of popular organization and deliberation that have flourished at the grassroots. But these accounts are not so attentive to the obstacles that are faced by barrio-based actors when they interact with state agencies. They also focus predominantly on groupings such as the Bolivarian circles, land committees, and communal councils that were formed under Chávez, excluding the long-term social movements that predate the Chávez government.

This book offers an alternative approach to the study of Venezuelan politics that explores the alliances, conflicts, and mutual empowerment of state and society. The relationship between society and the state is reciprocal: just as the strong figure of Chávez has given impetus and unity to popular organizing, so the creative movements fashioned in the barrios help determine the form and content of official politics. To see Chávez as an independent figure pontificating from above, or popular movements as originating in autonomous spaces from below, would be to deny the interdependencies between them that both constrain and make possible each other's field of action.

One of the other goals of this book is to comprehend the diverse histories and experiences of social movements under Chávez. Many commentators misrepresent those groups supporting Chávez as uniformly Chavista, when in reality Chavistas are only one tendency in a broad array of cultural, community, and political groups participating in the *"proceso."* José Roberto Duque defines the proceso as a parallel and underground movement that defends the Chávez government but which has its own trajectory independent of directives from the central government.[11] Many community organizers in the barrios do not identify as Chavistas, and they have alternative sources of identity that come from their barrio or parish (Barrio Sucre, Barrio Marín, 23 de Enero, San Agustín, Petare) and that form the basis of alternative social and community networks (Coordinadora Simón Bolívar, Cayapo, Radio Negro Primero, Ciudadela de Catía). These popular movements claim distinct genealogies that predate Chávez, including the clandestine movements against the 1950s military regime, the posttransition era of guerrilla struggle in the 1960s, movements against urban displacement and hunger strikes led by Jesuit worker priests in the 1970s, and cultural activism and urban committees of the 1980s and 1990s. These multiple histories are not adequately conveyed in reductive labels such as "Chavista rank-and-file," "Chávez supporters," or "Chavista movement."

The copious volumes of edited collections, books, and articles produced on Chávez's Venezuela have also failed to address the often painful contradictions and complexities of working-class life. As Daniel James has observed in the study of Peronism in Argentina, there has been a long-standing inability of academia to come to terms with working-class experience. The working class has either been mythologized or demonized, and working-class life has been simplified to fit the ideological parameters of the position being argued.[12] This book takes up James's challenge, and alongside histories of struggle and resistance in the barrios I include individual biographies that reveal the ambiguities of working-class life and the personal experiences of discrimination, redemption, and hope that underlie collective action.

INDIVIDUAL HISTORIES AND COLLECTIVE HISTORIES

My first night in Caracas, I stayed in a hotel in the middle-class suburb of Altamira. The next day I called Johnny, a contact from my sister Deepa, a journalist with WBAI radio (New York), who had spent some time in Venezuela the previous year. "Wait right there, I'm coming to get you," said Johnny. Next thing, a shiny green Nova pulled up outside the hotel, Johnny in the front and his wheelchair in the back. Johnny was a large, friendly, black Venezuelan man who had been left paraplegic after a car accident. I introduced myself using my nickname "Suyi," always easier than my full name. Johnny took me to the popular parish of El Valle, to the apartment that he shared with his *compañera* Yajaira, a middle-aged black woman from the parish of San Agustín. This was to become my home for the next month and over the years as I returned to Venezuela to do my field research.

Johnny and Yajaira lived in popular housing blocks (*bloques populares*), project-like buildings constructed by the government for barrio residents. I was to sleep on a small mattress on the floor in their spare room. The spare room was piled with boxes of papers, unironed clothes, dusty books, car parts, and other junk. Yajaira laughed nervously about how they hadn't cleaned out the room in years, but I said it was no problem. "I've lived in huts in the remotest villages of India, I've slept on park benches in Madrid, and on the floors of crumbling mansions in Cuba," I boasted. "I'll be fine." That night after all the lights were out, and I lay down to sleep, I immediately felt a small tickle on my arm. I brushed it off, but soon, I felt another tickle, and then another. Reaching for the light, I gasped in horror as I saw teams of winged cockroaches all over my mattress and the floor. I ran out of the room shutting the door behind me and went to the living room, where I perched anxiously on the couch. The lights from the small Christmas tree blinked on and off, and I considered my options. I couldn't wake up Johnny and Yajaira, not after all I had said about being so cool and unperturbed by the conditions of the room. They would take it as an insult, they would see me as a wimp. Maybe I was not cut out for this research, if I couldn't even deal with the cockroaches on my first night in the barrio. I dozed intermittently, jerked awake every now and again by the flashing lights and my own distressing thoughts.

The next morning Yajaira came out to make coffee and when she saw me on the couch, she shrieked, "Suyi, what happened?" When I told her the story she looked at me in horror, and exclaimed, "If that had been me I would have screamed so loud that it would have woken up the whole house and brought all the neighbors running." I was so relieved, we burst into laughter. The story of my night with the cockroaches would become urban legend. From then on, every time we saw a cockroach, it was an *amigo de Suyi* (friend of Suyi). Yajaira decided that if I was to stay in their house, we would have to clean the room out to get rid of all the cockroaches. She pulled two old, identical t-shirts and pants from the pile of laundry and said that she and I would form a cleaning cooperative, especially since Chávez was now giving money for cooperatives.

As I came to know Yajaira, I realized that this mixture of pragmatism and humor was how she dealt with many situations in her life, from the death of her mother from lack of prompt medical attention, to the shooting of her brother by gang members. As I heard the life stories of Yajaira and countless others, I saw how these qualities marked their entry into community organizing. Relying on your wits, stretching personal resources, and making jokes are at the basis of a model of sociability that has helped sustain urban social movements.

My third day in Caracas we were cleaning out the room, and I received my introduction to Yajaira and Johnny's life history. The morning extended into the afternoon, then the evening and the night, as we looked at photos and sifted through old papers, books, and souvenirs. We shared stories, moments of reflection, and laughs. There was memorabilia from Johnny's sporting career, including certificates, magazine clippings, and invitations abroad. I learned that after being left paraplegic from a car accident nearly thirty years ago, Johnny had embarked on a remarkable career as a long-distance marathon athlete. From one box, Johnny picked up an article from an American newspaper about his participation in the New York Marathon in 2001. The article said that Venezuelan athletes were being deprived of funds to attend overseas events under the Chávez government. Johnny said that he had tried to contact the press to tell them that this was not true, but nobody had wanted to hear his story. There were many papers on health care, diagrams of the body, and handwritten notes about disability.

In the evening, the neighbor Damarys dropped by and joined in the work. She picked up a book, dusted it off, and read the title. It was a Spanish translation of Alex Haley's *Roots*. Everyone in the room beamed in recognition. Damarys, a light-skinned black woman originally from the coastal region of Carupano, told a story about how she saw *Roots* on television with a young *negro* (black). According to Damarys, the young man burst into tears during this film about a black author's search for his roots in Africa and slavery. "He felt that the film really represented his experiences," she said. These questions of "roots" and belonging would recur throughout my time in Venezuela.

At one point, I picked up a wad of papers, with chapter headings on co-operatives. Yajaira sheepishly grabbed the papers of what was her un-finished college thesis. She told me that she had never finished college because her mother became ill and she had to abandon her degree and work as a street vendor in order to support her family. As we contin-ued into the night we came across banners, pamphlets, and flyers from Johnny's and Yajaira's years of community organizing. Johnny found some old bed frames and improvised a bed for me, while they told me about their work with street children in the parish of San Agustín. That night I col-lapsed into my new bed, with no cockroaches, and a glimpse into the lives of my new friends. I thought about the fragments, stories, and pieces through which we patch together our lives, make meaning of our present, and engage in action to fight for possible futures.

Over the years that I returned to stay with Johnny and Yajaira, I came to know much more about them. At night, we would stay up talking till late, exchanging stories about our day, about our lives, laughing, and getting to know one another as friends. I became close to Yajaira's nieces and nephews, who would often stay over, and the many friends from the neighborhood who would drop by. I came to know the local drug dealers and other characters such as the street vendors. Originally I had seen the house as a place to stay while I carried out my research on urban social movements. But I began to realize that these exchanges were a crucial part of the story that I was telling about the ways that larger political processes intersect with individual histories and individual lives. Yajaira's story helped me to see the personal reasons why someone might be motivated to become a community activist, what Chávez represents in her life and those around her, and how her individual experiences led her to build collaborations with others. While the historical archives offer certain accounts of local barrio histories, Yajaira's personal archives offer a different kind of interpretation, and both will be explored together in the early chapters of this book.

SOCIAL MOVEMENTS AND THE CITY

The barrios of Caracas, like the favelas of Rio de Janeiro, the periferia of São Paolo, the poblaciones of Santiago, and the villas of Buenos Aires, are places that have been formed by exclusion, rural-urban migration, and poverty. A visitor arriving to Caracas at night will see the sparkling lights of the shantytowns nestled in the valleys and hills of the city, but commercial tourist guides offer no directions to reach these areas and they are not present on visitors' maps. The Lonely Planet guidebook to Venezuela warns the traveler: "Don't venture into the shantytowns at any time of the day, let alone at night." This is not to deny that the money-making potential of the shantytowns is being marketed by resourceful entrepreneurs. In Brazil, following the commercial success of such films as *Cidade de Deus*, foreign tourists have been leaving the beaches and shopping malls of Rio to go on the increasingly popular "Favela Tours." But many of these tours are like safaris, where tourists remain in the safety of their buses or tour groups without having to engage with the realities of the residents' lives. Despite their connections to the outside world, the shantytowns remain in relative obscurity and isolation.

With the exception of Petare, a large, sprawling conglomeration of bar-

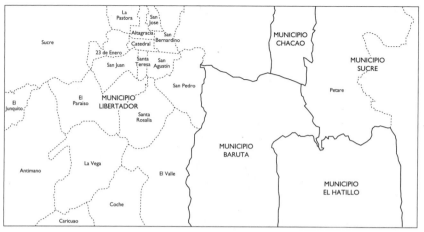

MAP 1 Municipalities and parishes of the metropolitan region of Caracas.
ORIGINALLY DESIGNED BY KAREN ALYDE PREN; REDRAWN BY BILL NELSON.

rios located in the far east of Caracas, most of the shantytown areas are in the western part of the city, known as the Municipio Libertador. Since my research was mainly carried out in the western parishes of San Agustín, 23 de Enero, and La Vega, I briefly describe them in this section. In the 2000 census, the population of Municipio Libertador was estimated at 1.9 million.[13] The rate of urbanization in Venezuela increased markedly during the twentieth century. In 2005, the percentage of the population living in urban areas was 93.6 percent, with around 13 percent of the population based in Caracas.[14] The country went from being predominantly rural in the early twentieth century to predominantly urban by the new millennium.

San Agustín is one of the older parishes, located close to the city center. The 2000 census lists its population as some 39,175, although this is an estimate. The actual numbers are probably somewhat higher due to the difficulty of accurately counting highly dense urban populations with a large number of squatters.[15] San Agustín del Sur is divided off from the more prosperous area of San Agustín del Norte by the river Guaire. Walking along the main avenue of San Agustín del Sur, one encounters a series of small bodegas selling groceries, cleaning products, and baked goods; religious shops with statues of saints and other mementos in the windows; and auto repair shops. Men sit outside on makeshift boxes, beer bottles in hand, laughing and making jokes. The pavement is jammed with a steady stream of pedestrians and street vendors selling popular snacks. Moving

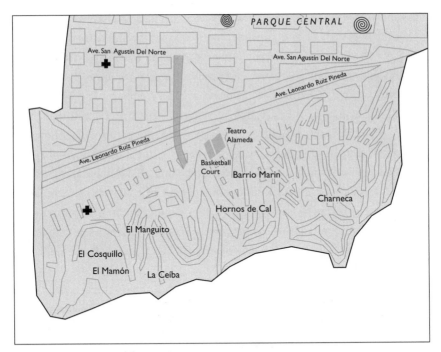

MAP 2 San Agustín parish. ORIGINALLY DESIGNED BY KAREN ALYDE PREN; REDRAWN BY BILL NELSON.

east along the avenue, there is a large basketball court on the left. On the right is a dilapidated theater known as the Teatro Alameda, which ceased functioning in 1965 and was recuperated by the residents in 2004 as a community cultural center. A lane behind the theater, littered with trash and syringes and reeking of urine, leads to a small square known as the Afinque de Marín, at the heart of Barrio Marín. Several houses face onto the square and there is a basketball ring to the right. On one wall of the Afinque, life-size murals of the original members of the 1970s-era local musical ensemble Grupo Madera give a sense of the cultural history of the sector.

Barrio Marín is unique among Caraqueño barrios for its old-style colonial houses with inner courtyards decorated with ornate grills and pastel colors; its wide stone streets; and street lights that begin to glow in the early evening. Some residents have the means to preserve these colonial houses, but most have watched their homes deteriorate in the humid climate as they are unable to pay for repairs. Between the tall facades of the houses, one sees the *ranchos* in the hills behind. The more precarious ranchos are made with wood or recycled materials and have zinc roofs and earth floors, while the consolidated ones may be multistory with brick walls, tiled roofs, and electricity. Leaving Barrio Marín and climbing several long, concrete staircases, one reaches the *cerro*, or upper barrios of the sector, such as Charneca, El Mamón, and La Ceiba. Interspersed among the precarious ranchos are rich vegetation, papaya trees, and overgrown grass; public water amenities for residents of the sector; a makeshift basketball court; and bodegas, where residents sell maltas, pasta, toothpaste, and soap from small windows of their dwellings. Salsa musicians gather in dark rooms to practice. Occasionally the clash of a snare or the rumble of a conga can be heard coming from a rancho. Reggaeton blares from small radios. The climb up to the cerro reveals views of large city skyscrapers, the Hotel Caracas Hilton, the downtown Parque Central district, and San Agustín del Norte.

Further west of the city, the parish of 23 de Enero is characterized by its militant murals and high-rise project buildings, built under the military ruler Marcos Pérez Jimenez. The 2000 census records 82,642 residents of 23 de Enero, of whom a little over half reside in the public housing buildings.[16] At one entrance to the parish, at Avenida Sucre, there is a large mural of Che Guevara next to a masked guerrilla, with the message "Welcome to 23 de Enero." Another entrance to the parish is from the metro stop Agua Salud, which lets out at a busy avenue with street vendors selling newspapers and fresh fruits, hawking trinkets, and offering telephone services. Buses and cars choke the busy street and collect waiting lines of passengers, headed for Monte Piedad. The street facing Agua Salud leads toward La Cañada. After five minutes on foot, one arrives at blocks 18 and 19, home to the militant, cadre-based organization Coordinadora Simón Bolívar (CSB). Their headquarters are in a reclaimed police station, painted in bright white, with images of Simón Bolívar and Che Guevara. Entering one of the residential buildings in La Cañada, the level of deterioration is immediately apparent. The paint is peeling, there are large patches of water damage on the walls, and the stairwell smells of urine. There is rubbish on the landings and here and there a rat scurries away. Climbing further up the street, one approaches the main intersection of Barrio Sucre, with its mazelike streets and small brick houses.

As a bus climbs to the sector Monte Piedad, the fifteen-story high-rise project buildings, set against hills and bulbous clouds, come into view. The

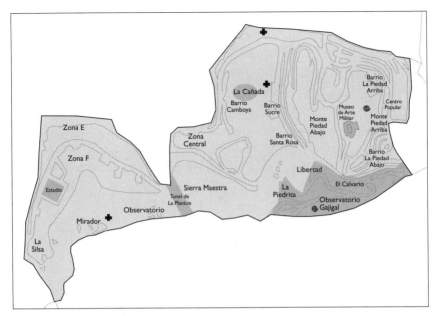

MAP 3　23 de Enero parish. ORIGINALLY DESIGNED BY KAREN ALYDE PREN; REDRAWN BY BILL NELSON.

facades of individual apartments appear as checkered squares of blues, whites, yellows, and pinks. Laundry hangs from the windows, fluttering in the breeze. The road winds through the hills in the approach to Monte Piedad Arriba, at the top of the hill. Here the Coordinadora Cultural Simón Bolívar (CCSB), a breakaway group from the CSB, have their headquarters in an old abandoned building. Facing the building is a long wall with a series of fierce images of indigenous chiefs. There are also murals of young men from the barrio who were killed in combat with the national guard in previous decades. The murals of fallen comrades, and bullet holes shot by security forces in the facades of the buildings during the 1989 Caracazo street riots, give the sense of being in a war zone.

To the south of these smaller, inner-city parishes lie the expansive and more recently urbanized popular parishes of El Valle, La Vega, Caricuao, and Antimano. La Vega is a large, mountainous parish, with about 130,886 residents living in an area of 13.3 square kilometers recorded in the census data.[17] A bus traveling from El Valle along the highway Cota 905 passes through a terrain of green hills with overgrown grass and trees and plants with rich foliage. It terminates at the Centro Comercial, a shopping center

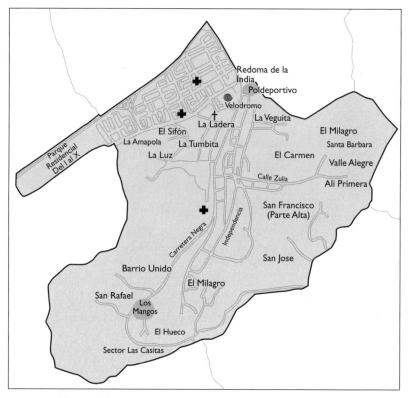

MAP 4 La Vega parish. ORIGINALLY DESIGNED BY KAREN ALYDE PREN; REDRAWN BY BILL NELSON.

at the entrance to La Vega. But the expensive boutique stores and fancy pastry shops in the shopping center are mostly for the wealthy residents of the neighboring El Paraíso. Stepping outside the air-conditioned environs of the mall, one encounters the bustle and noise of the barrio. Cars and buses sound their horns as they jostle to leave or enter the parish. Vendors line the street with large glass cases of sticky buns and iced donuts, surrounded by a halo of bees.

Taking the road to the left, one approaches Barrio Carmen and the headquarters of the Afro-centric cultural group Grupo Autoctono de la Vega. There is a large mural of Tupac Shakur, with a faint outline of Che Guevara's beret sketched in the background. On a large piece of metal someone has painted a portrait of Malcolm X. Further along this road is a small church and plaza, where fiestas of the saints are celebrated. Taking the road straight ahead and up from the shopping center, one passes several smaller barrios on the right, and then Las Terrazas de la Vega, a large newly constructed housing complex for middle-class families. Facing this complex is a barrio known as the "Carretera Negra." The barrio consists of a line of houses located along the main stretch of highway road, as indicated by its name, "Black Highway," and along three smaller lanes, Oriente, 24 de Julio, and Justicia. The buildings include an auto repair shop, a soup kitchen, and a small medical dispensary. Continuing along the same road, one finally arrives at the sector Las Casitas, the highest point. The air is noticeably more rarefied; on all sides there are views of rolling hills and vegetation. Some of the residents engage in small-scale agriculture. Every so often, the crow of a rooster punctuates the silence. A Catholic school with swing sets and brightly painted murals is set amid the lush greenery.

There is no sociological data on the barrios as a whole, but a World Bank study provides information about the parish of La Vega. It reveals that the average family size is 5.4 persons. The population of the parish is relatively young, with 32 percent under fifteen years of age. The average household income is the equivalent of US$409 per month. The study found that 45 percent of residents are employed in the informal sector, without job security or access to benefits. There are also pockets of extreme poverty, with the bottom 20 percent of residents earning only US$125 per month. The researchers found a similar socioeconomic profile in the area of Petare North, where they carried out another study.[18] Marital arrangements in the barrios are fairly informal and fluid. The rate of single-mother households in La Vega is high, at 38 percent.[19] Extended family structures are also common, with children being raised by grandparents or aunts. Although there is no data available on San Agustín and 23 de Enero, I also saw a high degree of informality, concentrated poverty, and single-mother households in these parishes.

For all their rich variety and diversity, the barrios of Caracas share similar histories of urban-rural migration, poverty, and marginality that differentiate and segregate them from the more affluent parts of the city. There is a strong contrast between the European-like cafes, wide streets, and secluded gardens of the middle- and upper-class neighborhoods; and the barrios with their bustling markets, improvised architecture, and the sounds of reggaeton and salsa coming from *minitecas*, or portable djays. As one observer noted, "The people of Prados del Este do not resemble those of El Guárataro, those of El Cafetal do not speak like those of Catia, the music that floats through the streets of Petare is not the same as that which passes through the upper part of La Castellana."[20] Moving between these different areas of the city is like passing through distinct worlds, each with its own aesthetic, norms of interaction, and street culture.

Since 1983, the two halves of the city have been connected through a subway system known locally as the *Metro*. Sleek, clean, and efficient, the Metro rapidly transports nannies, busboys, waiters, public servants, maids, gardeners, and students from their homes in the east of Caracas to the center and west of the city, and then back home at the end of the day. Those who live in the popular housing blocks, like Johnny and Yajaira, are more likely to be closer to the subway stops and have somewhat better access to services such as water and gas. By contrast, for those who live in the upper reaches of the barrio, in the ranchos, there is often a long wait for buses and less access to basic services. Despite developments that make it easier to traverse the city, the sharp inequalities between the east and west of the city remain salient, as do differences within the barrios themselves. The term "barrio" is technically used to refer to those poor, self-constructed neighborhoods that began as dispersed ranchos.[21] However, it has come to be used colloquially to describe poorer areas in general.

An important body of scholarship emerged in the 1960s to document and understand the problematic of urban segregation presented by shantytowns across Latin America. Some scholars sought to challenge what they saw as the "myth of marginality," debunking the idea that the shantytowns were peripheral and marginal to urban life.[22] Shantytown dwellers, they argued, were integrated into the life of the city and national politics through clientilist networks guaranteeing service provision in exchange for political votes and the struggles of neighborhood associations to improve their standard of living.[23] Contrary to notions of shantytowns as marginal zones or "cultures of poverty,"[24] these scholars argued that the urban poor were capable of social mobility, entrepreneurship, and political participation.

Revisiting these classical theories of marginality four decades later, a new generation of scholars reflected that the conditions of marginality that the scholars of the 1960s sought to challenge were being realized in contemporary societies.[25] Structural adjustment and neoliberal policies of the 1980s and 1990s produced classical features of marginality such as unemployment, a growing informal sector, and barter economy, as well as social exclusion and violence.[26] In addition to producing the conditions of marginality, with the advance of neoliberal restructuring, the idea of marginality has reemerged in the social imaginary of Latin American urban societies.[27] Intensified rural immigration to the cities, growing poverty and segregation, and rising insecurity have led to the criminalization of poorer sectors, which are seen to disrupt the order and health of the city.[28] In Caracas, the poorer areas are generally referred to as the *barrios marginales* (marginal barrios) or *zonas marginales* (marginal zones). Understanding this new geography of power and marginality in the city is crucial to understanding how it may also be the site for a new kind of politics.

Cities have played a major strategic role in contemporary processes of social change in Latin America, especially given the urban concentration of the population. According to Saskia Sassen, from the start of the 1980s the city emerged as an important terrain for new conflicts and claims by both global capital and disadvantaged sectors of the population concentrated in urban areas.[29] As emerging elite classes became increasingly powerful and transnational under processes of neoliberal restructuring, the urban informal working class has become the fastest-growing class on the planet.[30] Disconnected from the formal economy, lacking structures of unionization or access to social welfare, and stigmatized by the middle classes, the "new cities of poverty" are important sites for political organizing. The burgeoning population of an informal working class located in shantytowns and shacks on the margins of major cities has implications for the sociology of protest that have been largely unexplored.

In the wake of James Scott's characterizations of "micro politics" as everyday forms of resistance, scholars of Latin America have provided rich accounts of consciousness and culture among urban shanty dwellers in a neoliberal era. Authors focus on humorous storytelling, popular Christianity, spirit possession cults, evangelical Protestantism, and everyday debates as means by which the urban poor negotiate, challenge, and reproduce the conditions of marginality.[31] Others look at how emerging urban informal classes adapt new strategies to confront the retreat of the state and the lack of public services. In contexts of material hardship, Javier Auyero shows that clientilist practices may reemerge as a means of survival and problem solving.[32] As the state retreats from tasks of security and policing, urban residents step in to administer justice through vigilante lynchings.[33] But alongside these everyday forms of resistance and survival are also growing spaces for popular participation, where the urban poor have organized and asserted their rights. James Holston argues that the development of self-constructed neighborhoods on the peripheries of Brazilian cities fueled an "insurgent citizenship" as residents contested the conditions of segregation and illegality through which they were excluded from the formal city.[34] It is these kinds of social movement organizing in the barrios of Caracas that I attempt to describe in this book.

Urban social movements in Caracas are extraordinarily variegated and heterogeneous. There are militant cadre-based groupings that have roots in the guerrilla struggles of the 1960s, as well as collectives that operate through assemblies and mass actions, and cultural groupings based in music, song, and dance. These movements articulate together in "social movement webs," defined by Sonia Alvarez, Evelina Dagnino, and Arturo Escobar as "ties established among movement organizations, individual participants, and other actors in civil and political society and the state."[35] As the authors state, the metaphor of the web allows us to imagine "the multilayered entanglements of movement actors with the natural-environmental, political-institutional, and cultural-discursive terrains in which they are embedded."[36] Cultural, political, and identity-based struggles take place within defined spatial territories—the barrio, the plaza, the calle—suggesting the importance of public space in the formation of social movement webs. The contests over urban public space and the reclaiming of privatized areas are producing new means of public sphere, as arenas for deliberation and expression.[37] I distinguish urban social movements from political parties and trade unions by their basis in the networks of everyday life, their location in the space of the barrio rather than the party office or union hall, and their attempts to establish independent linkages with the state. While many contemporary trade unions tend to engage in concerns that are more narrowly economic—such as wages, length of the work week, and benefits—urban social movements see economic inequality as one dimension of the experience of marginality and have tended to couch their actions in cultural-symbolic terms.

At the center of these cultural-symbolic worlds are the *tambores*, or drums, that are part of a long history of black resistance. During slavery, plantation owners attempted to prohibit the African drums, as they were afraid of their power as a vehicle for covert communication and a call to insurrection. As the authorities attempt to police contemporary drumming rituals in urban fiestas, the drums are invoked as a symbol of defiance and survival. The title of this book, *Who Can Stop the Drums?*, references the question posed to me by a fiesta organizer. Yet the drums that I invoke are not entirely African; they speak to a cultural resistance that is also indigenous and more broadly Caribbean. As both sonic force and collective memory, the drums symbolize the potency of plural and diverse social movements.

Urban social movements are strongly engaged in cultural politics, a concept that scholars of "new social movements" such as Alvarez, Dagnino, and Escobar, among others, have elaborated. Standard theories of collective action within sociology and political science are often criticized for their lack of attention to the cultural dimensions of social movements, the discursive struggles in which they engage, and the construction of identity.[38] Cultural politics does not only refer to those groups explicitly deploying cultural protest or cultural forms. It also includes the attempts by social movements to challenge and redefine the dominant cultural order. While some movements are successful at negotiating and processing their demands at the institutional level—which makes them more visible to mainstream collective action theorists—others are engaged in a cultural politics that redefines the meaning of political culture, questioning not just who is in power but how that power is exercised.

THE HYBRID STATE IN A POST-NEOLIBERAL ERA

The specific configuration of social forces under Chávez is shaped by histories of the developmental and neoliberal state. In order to comprehend the constraints that face social movements as they construct alternative futures, it is important to outline the history and nature of the hybrid state that they encounter under Chávez.[39] While Chávez's administration has been broadly described as anti-neoliberal, I suggest rather that it is a post-neoliberal order, one where neoliberalism is no longer the dominant guiding policy, although it continues to surface in a range of conflicting rationalities and policies that are brought into an uneasy coexistence.

As others have pointed out, the historical experiences of state formation in Venezuela must be understood in relation to the exploitation of petroleum. According to Fernando Coronil, the state acquired its administrative capacity and finances while acting as a mediator between foreign oil companies and the nation in the early twentieth century, and gradually through its control of oil money it began to extend its centralized rule into education, private industry, transport, and communications, among other spheres.[40] Due to its oil largesse, the Venezuelan state differed from other peripheral states that were structured around the extraction and distribution of surplus value. For Coronil, what distinguished the Venezuelan state was its organization around the appropriation and distribution of ground rent.[41] This unique brand of rentier liberalism, based on the expansion of the state's oil rents, fused the republican ideals of Simón Bolívar with a common interest in the nation's subsoil. With the emergence of a liberal democratic opposition, "'sharing social power' was beginning to mean sharing political rights and oil wealth among the citizens of the same land."[42] As a result, the focus of political and economic struggles shifted to gaining control over the state apparatus.[43] As the party system consolidated during a brief coup in 1945 and after the 1958 transition to democracy, the ruling Acción Democrática (Democratic Action, AD) maintained a tight dominance, operating through a centralized and hierarchical party apparatus. AD made use of oil rents to expand and consolidate its political base.[44] Oil wealth produced a highly centralized state apparatus and hierarchical party system.

During the 1980s, Venezuelan politicians began to implement a series of neoliberal reforms that would dramatically redefine the character of the petrostate. Following the debt crisis of 1983 and a decade of growing poverty, unemployment, and spiraling inflation, presidents Luis Herrera Campíns (1979–84) and Jaime Lusinchi (1984–89) began courting foreign investors and borrowing to maintain social spending.[45] Following Herrera Campíns and Lusinchi, newly elected president Carlos Andres Pérez (1989–93) railed against the International Monetary Fund (IMF) and other international lending organizations in his inauguration speech on February 2 1989. Just a few weeks later he announced a neoliberal packet, known as El Gran Viraje (the Great Turn). Under pressure from foreign creditors to implement an IMF-style austerity program, he dismantled protections, deregulated prices, and reduced social spending. Pérez turned away from a national market artificially sustained by oil rents toward a global market.[46] He attempted to open up the state-owned oil company Petróleos de Venezuela (PDVSA) to foreign investment, but this was only achieved by his successor Rafael Caldera (1994–98).[47] In the neoliberal era, argues Coronil, the free market and not the state was seen as the rational means to achieve modernization.[48] The state control of oil was seen as an impediment rather than a tool for progress.

However, the neoliberal narrative about markets as the source of advancement did not resonate strongly in Venezuela. An early indication of this was the Caracazo, a series of protests and riots which came weeks after Pérez announced the Gran Viraje. Two subsequent coups, one in February 1992 led by an army colonel, Hugo Chávez, and another in November that came from high-level officers, signaled a continuing rejection of the neoliberal project. Nearly ten years after the Gran Viraje was announced, Chávez was elected to office on an anti-neoliberal agenda, with plans to rewrite the constitution. From the beginning of his tenure in office, Chávez linked his new development strategy with a redistribution of the oil wealth. According to Dick Parker, the government strengthened the Organization of Petroleum Exporting Countries (OPEC), contributing to an increase in oil prices. In the early years of Chávez's administration few changes were made to PDVSA. But following participation by oil executives in a work stoppage that preceded the coup against Chávez in April 2002 and a lockout and dismissal of 18,000 employees in December, Chávez made internal structural changes to the oil company, giving his government more leverage over funds. Foreign investment and increased production continued, although modified, but internal services were increasingly provided by worker cooperatives and PDVSA expanded its social programs.[49] Chávez's language harked back to earlier eras of rentier liberalism, and the sharing of the oil wealth.

Chávez has consistently drawn strong popular support for his return to a policy of capturing and redistributing oil rents, but his project confronts a new stage of capitalism, where production and accumulation have been globalized. This has made it harder for individual nations to sustain independent polities and economies.[50] Any assessment of contemporary Venezuela must take into account both the national and transnational level at which the state functions. As Coronil has noted, the Chávez administration is torn by its desire to both subsidize gasoline on the local market and obtain international rents, while maintaining the global competitiveness of the oil industry: "While as the sovereign owner of the subsoil the state has sought to obtain ever-larger rents by increasing oil prices and regulating supply, as a capitalist it must seek to obtain profits through productive investments in the global market."[51] The insertion of Venezuela into a global order requires certain policy adjustments and concessions that do not always fit with the anti-neoliberal rhetoric of Chávez.

The debate over whether the Chávez government is pro-neoliberal or anti-neoliberal has also tended to revolve around its economic policy. Neoliberalism is typically understood as a set of economic policies that attempt to privatize and deregulate the economy in order to promote free trade, foreign direct investment, and export-oriented industrialization. Some argue that especially after 2001 the Chávez administration has pursued anti-neoliberal measures—establishing majority ownership over the oil industry, passing agrarian reforms, reversing the reduction of social spending, and assigning resources to health and education that envision universal coverage, despite the tight constraints of the international context.[52] Others contend that the Chávez government has pursued macroeconomic stability rather than confronting multinational capital,[53] and that despite Chávez's rhetoric there have been no ruptures with foreign creditors or oil clients.[54] But following Wendy Brown, I argue that we must look at neoliberalism as not just a set of economic policies but as a modern form of power, labeled by Michel Foucault as "governmentality."[55] Governmentality refers to knowledges and techniques that are concerned with the regulation of everyday conduct. Neoliberal governmentality involves the extension of market rationality, based on an instrumental calculus of economic utility, to all state practices, as well as formerly noneconomic domains.[56] As Aihwa Ong has argued, these rationalities and techniques can predominate even in contexts where neoliberalism as an economic doctrine is not central.[57] I suggest that this is the case in Chávez's Venezuela, a post-neoliberal formation that has adopted significant anti-neoliberal reforms, while its ongoing subjection to the requirements of a global economy has given impetus to neoliberal rationalities and techniques in a range of state and nonstate arenas.

In Venezuela, neoliberal rationalities were deeply etched into the visions of technocrats who tried to reorganize arenas of public and private life to meet global competition during the 1990s. Like the Chicago-trained economists known as the "Chicago boys" who implemented the neoliberal turn in Chile, Venezuela also had a group of select, foreign-trained economists who spearheaded the Gran Viraje. The Institute of Higher Management Studies (IESA) became the training ground and platform for a new breed of technocrats, business elites, and managers who would form the "Venezue-lan technocracy."[58] Known as the "IESA boys," these technocrats had privi-leged positions in the Pérez government, playing key roles in public and private enterprises. According to Miguel Angel Contreras, the term "tech-nocratic" refers to a culture of technical decision making by specialists rather than through a process of democratic debate and consultation.[59] In the name of fighting bureaucracy and corruption, state institutions were scaled back and their operations were often linked to the priorities of the market and international lending agencies. While some institutions—such as media and cultural agencies—have undergone changes of personnel and policy under Chávez, they continue deploying market logics as they appeal to funders and corporations, even as they pursue their commitment to a pro-poor agenda.

I define a post-neoliberal order as a hybrid state formation that has mounted certain challenges to the neoliberal paradigm but which remains subject to the internal and external constraints of global capital. Some might argue instead that the Chávez government is "neo-neoliberal," given its continuities with the past. The Venezuelan economy continues to be dependent on a boom-bust cycle of fluctuating oil rents and an export-oriented model of development. It faces unfavorable external conditions due to the strength of fiscal austerity policies across the rest of the conti-nent. Despite Chávez's rhetoric, it is unclear whether his policies are actu-ally creating an anti-neoliberal challenge that could counter the influence of the United States or the strength of the global market.[60] But at the same time, the Chávez government's policies of land and resource redistribution, social welfare intervention, and restructuring of trade to promote joint ventures and "fair trade" bilateral agreements are incompatible with a neoliberal agenda. As the financial resources and influence of the IMF have entered into decline, Venezuela has offered alternative sources of credit to countries like Argentina to pay off their debt, as well as giving loans and oil subsidies to other countries in the region, without the conditions imposed by the IMF.[61] Chávez has nationalized the telephone company CANTV, the steelmaker SIDOR, regionalized electricity companies, remaining privately controlled oil fields, and foreign cement companies. Although these na-tionalizations were fairly moderate, in that they reversed privatizations that took place under previous governments or gave the state majority rather than minority stakes, they were symbolically important and financially lucrative for the state.[62] The Venezuela case contains both continuities and ruptures with the past. For the most part, new policies and orientations are being fashioned from within neoliberal state institutions, bounded by but also reshaping those institutions. The "post" in post-neoliberal does not intend to imply that neoliberalism has been superseded but rather that the state is grappling with the legacy of neoliberalism, responding to and at times providing alternatives to the neoliberal model.

In contrast to the ideal type formulations of neoliberalism as a set of economic reforms that were adopted uniformly across third-world debtor nations, there is a growing sense that neoliberalism is a "moving target, subject to hybridizations" and that it consists of "different rationalities and techniques, often working at odds with each other."[63] Neoliberal governmentality is just one modality of power working among others. In Venezuela under Chávez, neoliberal rationality fuses with a rentier liberalism in the contours of a hybrid state formation. The task of ethnography is to identify the scope of liberal and neoliberal logics as they come into collision with new forms of collective action. It is often the disjuncture between anti-neoliberal rhetoric and market-based rationalities that opens a space for critique by social movements.

This raises the specter of not just a post-neoliberal order but a post-neoliberal social imaginary, where alternative visions are being put on the agenda by social movements. According to Alejandro Grimson and Gabriel Kessler, the post-neoliberal imaginary refers to the new contestatory narratives and forms of collective action that are dislodging neoliberalism from its quasi-hegemonic position.[64] As Nancy Postero has argued, the emergence of alternative and collective responses to neoliberalism shows the limitations of theories of neoliberal governmentality, which have tended to focus mainly on the production of consent to regimes of structural adjustment.[65] We need to combine Foucauldian theories of governmentality with a Gramscian notion of hegemony, in order to account more fully for the contested nature of power.

EVERYDAY WARS OF POSITION

Just as in earlier eras of Venezuelan politics, class struggle in a Chávez era has centered on the state and access to the state. The difference with earlier periods is that the unifying nature of the state as a force that claimed to stand above and bring together different classes has been disrupted with the appearance of a polity divided by race and class.[66] Sectors of the poor and marginalized majority have aligned themselves with Chávez in order to wrest control of the state—and its considerable oil resources—away from the hands of multinationals and the privileged, transnational elites. Ongoing struggles for control over the state apparatus include the general elections of 1998, Chávez's standing for reelection in 1999 under a new constitution, and the general elections of 2006, as well as responses from the opposition who orchestrated a coup in April 2002 and attempted to legally remove Chávez from office through a recall referendum in August 2004. Urban social movements were central participants in these battles.

But beyond these larger struggles over the state apparatus, I argue that the structures and discourses of exclusion are being contested in a range of quotidian sites, through everyday wars of position. My formulation "everyday wars of position" combines Antonio Gramsci's term with James Scott's concept of "everyday forms" of resistance and "lo cotidiano," (the everyday) invoked by social movements themselves, in order to describe the multiple battles that they participated in daily on numerous fronts. Although Gramsci was concerned with hegemony in a negative sense as domination, he was also interested in hegemony in a positive sense, looking at how subordinate populations employ wars of position to remake their material and social worlds. He used the military metaphor "wars of position" to describe political struggle between classes. In contrast to the Leninist notion of a vanguard party that would lead the working classes to victory, Gramsci sees conflict as being fought out in the trenches of society, where incremental changes could help to shift the relation of the forces in conflict and build counterhegemonies.[67] Alongside contests over the state apparatus, this book shows the everyday battles in sites of civil society, culture, and media. And instead of looking only at confrontations between Chávez and the opposition, my study suggests more complex dynamics of power and contestation as urban social movements clash with the instrumental rationalities of the post-neoliberal state.

As the urban poor mobilized in defense of their rights and took to the streets during the 1990s, they challenged an exclusionary notion of civil society. The shrinkage of the state as a result of neoliberal policies had led to the growing focus on civil society as the arena of social action. After Chávez was elected, middle-class sectors and business elites constructed themselves as an organized and oppositional "civil society," while they vilified barrio residents as "uncivil society." In response, cultural groupings in the barrios organized festivals and cultural events and painted murals where they sought to define their identity on their own terms, using the past as a reservoir of images and symbols. Through celebrations of the fiesta of San Juan organized by Totoño, El Gordo, and the Grupo Autóctono, and murals of indigenous chiefs and the popular Simón Bolívar painted by La Piedrita and the CCSB, barrio residents put forth a local historical narrative of identity and belonging that challenged the universalistic pretensions of civil society. Under the local administration of opposition mayor Alfredo Peña, barrio residents faced police harassment and intimidation as they tried to organize their fiestas.

Another battlefield opened up on the level of media and access to information. Cutbacks to the public sector had involved substantial deregulation of the media: the Pérez and Caldera administrations had expanded concessions to media corporations, leading to the centralization of the media in a small number of private conglomerates like the Cisneros group and the 1BC group of Phelps-Granier. These groups defended against attempts at media reform, arguing that regulation of the media was an attack on the citizen's right to information.[68] Media monopoly edged out smaller and regional media outlets, linking all networks by chain to a small group of corporations. Following Chávez's election as president in 1998, and especially during the lead-up to the coup in April 11–13, 2002, the private media ran a fierce campaign to discredit him. On April 11, 2002, the leaders of the coup took the government-owned station Channel 8 off the air, the private media falsely broadcast that Chávez had resigned, and then ran its regular broadcast with no further information. Community radio and print media played an important role in releasing news about the coup and restoring Chávez to power on April 13. For many this was a wake-up call to develop their own local forms of media in the face of corporate consolidation and ownership of mass media.

Barrio-based groups started up their own radio stations or consolidated existing ones. Community radio collectives took advantage of their high locales to compete with mass media for airspace, and they made creative use of text messages, Internet, and local networks of communication to build a following. The idea that media should be locally managed, collectively owned, and facilitate a plurality of viewpoints was counter to the homogenization and concentration of media that had occurred as a result of media deregulation and privatization.

In their everyday battles with the opposition, the private media, and the police, urban social movements drew on the symbol of Chávez to bolster their position. As they created new forms of sociability, alternative cultural representations, and locally managed forms of media, these sectors allied themselves with Chávez. They made frequent reference to the constitution of 1999 to justify their rights to resources and claims over public space. The Chávez administration in turn sought to promote these movements through legislation and funding. Following the coup in 2002, Chávez gave substantial money toward the development of community radio stations. After the Chavista mayor Juan Barreto replaced Peña in 2004, he also began to give greater funding to local cultural groups. Government support was partly responsible for the flourishing of media and cultural activities at the grassroots level.

But closer collaboration between urban social movements and the state brought into relief the contradictions of the post-neoliberal state, as social movements collided with the instrumental rationalities of bureaucrats. Fiesta organizers and theater activists were subject to strategies of incorporation by arts administrators who saw culture as a tool for promoting economic growth and ameliorating social problems. Community media producers protested the neoliberal rationalities of state media agencies that required them to justify the costs and benefits of investment in their projects. The instrumental logics that guided state agencies were not only neoliberal; they also included liberal strategies of political incorporation. As Scott has argued, utilitarian rationalities are a feature of modern statecraft, observed in a range of sites and historical eras.[69] In making my argument, I am not conflating the instrumental logics of political incorporation and neoliberalism. Political incorporation was associated with earlier periods of national-populism, when state sponsorship was geared toward ideological goals of national unity and building clientilist linkages between state and society. Neoliberal rationalities are linked to the era of the 1990s when all aspects of social and political life were made subject to the market. Both of these logics appear and combine under the post-neoliberal state, and they may share elements in common, but they are distinct from one another in both goals and consequences.

I do not advocate an antistate position either. Given a situation of increasing global inequalities and marginality, the alliance between progressive social movements and left-wing states is more important than ever. What I am criticizing is the hierarchy and verticality that characterizes the instrumental approach of the state at certain moments. Tania Murray Li calls this the "will to improve," as a "hierarchy that separates trustees from the people whose capacities need to be enhanced, or behaviors corrected."[70] It assumes that those making the interventions are experts with the power to diagnose and design solutions for beneficiaries. It is not only state administrators who are guided by this will to improve— the tendency also appears among Chavista political parties and the vanguards of social movements themselves.

In contrast to this hierarchical relation, I look to state-society alliances where social movements access state power from the bottom up. In Bolivia, as Forrest Hylton and Sinclair Thomson argue, "impressive popular power has flowed from the bottom up, setting the parameters for national political and economic debate and putting in place authorities at the national as well as regional and local levels."[71] Alliances forged soon after 2000 against the privatization of water (the Water Wars) and for the nationalization of gas (the Gas Wars) provided a strong base from which to contest state power and eventually bring the indigenous leader Evo Morales into office. The partnership between the Chávez government and social movements in rewriting the constitution and instituting poverty alleviation measures is likewise an example of such fruitful state-society collaboration. Rather than seeing themselves in opposition to the state, social movements have employed a position of what the Aymara sociologist Pablo Mamani has called "strategic ambiguity," identifying themselves as part of the state in order to highlight the new forms of access and inclusion that have opened up, but maintaining a sense of their autonomy to be able to put pressure on the state where necessary. This monitoring of the state from below holds the potential for realizing a substantive democracy—a much deeper and more participatory form of democracy than the periodic elections and separation of powers touted by advocates of procedural democracy.

Within everyday wars of position, the heterogeneous set of urban movements are located differentially vis-à-vis the state. State-promoted organizations like the Bolivarian Circles, the Unidades de Batalla Electoral (Units of Electoral Battle, UBES) and the Unidades de Batalla Social (Units of Social Battle, UBSS) have emerged at specific times, proliferated, and then dissipated. While these groups, bolstered by significant state resources and state media promotion, may constitute the majority of barrio-based organizations, they are more dependent on the state for their existence. By contrast, urban social movements have longer histories that mostly predate the Chávez government, and they have internal structures of decision making and finances that are independent from state directives. The CSB and Catia TVe have managed to maintain some autonomy, while successfully bargaining for resources from the state and influencing officials at the highest levels. Cultural groups such as the Grupo Autoctono, the cofradía of San Juan, and Itagua have made important gains in providing alternative cultural representations and defining a new model of sociability at the basis of social movements. Those such as Itagua who have made alliances with community media and barrio assemblies have found a means to further develop and project their work. Barrio assemblies in La Vega and community radio networks that emphasize plurality and internal democracy have been most successful in building power from below.

Yet as urban social movements face directly the contradictions of the post-neoliberal state, the divisions among them have become more apparent. Various community media groups, together with cultural groups and local assemblies, have sought to build alliances from the ground up to protest their continued exclusion from the airwaves by state regulatory bodies and the exploitation of natural resources in indigenous populated areas, and to support rural land occupations, among other issues. By contrast, those groups such as Catia TVe, which are more closely aligned with the government, have emerged as brokers and intermediaries, trying to channel discontent from more critical social movements and urging moderation.

ETHNOGRAPHY IN THE CONTEXT OF POLARIZED POLITICS

The nature of my field research on urban social movements that is the basis for this book was less a disinterested inquiry than an attempt to document the lives and histories of ordinary people in a moment of extraordinary social and political change. Like Jeffrey Gould in Nicaragua during the Sandinista era, I found that people would present me to others as someone who was "helping us to write the history of our struggle."[72] Like

Lynn Stephen, I felt that the people I was studying were often friends and collaborators rather than the traditional "informants."[73] Clearly, I was doing more than simply recording the struggles of people in the communities, and my own critical approach did not always coincide with the views of people I was working with. There was also an issue of power relations, as I would decide which voices to represent in my book and how to represent them. I could share in the lives and experiences of my friends, but I was privileged with the ability to move back and forth between the barrios and the first world when I chose to do so.

In a context of vibrant and growing social movements, I found that I had to develop alternative forms of investigation. The traditional ethnographic study focused in one barrio or sector was not possible, as I was continually meeting people who wanted me to visit their sector and see their work. I also realized that residents of each barrio or parish participated in what the popular historian Freddy Hurtado described to me as the "mythification of the barrio," where activists would magnify the rebelliousness and radical history of their own barrio in comparison to others. I was interested in looking comparatively at different sectors, but the classic comparative style of focusing on two or three barrios was also limiting. It became apparent to me that I could get a fuller understanding of how barrio organizations participated in the contemporary historical juncture by looking at a range of organizations, how they interacted with each other and the state, and the broader linkages as well as differences between them. I did spend most of my time working with groups in the parishes of San Agustín, La Vega, and 23 de Enero, in addition to the parish of El Valle where I was staying, although my sites of research often extended beyond these. As I moved among the barrios of Caracas, I realized that these worlds within the shantytowns were an interconnected whole, and selecting one research site would be an artificial enterprise.

Open-ended interviewing was a central method of my investigations. Over the course of my research, I interviewed about 150 musicians, muralists, cultural leaders, barrio residents, *cronistas populares* (popular storytellers), movement leaders and activists, community media activists, local politicians, and directors of institutions. These interviews yielded crucial insights for my investigation, yet they had certain limitations. One problem was that the majority of my interviews tended to be with men. As movement leaders, politicians, and bureaucrats, men had more practice in answering standard interview questions than women, who often held back during interviews. Yet women constituted the majority of social movement participants. Another problem was that people would often give me standard answers to questions, rather than the rich and detailed narratives I would have preferred.

Ethnography was helpful in countering some of these problems and in exploring the internal dynamics of urban social movements. I found that it was by spending time with activists in their homes and attending meetings, protests, and cultural events that I was able to become a part of their daily activities and make observations that were not readily apparent through my interview material. This kind of research gave me access to women's worlds; as we joked and worked in the soup kitchens or cooked meals together, I came to learn about them in ways that standard interviewing did not allow. I participated in and recorded celebrations of popular fiestas, assembly meetings in the barrios, and radio programs. I also carried out library and archival research in the Universidad Central de Venezuela (Central University of Venezuela, ucv), the Biblioteca Nacional (National Library), and the Folkloric Institute (fundef), with the help of a local research assistant, Victor Santos. We consulted historical and archival materials in order to build a picture of the development of urban barrios and their ethnic and racial makeup. The combination of these methods helped me to counter some of the limitations I faced with standard field techniques, and it enriched the scope of the research.

Investigating social movements and politics in the midst of such a polarized context as Venezuela under Chávez, one is bound to be forced to articulate one's own position on the political situation. I was constantly questioned by people on both sides of the political spectrum: Whose side are you on? Are you a Chavista? I had to maintain a fine balance between saying what I thought people wanted me to say in order to collect the information I needed, or describing my own thoughts, complex and evolving as they always were. While my own feelings about the Venezuelan situation did not often fit into established categories, I also realized the importance of staking a position, so that people knew where I stood and how the material I was gathering would be used when I returned to the United States. I let people know that I was supportive of "the proceso." Like many of those I came across through my work in the barrios, I was ambivalent about the top-down aspects of the Bolivarian revolution. But I identified with and supported the work of the many men and women who saw themselves as constructing a new society through many fronts, with electoral politics itself a crucial battleground.

My own academic and racial background often positioned me for others. My prior experiences living and carrying out field research in Cuba were a stigma for some opposition types, given the close relationships between former Cuban president Fidel Castro and Venezuela's Chávez. When polite, middle-class fellow passengers on the flight from Newark to Caracas asked what I do, and I mentioned my Cuba experience, at best the conversation would turn to one of cordial disinterest, and at worst open hostility. By contrast, for social movement leaders and activists in the barrios, this previous work gave me credibility and helped to reduce suspicions of me as a foreigner. Among my barrio friends I could sense both a level of discomfort with my status as an outsider and a close familiarity, which were expressed in alternate joking references to me as a "gringa australiana" working as a spy for the FBI, or the "chica" from la India ("La India de la Vega," Yajaira would say in squeals of laughter, referring to a landmark, the Redoma de la India, at the entrance to La Vega).

My brown skin helped me blend in to the poorer urban communities where I lived; I was often taken for a Venezuelan person from the barrios. I could move from one barrio to the next with ease, but I sometimes encountered problems when I went to the middle-class and upper-class areas of Altamira and Los Palos Grandes. On one visit to meet an anthropologist colleague in the higher-income neighborhood of San Bernardino, I lost my way, but none of the white, upper-class women in the street, with their Gucci handbags and Chanel suits, would even look at me when I tried to ask for directions. When I discussed the incident with my anthropologist colleague and several sympathetic white colleagues back in the States, they dismissed it; it was not racism but because I looked like "a hippie from the UCV."[74] By contrast, when I told my friends in the barrio, they understood the racism and elitism that I had experienced, as it is a factor that shapes their everyday lives.

I felt that people were eager to invite me into their homes, their barrios, and their movements, because of their need for visibility and their desire to make their stories known. Given the one-sided media coverage of Venezuelan politics in the foreign press, many activists looked hopefully to my work as a way of countering this publicity by showing something of the other side. I struggled to find a way to reconcile what I myself believed was a crucial task of making this information accessible to a nonacademic public and the limitations of academic work in the United States, where articles in journals and books with academic presses are often read by specialized audiences and may take years to be published. During my field research trips, I began to put together short reports that I sent back to my friends at WBAI radio to put on the air. I worked with young people at the community radio stations in Caracas to put together their own reports to send back to the United States. I also began to write short articles for on-line magazines and English and Spanish-language local newspapers. When I returned to Venezuela, I would bring copies of these pieces and translate them for the activists. This gave me a sense of giving back something tangible to the communities and being a part of the process of social transformation in which they were engaged.

But at the same time, people in the barrios were eager to know about social justice movements and struggles in the United States, and they continually challenged me to think more about my own location and activism back home. When I first met Palmiro, he said to me, "You spend all your time in Caracas with *los negros* from the barrios, but what kind of people are your friends back home?" At an *intercambio* (exchange) organized by a community leader in La Vega, the women of the barrio wanted to know why I traveled to Venezuela, Brazil, Ecuador, and Cuba to learn about social movements, rather than building a social movement in my own country. And another leader from 23 de Enero, Gustavo Borges, pointed out that to do truly collaborative work and exchanges, we foreigners needed to have a base in local communities back home. My barrio friends were critical of the middle-class researchers and solidarity activists who flocked to the newest revolutionary opening.

These were all questions that I struggled with over the years that I visited Venezuela, something made particularly hard by the race-class dynamics and privileged world of academia itself. On coming home from my trips to Venezuela, I began to investigate and get involved with the growing immigrant workers' movements in New York City, working as an organizer with New York Construction Workers United (NYCWU). I was taken with Greg Grandin's idea that the immigrant rights movement was the northern front of a rising insurgency in the south. On return research trips to Venezuela, I noticed that the dynamic of my relationships with people changed;

as we exchanged ideas about organizing, we compared the vilification of immigrant workers and barrio residents, and I gave them access to information that was not readily available. I noticed that with my growing activist involvement back home, the research became less a one-way street and more a collaborative exchange of ideas and information. Of course, I have certain privileges that allow me to be an intermediary and to traverse the globe, while for the urban and working poor those boundaries are more impenetrable than ever. But I hope that one day the interchanges can be directly between the construction workers and domestic workers who are campaigning for their rights and recognition on the streets of New York and their counterparts in Venezuela and elsewhere. I have written this book in that spirit of interchange and mutual learning, and in anticipation of many more conversations to come.

This book is divided into three main parts. Each part moves from a larger, general picture of histories and movements, to the local level, using life histories and specific cases. Part I presents individual and collective histories of the barrios, from the era of guerrilla insurgency, community-based activism, and cultural movements, followed by the debt crisis and neoliberal reforms, to the Chávez period. Chapter 1 explores the self-making of contemporary urban social movements from the 1960s through the 1980s, tracing their genealogy through movements against the dictatorship, urban insurgencies, nonviolent mass action, and cultural resistance. In chapter 2, I address the reshaping of everyday life during the neoliberal era of the 1990s. I look at the making of a neoliberal state, and how this dramatically transformed the state-society relationship, creating a growing divide between the shantytowns and the outside polity. I explore the coming to power of Chávez, contrasting his specific policies and programs with those that preceded his presidency. While chapters 1 and 2 present collective histories and structural analysis of events, chapter 3 narrows the focus to the individual life history of Yajaira, a black woman from San Agustín. Her narrative can present certain insights into how these events were lived and experienced.

Part II moves on to look at various sites where urban social movements are contesting the structures and discourses of exclusion since Chávez has come to power. Chapter 4 describes the religious fiestas and murals in the barrios of Caracas, and examines the ways in which they are providing alternative social imaginaries to the exclusionary discourse of civil society.

Chapter 5 focuses on the movement of community media, and how it is providing opportunities for barrio residents to access the airwaves in the face of media consolidation. Chapter 6 looks at the takeover of an abandoned theater by a group of residents in San Agustín, and its transformation into a culture house. The chapters explore the creation of alternative forms of cultural identity, the resignification of public space, and the deployment of historical memory by social movements. These movements have been encouraged and funded by Chávez. But each of these chapters also discusses the obstacles that these movements encounter as they interface with the policies and rationalities of a hybrid post-neoliberal state.

Part III addresses the attempts of urban social movements to build more enduring structures of representation and accountability from the bottom up, as a way of pushing forth their agenda. In chapter 7, I look at the new coalitions being formed between urban and rural sectors, as they put forth a deeper critique of the post-neoliberal state. Through marches against coal mining in Zulia, social movements built new alliances to provide an accountability from below. I also look at the internal dynamics of these alliances—including gender and regional inequalities, paternalism, and hierarchy that are present—and the struggles of social movements to address issues of their own internal democracy. The final chapter ends with a consideration of the comparative dimensions of the Venezuela case, the role of cities in a new kind of politics, and a speculation on what post-neoliberal futures might look like.

A NOTE ON NAMES

I thought a lot about the convention of anonymity that is usually followed by ethnographers to protect the people that they work with. I agree with the sentiment expressed by the anthropologist Nancy Scheper-Hughes that "anonymity makes us forget that we owe our anthropological subjects the same degree of courtesy, empathy, and friendship in writing that we generally extend to them face to face in the field, where they are not our subjects but our companions and without whom we quite literally could not survive."[75] Rather than decide on my own whether or not to make someone in the book anonymous, I wanted to leave the choice to my collaborators, especially those who appeared frequently. This introduced some difficulties because the book is written in English, and since my collaborators do not read English, they had no idea how they were being portrayed. The unwieldy solution was for me to translate portions of the manuscript, either in written form or verbally, for my collaborators. This led to some challenging discussions, as I was asked to remove or rework certain sections and my interpretations were questioned. In the end, all the collaborators who read the text expressed a wish to be fully identified. The process deepened my own understanding and the resulting text is more of a co-production than might otherwise have resulted.

In the case of those who did not read the manuscript, I used the real names of social movement leaders such as fiesta organizers and community radio directors who were well-known and public persons. I changed the names of administrators, drug dealers, and the residential complex where I lived, to avoid subjecting individuals to scrutiny or harassment. All of the other places and the dates are real.

I INDIVIDUAL AND COLLECTIVE HISTORIES

The histories of the urban shantytowns are marked on their physical spaces and preserved in the names of the barrios and the memories of their residents. On the central wall of the "Afinque de Marín," a historic meeting place in Barrio Marín of San Agustín, there is a mural of the members of the radical musical ensemble Grupo Madera. Most members of the group died in a tragic boat accident in the Orinoco while on tour in 1980. On one side of the mural are images of three of the Ramos sisters, with their Afros, hoop earrings, and African head wraps. In popular lore, it is said that when their boat was sinking, the three sisters held hands and jumped together to their death. Above this and on the other side of the mural are the musicians in action, dancing, laughing, playing the guitar, immortalized forever as youthful and vibrant as when they were alive.

In the zone bordering the Avenida Sucre in 23 de Enero, many buildings show the bullet marks from the tragic days following the Caracazo, when widespread popular riots were faced with massive state repression. As residents describe it, the large project-like buildings in Monte Piedad and the Zona Central looked like colanders after the attack. The buildings, blocks, and walls of the parish bore the marks of the brutal offensive launched by the security forces and were a stark reminder to residents of the neighbors, cousins, friends, and other family members killed in the crossfire.

The walls of Monte Piedad Arriba contain portraits of young men who have died in prison or were killed by security forces. One portrait of a young man named Cheo contains the following phrase: "Jail is the place transformed into a school where the revolutionary deepens their ideas to later make them into reality." Another portrait of an activist, Carlos Vielma, has the caption "Those who die for life cannot be called dead," a quote from the revolutionary Venezuelan folksinger Ali Primera. Through murals, barrio residents commemorate the dead and incorporate their memory as part of their present.

Historical memory and narratives of resistance are central to the self-making of contemporary urban movements. Community leaders in the barrios trace their genealogy from the clandestine movements against the military regime in the 1950s, through to the period of guerrilla struggle in the 1960s, the cultural activism of the 1970s, and the emergence of new forms of urban resistance in the 1980s. At the same time, urban movements have participated in shifting clientelist relationships with the state, fostered over three decades of a redistributive welfare state, passing through a neoliberal state, and refashioned under Chávez. The approach of contemporary urban sectors to the Chávez government contains these elements of both autonomy as grounded in histories of local struggle and mutual dependency that has evolved over time. We can more fully understand this contemporary dynamic by exploring the formation of urban social movements in the barrios and their embeddedness in local political histories.

MIGRATION AND THE FORMATION OF THE BARRIOS

Caracas initially underwent some degree of urbanization under the administration of Antonio Guzmán Blanco (1870–88). But it did not experience comprehensive urbanization until the 1930s, by which time most other Latin American capitals had already been consolidated.[1] Following the Federal War of 1859–63, the Venezuelan coffee economy expanded rapidly, making Venezuela the world's third-largest coffee exporter by 1890.[2] However, as the historian Arturo Almandoz describes, Caracas was mostly a commercial and bureaucratic outpost for the coffee and cocoa exporter until the emergence of the oil economy in the 1920s.[3] Oil fueled certain administrative, legal, and infrastructure reforms in the capital under the administration of Juan Vicente Gómez (1908–35).[4] The shift from coffee production as the economic base of the country to an oil economy also encouraged migration from rural to urban areas.

One of the first working-class neighborhoods to emerge in the west of the city was San Agustín del Sur. The architect Luis Roche was responsible for the elite, middle-class urbanización San Agustín del Norte in the 1920s. At this time, San Agustín del Sur was a *cerro*, a hillside dotted with make-shift homes. The majority of migrants residing in the cerro came from the predominantly Afro-Venezuelan, coastal regions of the state of Miranda. According to the local popular historian Antonio "Pelon" Marrero, the sectors forming in the cerro took their names from the trees and fruits found in their area: La Ceiba, La Charneca, El Mamón, El Manguito, and Los Almendrones.[5] As urbanization proceeded in San Agustín del Norte, Roche began to claim the central avenue of San Agustín del Sur to house his construction workers, mostly Portuguese and Italian immigrants.[6] Given growing demand for housing, the Banco Obrero was charged with the construction of housing in San Agustín del Sur during the 1920s, and they also built passageways in La Ceiba, Manguito, and Mamón, which were inaugurated in 1932.[7] Other areas being developed in the west of Caracas included the upper-class enclave Cuidad Nueva (New City), now known as El Paraíso.

Prior to the 1920s, the east of the center was mostly *haciendas*, or large plantation estates, and hills covered with forests of trees. The expansion of Caracas toward the east was boosted with a decree passed on April 19, 1920. As middle- and upper-class groups sought to escape from the increasingly populated center, the former haciendas in the east were urbanized. Roche, along with other entrepreneurs such as Santiago Alfonzo Rivas and Juan Bernardo Arismendi, was responsible for the construction of areas such as La Florida, El Recreo, and Los Palos Grandes.[8] As these development projects proceeded and trees were being cut down, sawmills were built along the principal avenue of San Agustín del Sur in order to process this wood.[9] The wood factories were run by Jewish immigrants, who brought the technology of wood processing.[10] These factories were an important source of work for the working-class residents of San Agustín del Sur. Another source of work was the mortadella factories; the technology of meat processing was brought by the Italian immigrants. Marrero told me that mortadella was a distinctly working-class meat associated with San Agustín del Sur, as compared with the ham that was eaten by the middle classes in San Agustín del Norte. Factories were also constructed in other parts of the city. In 1907, the National Cement Factory was built in La Vega. The establishment of the cement factory served as a pole of attraction for other industries, incorporating migrants into industrial production as factory workers.[11] A curtain factory was built in 1920, followed by a confectionery factory in 1938. Rural migrants who came to the city found jobs in these factories.

The expansion of oil production also began to increase the pace of urbanization, albeit indirectly. Charles Bergquist describes how during the labor-intensive period of oil exploration, drilling, and construction of facilities, large numbers of workers were drawn away from agricultural work and into remote oil zones. Even as labor demand in the oil fields began to decline during subsequent phases of production, oil production was stimulating economic development in the oil zones and agriculture suffered. Meanwhile, the increasing volume of foreign trade due to oil production financed a growing bureaucracy, local commercial services, public works, social programs, and development programs in the capital city of Caracas.[12] As agriculture declined, rural migrants came to Caracas for jobs in the public sector, public works programs, and the service industry.

Caracas experienced its first major wave of rural migration in the 1930s.[13] Migrants to the city came from all across the country, from the Andes, Miranda, Aragua, Yaracuy, and Sucre among other regions. As the chronicler Rafael Quintero recounts, the migrants would arrive at the Nuevo Circo Terminal, a few minutes' walk from San Agustín.[14] They would be picked up by a relative or friend, who would house them for a few days. Then they would begin to construct their own *rancho*, a precarious zinc roof house with walls of carton, cardboard, or wood, and they would buy chickens and pigs to raise. In this way, rural customs and life gained a foothold in the city.

One of the central institutions of barrio life was the *bodega*, a small grocery store up in the cerro. According to Quintero, "There you could obtain almost everything: from salted fish to fruits and nuts, pots, pans, skillets, kerosene for cooking (in that time there was no gas or electricity), coal for those who didn't have kerosene cookers, beans, platanos, potato, yucca, sweet potato, red and white onions, mortadella, sardines and tuna in cans."[15] The bodegas were the center of barrio life because of the goods they provided and their generation of economic activity. But they were also spaces of social interaction: "the place to comment on the happenings of the barrio, the latest fight between Teófila and her husband where 'they destroyed all the pots and plates around, and I don't believe it, but they say she left with one of her cousins for Cochecito.' "[16] People would gather at the bodega to catch up on the latest gossip. The bodega owners were also known to give goods on credit to those without funds, or loans for medical emergencies. Later, during the years of the insurgency against the dictatorship, bodega owners sympathetic to the cause aided in the formation of guerrilla units.

After the death of Gómez in 1935, his vast landholdings were inherited by the government. As a result, much of the land upon which newly arrived residents constructed their houses was the property of the government. Some owners laid claim to the property, while others bought their parcel of land from the municipality. But these were a minority, and most barrio residents were technically squatters.[17] By 1936, special laws were enacted to organize the Federal District of Caracas and the federal territories. The Organic Law of the Federal District passed in 1936 outlined the new structure consisting of the Departamento Libertador and the urban *parroquias*, or parishes, which consisted of Catedral, Santa Teresa, Santa Rosalía, Candelaria, San José, La Pastora, Altagracia, San Juan, San Agustín, Sucre, and the outside regions of La Vega, El Valle, El Recreo, Antímano, and Macarao.[18] From 1501, the Spanish Crown had divided the capital city into "ecclesiatical territories" known as parishes and controlled by priests.[19] In the Constitution of 1811, the parish was also given a civil and political-administrative character.[20] The recognition of new urban parishes in 1936 marked an important phase in their consolidation and development.

A second major wave of immigration took place in the 1950s, under the rule of the military leader Marcos Pérez Jiménez (1950–57), who took power after a brief period of democratic rule. Pérez Jiménez's seven-year presidency was a period of rapid economic growth during which there was a doubling of oil production. Pérez Jiménez pursued a policy of the New National Ideal, investing large amounts of capital in urban infrastructure.[21] The luxury hotels, major highways, monuments, and university campus constructed by his administration were projected as symbols of modernity and progress.[22] The government demolished several existing communities of ranchos, banned the construction of new ranchos, and constructed popular blocks as a way of addressing the need for housing for rural migrant workers.[23] These popular housing projects were part of the National Housing Plan, directed by Carlos Raúl Villanueva at the Banco Obrero. On December 2, 1955, Pérez Jiménez inaugurated four groups of housing projects, which consisted of 13 buildings of 15 stories and 52 buildings of 4 stories, which contained 2,366 apartments. The buildings were built at the intersection of the center and west of the city, facing the Miraflores palace.[24] They were baptized "2 de Diciembre," a symbolic inauguration date that celebrated Pérez Jiménez's electoral coup of 1952.[25] The buildings were publicized as "preferential access for families living in the unhealthy ranchos."[26] Subsequent buildings were inaugurated in 1956 and 1957, and at the time of the transition to democracy in 1958 many were still uninhabited.

During the 1940s and 1950s there was a burgeoning movement supported by people in the barrios against the military regime. Party militants from Acción Democrática (Democratic Action, AD, or Adecos) and the Communist Party of Venezuela (PCV) built their support bases among popular sectors. At certain times the AD had a more confrontational antiestablishment stance than the PCV, which was more moderate in their critique of the military regime.[27] The parish of San Agustín played an important role in the demonstrations against the regime, for its location is close to the center of the city. Barrio Marín served as a refuge for AD leaders.[28] Luisa Alvarez, an older resident of San Agustín, recounted to me that La Charneca in San Agustín del Sur was a hideaway for AD-identified student activists from the nearby Universidad Central de Venezuela (Central University of Venezuela, UCV). The students would throw Molotov cocktails at buses and military tanks and then they would run back to hide in the cerros. San Agustín was known as "the most revolutionary parish of the capital, a real bulwark of Acción Democrática."[29] During its brief stint in power from 1945 to 1948, AD made use of state resources to harness popular support and further expand its base in the barrios.

By 1957, a combination of factors, including the exclusion of middle and ascendant sectors of the military from access to power, a growing centralization of political power in the hands of the government, and Pérez Jiménez's decision not to hold multicandidate elections, eroded its support bases and catalyzed a series of coordinated opposition efforts.[30] On January 23, 1958, military rule ended with the flight of Pérez Jiménez from the capital. On this same day, thousands of people took over the apartment complex 2 de Diciembre and renamed it 23 de Enero. Soon after, the area was functioning with hardware stores, grocery stores, bread shops, shoe shops, and even delis.[31] The fall of Pérez Jiménez and the brief military-civilian junta presided over by Admiral Wolfgang Larrazábal heralded a new era for barrio residents.

Over the period of the 1960s, AD consolidated its power and edged out other contenders for power such as the Communist Party. The fall of Pérez Jiménez led to chaos in the streets of the capital, as people clamored for jobs and condemned the oil companies for their support of the military regime.[32] In response, Larrazábal proposed an Emergency Plan, which provided a minimum wage to unemployed workers in Caracas and materials for public works projects in the barrios, leading to the third major wave of migration into the city.[33] The following year the Emergency Plan was replaced by the Plan of Extraordinary Works, which sought to address unemployment through major public works programs as well as to resolve needs such as housing, education, sanitation services, and transport. In order to channel the programs into the barrios, the government created Juntas Pro-Mejoras (Improvement Councils) and Centros Comunales (Communal Centers).[34] The Juntas Pro-Mejoras in the barrios were dominated by political parties, mainly the Communist Party and AD.[35] The juntas organized cultural activities in the barrios, giving resources to many aspiring artists who went on to garner greater national fame and recognition.

The Communist Party had notable support in the barrios for the role that it had played in the downfall of the previous regime, and it was part of the prodemocracy umbrella organization known as the Junta Patriótica (Patriotic Council), formed in 1957. In 1958 and during the first few years of President Rómulo Betancourt's administration, political parties signed pacts including the Pact of Punto Fijo, but the Communist Party was the only party excluded from these pacts. Terry Karl refers to Venezuelan democracy after 1958 as a "pacted democracy,"[36] because fundamental issues including a development model based on foreign capital, state intervention in processes of union bargaining, and heavy subsidization of the oil sector were decided before they could be open to public debate through the holding of elections.

Once in power, AD competed with other parties to win the support and patronage of barrio residents. The government used state resources to finance various new programs in an attempt to displace the Communist Party.[37] These plans were launched through the Central Office of Coordination and Planning (CORDIPLAN), the National Council of the Community, the Ministry of Sanitation and Social Assistance, the National

Institute of Sanitation Works (INOS), and the Foundation for the Development of the Community and Municipal Promotion (FUNDACOMUN).[38] The plans included self-help community projects that were heavily funded by the state.[39] The AD built up a vast network of support in the barrios, including Comités de Barrio (Barrio Committees) and Comités de Base (Base Committees). The AD government sought to utilize the Juntas Pro-Mejoras as instruments of rule.[40] The juntas were seen as conduits to the people, and those junta leaders who were less independent and saw the party interest as greater than the community interest lasted longest in power.[41] In the 1970s, the Juntas de Vecinos were added to these organizations, as local institutions designed to attract resources and distribute them locally.[42] Trade union and peasant organizations were also linked to the ruling party in a corporatist fashion, as the state intervened in collective bargaining in favor of the Confederation of Venezuelan Workers (CTV) and the Venezuelan Peasants Federation.[43] Most local organizations had links to political parties, and their demands for resources and services were channeled through the parties.

This early period inaugurated a new state-society dynamic that was to last for several decades. Samuel Hurtado Salazar describes this dynamic as centered on the redistributive role of the state: "The intervention of the state in the barrios does not occur via the market or private capital, but rather through the system of redistribution that is structurally related to the public sphere, defining the state as the center of political power."[44] Due to the largesse of oil income, the state had considerable leverage to address the social welfare needs of the barrio residents. The state was legitimated as the central place for solving all social problems and there was a "partyization" of all social and political life.[45] Moreover, the system of corporatist clientilism that emerged ensured that people's loyalties were not to their community or to the sector in which they lived but rather to the political party to which they belonged or sympathized.[46] This system had what Edgardo Lander calls a "populist-paternalist-clientilist character,"[47] in that all demands had to be channeled through the state and it created a dependency among the population on the state and political parties.

Most political scientists and sociologists have tended to see clientilism as a hindrance to the true functioning of electoral democracy, by encouraging the exchange of votes for favors, discouraging participation by social movements, and promoting party domination of political life.[48] Populism, as the direct, unmediated relationship between a ruler and the masses, has been linked to the development of patron-clientilism, partisanship, and corporatist bonds.[49] But others have argued that populism and clientilism can provide the vehicle for a more class-based, revolutionary politics. Eric Hobsbawm made the case for "populist legitimism" as a belief by the masses that the ruler represents justice, the people, and their way of life.[50] If the ruler failed to meet these expectations, the people would protest in order to defend their rights. Following from this analysis, scholars have talked about the "Peronist moral economy" in Argentina or the "Sandinista moral economy" in Nicaragua,[51] whereby patron-client relations enable a redistribution of wealth and provide a means of holding the leadership accountable and satisfying basic needs while at the same time containing conflict.

During the post-1958 period of national-populist rule in Venezuela under the AD, machine-based politics similarly created a space for questions of redistribution and inequality to be addressed through the state apparatus, thus controlling popular sectors and reducing social antagonisms. As in the case of Peronist Argentina of the 1940s, the urban working-class masses in Venezuela were to be incorporated into the polity as a recognized social force. This meant changes in the central idioms of everyday political language, with a greater emphasis on dignity of workers and limits on the power of the upper classes to control wealth and resources. In the moral economy of the national-populist period, the ruler was representative of "el pueblo" and charged with upholding its interests. Yet unlike the populist legitimism of the Sandinistas in Nicaragua, the populism of the Peronists and the Adecos was reformist rather than revolutionary in character. The AD sought to build a multiclass, reformist party, in pursuit of capitalist development together with propertied interests.[52] The leadership demobilized the working class and incorporated unions into the state, establishing collective bargaining as the only channel by which workers could exert pressure.[53] The exclusion of the left from agreements and pacts reinforced the shift of the AD toward a centrist political program.

While the clientilist political machine of the Adecos developed deep roots in Venezuelan society, there were sectors and groups in the barrios who were dissatisfied with the conditions of "pacted democracy." The exclusion of the Communist Party had serious repercussions for the stability of the future regime. There were also dissenting voices within the AD,

particularly among the militant youth who had participated in the clandestine struggle against military rule. In April 1960, the youth branch of
the AD left the party and formed the Movement of the Revolutionary Left
(MIR), allied with the Communist Party. The Cuban revolution under the
leadership of Fidel Castro had also taken place on January 1, 1959, and this
had an important impact in Venezuela and Latin America. Juan Contreras,
a community organizer who later founded the Coordinadora Simón Bolívar in 23 de Enero, related, "In this moment [1960s] people began to grow
beards, take up arms and go to the mountains; whether or not it was
justified they thought they could do what Fidel had done." Leftists and
revolutionaries formed small guerrilla units in the mountains and in the
barrios. In the period of the 1960s, there were many armed confrontations
as guerrillas tried to take power. The barrio 23 de Enero was the focus of
much conflict and urban insurgency. According to Juan, "The guerillas
placed themselves on the roofs of the buildings as snipers to confront the
armed forces of public order, such as the police, the political police, the
army, and the National Guard, and as a consequence many youth were
assassinated and persecuted." San Agustín was also important to the development of the guerrilla movement, and the barrios served as a refuge for
the insurgents. During these days the police would come combing the
barrios for insurgents; sometimes they would come in plainclothes, wearing a handkerchief for identification to avoid killing each other by mistake.[54] In La Vega, armed guerrillas carried out Robin Hood–type expropriations.[55] As had been the case during the earlier movement against
military rule, the barrios once again became the focus of oppositional
movements.

The 1960s were the most intense years of the armed struggle, the for-
mative years for many contemporary leaders of community organizations
in the barrios. "In one form or another we are the result of all of this history
that has to do with the parish," says Juan. "We, especially myself and many
compañeros who are today part of the Coordinadora, grew up seeing this.
We are the heirs of all these people, of all of this struggle that began in
those years and from a young age we were incorporated into the political
struggle." Some activists such as Edgar "El Gordo" Pérez in La Vega later
criticized what he saw as a "Cuban recipe for revolution" adopted by the
guerrillas. But the vision and the struggle of the guerrillas remained in the
memory of many barrio residents, particularly the young people coming of

age in that period. The partial autonomy of urban social movements was established during these years of armed struggle, especially in parishes such as 23 de Enero. Guerrilla activists forged an alternate pole of historical memory that existed alongside and in contrast with deepening clientilist relationships between barrio residents and the state.

PACIFICATION AND COMMUNITY-BASED ACTIVISM OF THE 1970S

The decade of the 1970s was marked by a shift away from the guerrilla tactics of the 1960s. In 1969, Rafael Caldera from the Christian Democratic party COPEI came to power. Caldera presided over what was known as the "pacification" of the guerrilla movements; this involved partially disarming the guerrillas, although some groups remained actively clandestine. The failure of the strategy of armed struggle was confronted in a range of ways: some groups went on to form political parties such as the Movimiento al Socialismo (Movement for Socialism, MAS), some created mass fronts, and others turned to a strategy of cultural activism. David Guss argues that the pacification of guerrilla groups after some ten years of armed struggle coincided with a growing interest in popular culture. In December 1970, a group of former militants held a three day conference, "Cultural Congress against Dependency and Neo-Colonialism." The conference was sponsored by the National Publicity Corporation (CORPA) and participants outlined a New Turn (El Nuevo Viraje) from armed struggle to cultural struggle. The conference heralded the role that was to be played by state-owned companies in the promotion of culture.[56] As the iron industry was nationalized in 1975 and the oil industry in 1976, there were more resources available for sponsoring cultural workshops, teaching and researching traditional music, and the promotion of musical ensembles. Many leftists themselves participated in this movement, calling for a "democratization of culture."[57] The turn away from armed resistance toward cultural struggle partly reflected the depoliticization of the left as a result of pacification. But at the same time, tactics of cultural resistance were woven into the continuing strands of community-based activism that sought to contest the ongoing segregation of the barrios.

Several community leaders in La Vega came of age during the protests and hunger strikes in the barrios led by Belgian *curas obreros* (worker priests). This period saw a growing divide between the established Church, affiliated with the Christian Democrats in power, and a movement of liberation theology started by the Catholic worker priests. The movement of liberation theology was a movement within Catholicism that emphasized the social justice aspects of Christianity. It developed in dialogue with Pope John XXIII and the Second Vatican Council, which had sought to respond to the contemporary challenges facing bishops. One of the foundational documents of liberation theology, "A Theology of Liberation: Perspectives," came from the Peruvian priest Gustavo Gutierrez in 1972. Barrio leaders were drawn to the radical Christian values of liberation theology, consciousness-raising techniques of Paulo Freire, and mass protest actions of the May 1968 worker-students strikes in Paris and anti–Vietnam War marches.[58] The involvement of the Belgian worker priests in La Vega gave strong impetus to the development of a Christian-influenced, mass-based politics in the parish.

Francisco Wuytack was a worker priest based in Barrio Carmen of La Vega. When he arrived in the barrio in March 1966, Wuytack noticed the poor conditions of schooling for the local children, who did not have adequate facilities above the third grade. In 1969, he helped organize a campaign for admission of barrio children to better schools in the neighboring urbanización of El Paraíso. Wuytack said to me, "I thought of entering them into other schools that had availability and I went to the Colegio San José de Tarbes in El Paraíso where there were twelve or sixteen students, but with space for twenty-five or thirty." When he asked if the children could attend this school, he was told that he was a dreamer. Wuytack returned several times with the children and their mothers, who were accused of being a disturbance and wanting to set fire to the school. Wuytack and the women stayed outside the school, singing hymns and chanting, but several were taken to prison and beaten. The activities helped the community to organize and realize the injustices it faced as compared with the neighboring sector of El Paraíso. The protests in El Paraíso were followed by a series of nonviolent protests to demand basic services in other sectors, such as highways, water, electricity, and schools.

In 1970, Wuytack organized a large mass protest outside Congress to demand a law against unemployment, also asking for unemployment benefits for those without work. The protesters denounced the fact that there were more than 7,000 young people unemployed in La Vega alone. The residents gathered in El Paraíso from various sectors of La Vega, and together with residents from other parishes such as El Valle and Antímano they marched to the National Congress. Some 1,200 people gathered for the demonstration. Reminiscent of peaceful mass protest, they formed a large chain of people to defend against police attack. But a special unit of the police, the Cascos Blancos (White Helmets), was deployed against the strikers and dissolved the demonstration with tear gas, arresting several protesters.

After this, Wuytack was hunted down by the police, but he fled several times and hid with the help of barrio residents. In June 1970, when Wuytack was giving a Mass in the small chapel of Barrio Carmen, several military personnel arrived in trucks and demanded that the people come out. Wuytack described it: "The people did not come out and more people came to the Mass. I prolonged the Mass. It was a popular Mass because there were many women who spoke, we sang, there was poetry. It was three hours. And finally the military or police left with their trucks." The next day the police came back and took Wuytack to Maiquetia airport, where he was put on a plane out of the country. Caldera publicly accused Wuytack of interfering in internal politics, and the ecclesiastical authorities approved his deportation, saying that he was organizing illegal street demonstrations.[59] The demonstrations and protests in La Vega continued after Wuytack's departure. In August 1976, following a landslide in the sector Los Canjilones, residents of La Vega mobilized under the leadership of another worker priest, José Antonio Angós. Many residents of the sector were buried alive as a result of the landslide, but the government did not send any rescue team. Hermelinda Machado and other women in different sectors of La Vega carried out major protests, blocking off the entry to La Vega.[60] The government used the tragic events as a means to propose a relocation scheme for barrio residents. In response, Angós organized a hunger strike along with the barrio residents.[61] The worker priests played an important role in stimulating protest and community activism in La Vega during this time.

Community organizers in La Vega such as Freddy Mendoza, Edgar "El Gordo," and Williams Ochoa recall the work of the worker priests as a crucial moment in their own formation. Their parents had migrated to La Vega, and they came to know each other as adolescents in the parish during these protest movements. Freddy says that he was present during the hunger strikes in Los Canjilones, along with El Gordo. Freddy recalls, "It was a hard struggle, the DISIP removed the strikers at two or three a.m.

in the morning at gunpoint and tossed them along the Cota 905."[62] These actions and others were part of the ongoing repression faced by barrio residents, who had no legal process or defense against the security apparatus of the state. After the hunger strikes these local activists began to participate in other struggles, such as the campaign to remove the cement factory of La Vega. The factory produced contamination for an area radius that covered over 1,500 people, leading to respiratory illnesses such as asthma, bronchitis, and lung disease. The campaign was successful and in 1981 the cement factory ceased production. This series of activities involved large numbers of residents and succeeded in uniting them around common demands.

Barrio residents in 23 de Enero had also begun to form sporting, cultural, and community-based organizations during the 1970s. The residents of the popular blocks engaged in similar protest actions as residents of other barrios. They made demands on the government to address the problems of the buildings and the sector, such as electricity, telephone services, and sanitation.[63] Alejandro Velasco argues that pacification under Caldera had created an opening for the kinds of community work that had been sidelined by both militants and the state during the guerrilla era: "An alternative current of activism gained force, one emphasizing community needs over political aims and resorting to unarmed, if not always passive, forms of collective action to achieve results."[64] Velasco describes the emergence of cultural groups such as Movimiento Social, Cultural, y Artístico (Social, Cultural, and Artistic Movement, MOSCA) in the Sierra Maestra sector, Como Gotas de Lluvia Sobre el Desierto (Like Desert Raindrops) in Zona E, theater groups, and drug awareness campaigns. There was a shift in focus from taking state power to collective action focused on local concerns.

In San Agustín, community-based activism emerged in response to government plans for urban remodeling. In his program of governance, Caldera offered to build 100,000 houses in order to provide a solution to housing problems.[65] In 1972, the area of Parque Central was created, which affected those in the barrios of San Agustín del Sur.[66] The government demolished the barrio of Saladillo, a barrio well known for its musical traditions of Gaitera.[67] Caldera promoted a housing program known as "the New San Agustín," which proposed to eliminate the ranchos and to build houses in the lower and middle ranges of the cerros, while the higher ranges of the cerros would become public gardens, uniting the Botanical Gardens and Parque los Caobos.

Through a state agency known as the Centro Simón Bolívar (CSB), the government expropriated the lower and intermediary territories of the Barrio Hornos de Cal and relocated the displaced to the Urbanización La Yerbera. But for the other residents who were to be displaced, the government intended to send them to Valles del Tuy, which would isolate them from their work and schools.[68] Young promoters from the CSB came to the barrio in an attempt to win support for their urban remodeling projects through social activities. They involved people from the parish in baseball teams, choirs, and musical groups such as the San Agustín Popular Choir. They helped barrio youth to edit a newspaper known as *La Realidad* and they organized spiritual retreats.[69] One leader from San Agustín, Jesús "Totoño" Blanco, recounts, "It was a form of getting into the community, so that the people would soften up, sell their houses, and leave. Then the government could demolish their houses and organize their project." But as barrio residents realized that the activities of the CSB were part of a program to displace them, they began to organize on their own.

A group of radical youth from San Agustín del Sur, inspired by Che Guevara, Ho Chi Minh, and Victor Jara, formed the club Wilfredo Carrillo, also known as the Committee against Displacement (Comité contra los desalojos). The committee began in the premises of an abandoned bodega, known as "La Palma," which the young people occupied, cleaned out, and painted.[70] As Quintero recounts, "They visited every street not only of Marín, but in the whole parish, with slides, forums, clear explanations of the objectives and plans for relocation, and with theater. They connected with other similar movements in La Vega and La Pastora, and there were repercussions in the whole of Caracas from what they did here."[71] Residents across the parish became involved in the activities of the young people, and they raised money through raffles and games. The committee proved that the price being paid for each square of land was not that indicated by the Municipal Office of Urban Planning (OMPU). Nevertheless, the CSB continued demolishing sections of La Charneca and Hornos de Cal, and they constructed two buildings, which were not available to barrio residents due to their high prices. The committee continued to protest and finally the work of the CSB was paralyzed, leaving mutilated barrios, open sewers, water shortages, and ruins. One of the biggest casualties of this urban remodeling was the industrial sector north of the main avenue. The CSB had purchased the businesses and sawmills of this sector, which were later abandoned.[72] The remodeling plan was a disaster, and it betrayed the hopes of those who had hoped for positive change.

Carlos Andrés Pérez from AD came to power in 1974 and in his V Plan of the Nation he continued his predecessor's plans for urban remodeling and displacement of barrio residents.[73] But during this period the movement of community resistance in San Agustín grew stronger and was based around the movement "El Afinque de Marín," started by the Grupo Madera in 1977. The members of the Grupo Madera were musicians from different barrios of San Agustín del Sur who worked in salsa orchestras and other musical groups. The members of Madera began to investigate the black movement in Venezuela, and some went back to their place of origin in Barlovento to carry out research on the African slave trade and the distinct places in Africa from which slaves were brought to Venezuela. Others carried out research on salsa music and other musical genres in Venezuela. Members of the group went to the library of the UCV to research fiestas and popular traditions. The group began to perform and create fusions of these "autochthonous" Venezuelan traditions, from guaguanco to Yoruba chants.[74] The Grupo Madera was part of a vibrant cultural revival; similar groups were also started in other barrios of Caracas, among them the Grupo Autoctono, founded by Williams Ochoa in Barrio Carmen of La Vega in 1974. The Grupo Madera was symbolically associated with the small plaza of Barrio Marín, behind the Alameda Theater, where they practiced, held jam sessions, and performed large concerts for barrio residents. At that time, Jesús Blanco, Totoño's father, noted, "Look how these kids *afincan* [get down]."[75] From this phrase came "El Afinque de Marín," as the name of the small plaza and by extension of the movement that formed around the Grupo Madera.

Grupo Madera was a radical cultural movement concerned with building solidarity and unity among the members of the barrio and with other groups nationally. According to Nelly Ramos, one of the surviving members of the group, the members of Grupo Madera wanted to create an artistic project of quality and dignity, as well as to "forge an ideological consciousness . . . above all, to give incentive to all the participants to define their corresponding role as the protagonists of a cultural response that was emerging in the heart of the community."[76] The Grupo Madera created a free school for children of the parish, known as Maderita; they took all decisions related to their work in popular assemblies; and at the same time, their music garnered national and international attention.[77] They were part a broader current of socially committed music, or protest music, during this era, which included the nueva trova of Silvio Rodriguez and Carlos Varela in Cuba, the nueva canción of Victor Jara and Violeta Para in Chile, and the civil rights song movement in the United States.

Grupo Madera sought to revive a sense of black pride and dignity. One of the members, Alejandrina Ramos, reinterpreted a poem by the Venezuelan poet Miguel Otero Silva, "El Negro Lorenzo," in a composition known as "Ritual," or "La Negra Lorenza." The subject of Ramos's song composition is the black woman: while Otero Silva's "negro" is the slave of all, Ramos's "negra" is slave to men as well. The reworking of the song with the black woman as the subject points to the intersectionality of race, gender, and class oppression and attempts to overcome this oppression: "Black woman, slave of all, I am no-one's slave." With their natural Afro hairstyles and African clothing, the black women of Grupo Madera launched a struggle of cultural resistance, what the song refers to as "rebelde el pelo," or "rebellion of hair." Grupo Madera reclaimed black subjectivity and revindicated black culture as the basis of an autochthonous culture.

The rural is a significant trope of rebellion and roots in the music of Grupo Madera. In the song "Ritual," "Negra del tuy," refers to the southwest region of Valles del Tuy, the origin of many migrants to San Agustín. Agricultural labor in the cane fields is also presented as a symbol of honest labor and revolutionary spirit. In another song, "Compañeros," they sing: "The land that you cultivate is your present / In the future it is your wellbeing / Don't abandon the land *compañero* / And history will thank you." As they traveled back to Barlovento and other rural regions in Venezuela, Grupo Madera sought to reengage with their rural roots; in contrast to the indignities and harsh realities of urban life they saw the rural as a place of refuge and hope. But the urban context was the source of their identity, and in their song "Canción con todos" (Song with all), they refer to Barrio Marín: "From this barrio has emerged my feeling and my expression that I show you now." In contrast to the stigma associated with being of African descent and from the barrio, the musicians of Grupo Madera sought to revindicate race and place as the basis for their movement.

These vibrant social movements in the barrios suffered some setbacks in the early 1980s, under the administration of Luis Herrera Campíns. In August 1980, several of the members of Grupo Madera died in a tragic boat accident that many believed to be a deliberate act of negligence on the part of the government. The Grupo Madera had been invited to come to the Amazonas by the Ministry of Youth in the Amazonian Federal Territory. As the boat crossed the Orinoco River during a turbulent storm, it sank, and eleven members of the group drowned. The journalist Alexis Rosas confirmed the suspicions held by many community activists of government involvement in the accident. Rosas says that there were too many indicators of negligence for the accident to be fortuitous: the captain of the ship was drunk and during the accident he abandoned the ship rather than organizing a rescue, and the life vests were locked up in compartments. Knowing that crossing the Orinoco in winter required a captain with expertise, the ministry had put the lives of the group in the hands of an inexperienced sailor.[78] After the accident, the president of the Youth Ministry, Charles Brewer Carías, protected the captain by concealing his identity. For the residents of San Agustín del Sur, this was a sad moment. As one resident noted, "Everyone identified strongly with this tragedy and it was very painful. We held vigils in the houses of some families of the group, to await further news . . . The amount of people was impressionable, the plaza filled as though there was a meeting or a march. And everyone was there crying and singing the songs and paying homage to them with coffins and later we accompanied them to the cemeteries." The Madera tragedy marked a moment of decline for some sectors of urban popular movements and was followed by a growing middle-class involvement in politics during the 1980s.

THE EMERGENCE OF THE NEIGHBORHOOD MOVEMENT

The 1980s saw the growth and consolidation of the neighborhood associations (*asociaciones de vecinos*), a self-help and cross-class movement of residents organized to resolve local problems. The neighborhood movement had emerged among middle- and upper-class sectors in the early 1970s as a means of defending the interests of these sectors against political parties and mayors.[79] In 1971, fourteen wealthy neighborhood associations founded the Federation of Associations of Urban Communities (FACUR).[80] One of the aims of the neighborhood movement was to challenge city construction projects that violated official ordinances such as the installation of commercial shopping centers in residential areas or the elimination of green areas.[81] Neighborhood movements initially consisted of advocacy groups that represented the shared interests of the middle- and upper-class residents of the sector.

The middle and upper classes began to play an important role in politics during the 1980s, especially given the declining legitimacy of political parties resulting from internal problems and corruption. In 1978, middle-class groups secured the passage of a law known as the Organic Law of Municipal Regimes (LORM) that gave neighborhood associations rights of exclusive representation of their communities and also encouraged municipalities to form new associations.[82] Following this ordinance, there was a boom in neighborhood movements among different social sectors and regions of Venezuela. Given the reduced resources available through political patronage to satisfy the subsistence needs of the poor, the neighborhood movement began to spread to the barrios.[83] But unlike the middle- and upper-class neighborhood movements, the neighborhood associations in the barrios functioned in a similar way to the Juntas Pro-Mejoras and were strongly dominated by the AD.[84] In La Vega, fifty-six neighborhood movements were grouped into a Front for Integration of the Community (FREINDECO), which was said to be an initiative of the AD.[85] As did previous committees and organizations, the associations channeled local demands through political parties.

The neighborhood movement was promoted as the dominant model of citizen participation during the 1980s. According to Lander, the neighborhood movement proposed a "new concept of citizenship" that was critical of clientilism, citizen passivity, and the involvement of political parties and the state in every aspect of community life. But as Lander goes on to argue, "The prototype of the good citizen is a neighbor of the middle-upper classes who organizes in defense of their property." Popular sectors are not seen as citizens with equal rights but as potential threats to property and security.[86] In this model, citizenship is linked to property and has as its ends the defense of property and the preservation of the privileges of middle-class urban spaces. Barrio neighborhood groups uncritically adopted the approach of the middle-class groups in relation to problems such as delinquency. For instance, one barrio-based neighborhood movement in Los Erasos called police to hunt down wayward youth, followed by a "re-education" campaign, rather than probing the structural causes of crime and delinquency.[87] Neighborhood movements in the barrios favored this kind of "law and order" approach, as compared to a more radical analysis of social conditions.

Other middle class–led movements such as the feminist movement also grew during this period. Like the neighborhood movements, feminist groups sought to establish independence from party politics. During the early 1980s, the professional women's organization Venezuelan Federation of Female Lawyers (FEVA) organized a campaign to reform the Civil Code. The campaign sought equal rights for wives and husbands regarding property and divorce, and equal rights for children born out of wedlock.[88] The success of the reform, passed by Congress in July 1982, was due to the coalition-building and broad tactics applied by the women. Some of the reform provisions did affect poor women, who were organized in groups known as Círculos Femeninos (Feminine Circles). But as Elizabeth Friedman notes, "Most of the reform provisions reflected a middle- or upper-class perspective—for example, because poor women rarely got married, they would not benefit from a changed divorce law, and their partners usually did not have property to share or inheritance to leave."[89] These class biases were also reflected in later campaigns, such as the campaign to reform the Labor Law. Since most of the reform leaders were middle- and upper-class women who relied on domestic labor, the rights of domestic workers were not included in the campaign.[90] While efforts in women's organizing did impact poor women somewhat, these campaigns were more focused on the demands of middle-class, professional women.

DECENTRALIZATION AND NEW CHANNELS
OF POPULAR PARTICIPATION

The tendencies toward decentralization in the 1980s, from which the middle-class neighborhood movements emerged, had various contradictory effects. Decentralization was carried out as part of a package of neoliberal reforms that will be explored in detail in the next chapter. It went hand in hand with privatization; as public services were dismantled, they were turned over to private enterprises or they were handed off to municipal governments, without the corresponding resources. Under the 1978 LORM, municipal governments were entrusted with the administration of a range of basic services, including aqueducts, drainage, electricity, gas, transport, fire and emergency services, and police.[91] In 1984, the Presidential Commission for Reform of the State (COPRE) proposed a slate of reforms that, in addition to transference of powers from the central government to regional and municipal levels, sought reforms of the judicial system, the electoral system, political parties, and the civil service.[92] The passing of the New Organic Law of Municipal Regimes in 1989—an elaboration and reform of LORM—gave greater fiscal independence to municipalities. Within two years, four new municipalities were created in wealthy areas—Sucre, El Hatillo, Baruta, and Chacao. The concentration of resources in these areas, as a result of their higher tax base, exacerbated the uneven development of the city.[93] Given the unequal resources between rich and poor municipalities, decentralization often reinforced economic segregation.

At the same time, the greater focus on local and regional units of government marked a shift away from traditional corporatist structures of mediation and allowed new power bases to emerge. In the wake of the unsuccessful coup attempts launched by Chávez in 1992, the proposal by COPRE to replace centrally appointed regional officials with directly elected ones was finally passed. This move strengthened the position of mayors and governors from alternative political parties. During the December 1992 gubernatorial and mayoral election, opposition and alternative parties including COPEI, Causa R, and Movimiento al Socialismo (MAS) won heavily in local and regional elections. But the high abstention rates of up to 50 percent also pointed to the apathy of voters.[94] The CTV, which had been a central channel for mediation between the state and organized workers, declined in importance as its natural constituency of workers shrank and it gradually made unofficial alliances with pro-neoliberal administrations.[95] As established corporatist institutions like trade unions and parties lost power, there was greater space for unaffiliated barrio-based organizations to build their bases. Juan Contreras suggests that policies of decentralization and the changed administrative configuration of the country gave a new impetus to the "parish" as a unit of citizen power.[96] Community activists such as Juan began to talk of "popular power," as "a space capable of producing values and goods locally, which imply processes of negotiation between actors who generate relations of power in function of the production and distribution of wealth and power."[97] The broader crisis of the political system, and the importance of cultural and community work from previous decades, contributed to the development of a politics strongly grounded in the local.

By the period of the mid-1980s, a movement of barrio-based organizations had begun to emerge in contrast to the neighborhood associations that were linked with a middle-class agenda. During the 1980s, barrio sectors were strongly impacted by the debt crisis and subsequent currency devaluation, which led to rising unemployment, a drop in the value of real salaries, growing poverty and inequality, an increase in violent crime, and a marked deterioration in public services.[98] These conditions highlighted the distinct concerns of popular sectors and the need for independent action to address those concerns. As Holston describes in the case of the community organizations in Brazil such as the Society of Friends of the Neighborhood (SABS) and Christian Base Communities (CEBS) that broke away from clientilist relationships with the military government in the 1980s,[99] barrio-based organizations in Caracas also developed new forms of civic participation demanding equal rights to the city, claims to resources, and access to basic services of the legal city. Their demands were not processed through the established channels of mediation such as parties, neighborhood associations, and trade unions but rather through new collectives with their roots in longer-term social movements. Barrio-based organizations engaged in strikes, hijackings of public vehicles, and other protest actions that were outside the repertoire of the more advocacy-oriented neighborhood movements.

One example of a barrio-based movement that incorporated direct action tactics was the Grupo de Trabajo La Piedrita (GTLP), in the sector Arbolitos II of 23 de Enero. The group was born on December 26, 1986, as a result of several popular assemblies in the sector. One member of the group, Valentín Santana, says that they took the name La Piedrita (Little Stone) from the local name for the sector where they live, but also because "a little stone in your shoe irritates you, so we wanted to become the irritation of the barrio so that people would organize." La Piedrita sought to rescue spaces taken over by narcotrafficking, through the organization of popular fiestas and the cleaning up of public spaces for their use by the community. In homage to Che Guevara, the group organized a brigade known as Ernesto Guevara de la Serna. The brigade painted murals in the barrio that commemorated those martyred at the hands of gangs or security forces, promoted political awareness, called attention to issues, and helped formulate complaints. The murals became an important tool of the organization. One of the main muralists of the group, Nelson Santana, said, "If they killed one of our compañeros or if we wanted to protest something with a compañero from another sector, we would go and paint a mural." At the same time, as Velasco describes, La Piedrita had an armed presence in response to police violence, drawing on the repertoire of 1960s groups such as the Tactical Combat Units. According to Velasco, the case of La Piedrita helps to demonstrate the ways in which direct action and community work were being synthesized in the parish.[100] This period saw a convergence of the radical tactics from guerrilla movements of the 1960s with the locally oriented collective action of the 1970s, which found its eventual expression in the formation of the militant, cadre-based organization Coordinadora Simón Bolívar by Juan Contreras and others in 1993.

Newspapers were an important tool for consciousness raising and community work. La Piedrita's newspaper, *La Piedrita*, lasted for over eight years. Community activists in La Vega started the newspaper *La Vega Dice*. Freddy Mendoza says that the newspaper had two aims: "one, community work directly in La Vega, and two, a front at the level of the workers of Yaguara and the industrial sections of Antímano and Carapita." Due to their work with the unions and the newspaper, the community activists won several elections in the unions and local government. During this period, Freddy, Edgar "El Gordo," and other activists of La Vega formed several joint coalitions. In 1986, they made alliances with residents of the neighboring parish of Caricuao to prevent the relocation of the Retén de Catia prison from the parish of Catia to the elevated sector of Las Casitas. They were less successful in halting the construction of a cemetery and had to leave the zone at the last minute. These leaders began to work more within their own sectors in activities such as dance, theater, baseball, and softball. El Gordo helped found a cultural group known as Grupo Caribes de Itagua in his sector of Las Casitas, in the highest part of La Vega. This group also worked with children of the barrio, in sports, music, and cultural activities, linking cultural work with social work in the community.

Just as in the decade of guerrilla activity and the struggles against displacement, the community-based activism that emerged in the mid-1980s asserted the political presence and power of the urban poor, differentiating them from the state and middle-class sectors. The barrio itself came to be a symbol of urban life and struggle, as barrio residents fought for dignity, respect, and recognition.

CONCLUSION

Contemporary urban social movement leaders locate themselves within histories of guerrilla insurgency, locally based collective action, and cultural resistance over a period of several decades. Juan Contreras noted, "We came from all this struggle, it has produced five generations in this barrio who have thought about transforming the country: the generation of the 1960s, the 70s, the 80s, the 90s, and the generation of the first four years of the twenty-first century. That is, five generations who have thought about change by different paths, the electoral path, the peaceful path, and the path of arms." Over this period, a state-society dynamic of patron-client relations also emerged alongside a redistributive welfare state, as another path by which barrio residents engaged the political system. The history of popular organization in the barrios has been an interplay of independent action and linkages with the state, and the fashioning of creative strategies inside, outside, and against the political system.

The distinct orientations of contemporary community-based organizations were shaped throughout half a century of political engagement. Some activists retained their belief in the need for revolutionary armed struggle and they defended this vision even during the process of pacification. Others, influenced by liberation theology and nonviolent mass action techniques of the Belgian worker priests, began to turn away from armed struggle. The cultural resistance tactics of the Grupo Madera also profoundly shaped the orientations of subsequent cultural groups that followed its demise. Culture as a means of protest and community mobilization and a vehicle for the expression of identity has become a vital part of barrio-based movements. But as Contreras notes above, many community-based organizations reflect a synthesis of diverse strategies honed over several decades of self-criticism and resistance. The combined emphasis on consciousness raising, community-based work, and radical direct action is a hallmark of many contemporary barrio organizations.

During the neoliberal period of the 1990s, community-based movements faced a situation of declining welfare and unemployment, along with growing inequality, violence, and segregation. Given the large vacuum left by the retreat of the state from the barrios, gangs and informal networks emerged in its place as means of protection, subsistence, and survival. Chapter 2 looks at changing state-society relationships during the neoliberal era and the emergence of a new geography of exclusion.

"Epa-le, Johnny!" shouts Yorman, a lanky, brown-skinned young man who flicks away his cigarette and comes up behind Yajaira and me to take over control of Johnny's wheelchair and push him up the ramp that leads to the front gate of our apartment building.

"Epa-le, Yorman!" says Johnny, relieved that he will not have to struggle up the ramp, at midnight, when he is exhausted.

Orlando, Yorman's smoking buddy, holds the gate open for Johnny as we enter into the apartment complex, and there is another round of greetings as we see Iván, Bao, and Yancry, smoking in the cool darkness of the open patio beneath the apartments.

"Epa-le Johnny, hola Señora Yajaira." The young men then nod in greeting to me, and I nod my head back. Yorman, Orlando, Iván, Bao, and Yancry are the local drug dealers in the Residencia José Felix Ríbas, Sector III of the popular Caracas parish of El Valle. When I first began doing my field research in the barrios of Caracas, residing in the home of Johnny and Yajaira, I was aware that I could move freely in Sector III because the local drug dealers had seen me with Johnny. Johnny, who has been a paraplegic for thirty years following a car accident in his youth, commands respect in the eyes of the dealers because of the energetic way he lives his life. He is a community activist who works with street children and he has a special rapport with the drug dealers and street children of Ríbas, where he has lived for many years. The dealers understood that I was in the barrio as Johnny's friend, and when I arrived home in the morning or night, they left me alone because they knew who I was. The same went for Yajaira, Johnny's *compañera*, who had moved from Barrio Marín in San Agustín to live with Johnny in El Valle a few years earlier.

The Residencia José Felix Ríbas is a complex of housing projects constructed for victims of the flood tragedy in the neighboring town of La

Guaira, which left over 10,000 dead and 150,000 homeless soon after Chávez came to office in 1999. Former residents of La Guaira came to live in the city and remake their lives and homes in these rapidly constructed housing blocks. After several years of living in the blocks, the residents still had no cooking gas; there were frequent problems with water leakage and plumbing; a lack of sanitation services produced cockroaches and rats; and in four years the complex system of gang control and drug dealing that characterizes every major barrio in contemporary Caracas had evolved.

Unlike the gated communities in the east of Caracas, with doormen and security guards outside the front of the complexes and then several bolted security gates leading to the apartments, the popular residencies have few security gates. In Ríbas, there are two main gates, one in the north of the complex and one in the east. Each building also has its own gate that leads onto an open patio. The eastern gate of the complex serves no real purpose, as it is surrounded by low and broken-down walls, which the younger residents easily jump over to get in and out. The northern gate is monitored by the drug dealers, who have their "business" in a small shack at the side of the gate. Moreover, the outside and inside gates are never locked, because only one resident per household has the gate keys. When I began to stay with Johnny and Yajaira, they gave me a key to their front door, but I had no gate keys, and I did not need these. There is an unspoken agreement among residents that when you open the gate you leave it resting on the frame rather than pulled locked, so that people can come in and out without keys.

A middle-class acquaintance visiting me once from the east of Caracas was shocked at this "poor security," but what he did not understand was that security for the residents of Ríbas does not lie in the locks on the gates but rather in the gangs that control the territory and monitor who goes in and out. In the barrios, the concept of public space is entirely different from the middle- and upper-class gated communities and condominiums, known as *urbanizaciones*. While most middle-class residents have few common areas for public interaction and recreation, the streets, patios, and doorways of the barrios are generally crowded with children playing baseball, girls and boys flirting, women gossiping, and men playing dominoes or smoking. What underlies the relative sense of security in public spaces are the arrangements between sets of competing gangs in the sector, who have marked out their territory and delineated their responsibility for their area. At times the gangs even display a sense of commitment to residents of the community. The gang leaders and drug dealers of Ríbas are generally on hand to assist Johnny up the ramp and through the gates, to help him push his car when it breaks down, or to help Yajaira carry home her groceries.

But this balance is extremely precarious and residents tend to stay home after about ten at night, when violence may erupt between competing gangs. The large holes blown by a bazooka in the façade of the local shopping mall across the road are testament to the kinds of artillery found in the barrio. Most of the time the residents joke about these intergang exchanges; when the gunshots begin, the residents pretend not to notice and if asked they generally use the euphemism of *fuegos artificiales*, or firecrackers, to refer to the shooting. Violence has become routinized in the lives of the residents. Sadly, these kinds of shootouts can happen even during the day; they can erupt out of nowhere, and innocent residents can get caught up in the middle of a situation and be hurt or killed. This is more often the case when the police become involved. The corrupt and inefficient nature of the police force means that they are sometimes bought off by gangs, or they do not have the resources to attend to complaints in the barrios, but they frequently make incursions into the barrios, disrupting the relative equilibrium established by the gangs.

One afternoon on my way home, I was stopped by a police officer at the outside east gate of Ríbas and told that I could not enter. Several neighbors were standing around, trying to find out what was going on, but the police had cordoned off the area for nearly two hours. When I could finally get inside to my building, I saw that there was fresh blood on the ground in our open patio. Victor, the four-year-old boy from the apartment next to ours, came over and told us that the police were chasing a gang member who had come running into our building complex, knocking on all the doors to be let in. Victor's *abuela* opened the door. The police shot the young man right there, on the doorstep of Victor's house, in front of Victor and his abuela.

Everyday violence is one of the most pervasive indications of how neoliberalism reshaped the contours of society. Neoliberal policies, consisting of the privatization and deregulation of state enterprises, trade liberalization, and the flexibilization of labor markets, were introduced into Venezuela during the period of the 1990s. The retreat of the state from social welfare and service provision, and its greater orientation toward an international market, left popular sectors to fend for themselves in a situation of growing desperation and impoverishment. Large-scale unemployment and poverty led to the proliferation of street gangs, violent crime, and the illegal drug trade as a means of survival. But as Jean and John Comaroff argue, rising criminality in postcolonies is not simply a response to the poverty and scarcity produced by structural adjustment. Rather, it is part of a much more troubled dialectic of law and dis/order, whereby criminal violence appropriates the rule of law and operations of the market, creating parallel modes of production, social order, and governance under conditions of deregulation and privatization.[1] Nor is it the case that under neoliberalism the state simply disappears. While the state retreats from its role as a benefactor and protector, it reenters as a repressive force, carrying out sporadic raids against barrio residents.

In this chapter, I look at the changing nature of the state in Venezuela during the 1990s and early years of the new century and the shifting dynamics of state-society relations. I explore the impact of neoliberal reforms on the relationship between the state and the urban barrios, and I consider the social effects of neoliberal reforms. The chapter goes on to outline the transition to a post-neoliberal state under Chávez, with certain key areas of social policy governed by principles of welfare liberalism, and others subject to the market.

THE MAKING OF THE NEOLIBERAL STATE: 1989–98

Marginality and the violence of contemporary urban life are related to processes of growing urban segregation, a deterioration in the conditions of public services, and the transition from a protectionist to a neoliberal state. The insertion of Venezuela into a global order required new forms of efficiency and competition that put pressures on the state-based developmental model pursued by previous governments. The shift of resources away from infrastructure, health care, education, and other social services led to a sustained increase in social inequality. These changes were also racialized, with those at the bottom of the social scale—mostly the black, indigenous, and mixed-race population who form the majority—hit hardest by the changes.

After the collapse of the military dictatorship in 1958 and the transition to democracy, the new Acción Democrática (AD) government pursued strategies of Import Substitution Industrialization (ISI) and prioritized social welfare. Héctor Silva Michelena refers to the period of the 1960s and 1970s as one of economic expansion and redistribution, where the economy generated oil wealth that could be used to increase social spending, provide subsidies for basic goods, and pay high wages to the working classes.[2] But after 1980, this pattern was interrupted by a decline in oil prices and an increase in international borrowing costs.[3] On February 18, 1983, otherwise known as "Black Friday," the currency collapsed, leading to a period of depreciation, hyperinflation, and economic stagnation.[4] The crisis produced by Black Friday was related to massive spending, illegal use of state funds, and unrestrained foreign borrowing, which had increased from $9 billion to nearly $24 billion under the administration of Luis Herrera Campíns during the early to mid-1980s.[5] As a response to rising interest rates, the government of Herrera Campíns devaluated the currency and initiated a set of controls over the economy to prevent the massive flight of private capital.[6] Yet during the administrations of Herrera Campíns (1979–84) and Jaime Lusinchi (1984–89), the economy continued to experience high inflation, disequilibrium in the principle macroeconomic indicators, a deterioration in public-sector salaries, the flight of private capital, and internal and external indebtedness.[7]

Despite his populist, anti-IMF rhetoric during the 1988 election campaign, when Carlos Andrés Pérez attained the presidency in 1989 he declared his plans to adopt neoliberal austerity measures. On February 16, 1989, just a few weeks after his inauguration, Pérez announced the Gran Viraje (Great Turn), a program that sought to dramatically reshape and restructure the economy, political institutions, and cultural foundations of Venezuelan society. The program consisted of austerity measures such as dismantling government subsidies to local industries, deregulating prices, privatizing public enterprises, and reducing social spending. Through these measures, the government sought to increase the competitiveness of Venezuela in the global economy through the growth and diversification of exports and to reduce the role of the state in the domestic economy.[8] But Pérez underestimated the widespread opposition to these proposed reforms, and within ten days the initial measures had sparked the largest anti-austerity protest in Latin America, which came to be known as the *Caracazo*.

Soon after Pérez's announcement of the neoliberal measures, in anticipation of the removal of subsidies and competition, local manufacturers cut back on production. Sellers hoarded goods in order to drive prices up, causing shortages and a growing anger among the urban poor. Subsequently, on February 26, the government announced that gas prices would double in accordance with global market prices. When people went out to catch public transport to work on the morning of Monday, February 27, they found that bus fares had doubled. Protests against the fare increases in the town of Guarenas outside Caracas and at the Caracas bus terminal soon spread across the city.[9] Fernando Coronil and Julie Skurski argue that the decision to raise gas prices in an oil-exporting nation was seen as a violation of the imagined shared ownership of the country's petroleum resources, a rupture of the moral bond between state and pueblo.[10] Men, women, and children came down from the cerros in large numbers to participate in a *saqueo popular* (popular looting) of grocery stores and processing plants. By six in the evening, the main arteries of the city were blockaded, and there was no transport, forcing protesters to return home by foot. With no authorities on the scene, the looting continued into the night. In the early hours of February 28 the army was dispatched onto the streets and there was a massive and violent crackdown. Thousands of people were killed or wounded in the streets by the armed forces, and others stayed terrified in their homes.[11] State violence reimposed conditions of stability and set the groundwork for a new order.

Despite some adjustments and delays, the original neoliberal package was implemented through most of Pérez's presidency.[12] The first stage of the reforms in 1989 included cuts in public spending and trade and financial-sector liberalization. There were successes in reducing imports, but the economy contracted by 8.6 percent and poverty rose over 20 percent. By 1991, oil prices had risen, which led to higher economic growth, but poverty continued to rise dramatically.[13] The Privatization Law in 1992 set the groundwork for privatization of key industries. Over the years 1989–93, the market came to play a much more prominent role in the economy as the state was scaled back.

Under Pérez, there was a transition from a protectionist to a neoliberal state. A combination of external pressures and internal political realignments produced changed roles for the state and new modes of governance under neoliberal regimes. But in contrast to the scholarship that refers to the eclipse or decline of the state,[14] there is growing evidence to suggest that the "nation-state" is simply being rearticulated as the "neo-liberal nation-state."[15] The state takes on new functions as representative of global economic forces in the national realm and a terrain of competing interests as domestic groups raise their demands.[16] The VIII Plan of the Nation, devised under Pérez, has a section titled "The New Role of the State." It states, "The new strategy requires a strong and efficient state that promotes competition and stimulates the expansion and consolidation of a modern market economy."[17] In Venezuela, the orientation toward private initiative and a global economy was channeled through the state, as powerful economic groups such as the media corporation Cisneros group used their local political connections to deepen their involvement in international markets.[18] In contrast to the protectionist state, which is described in the VIII Plan as a "direct participant in private economic activity," "discretional and centralized distributor of oil rents," and "inefficient administrator of social wealth," the neoliberal state should be a "promoter and efficient regulator of private activity," "generator of adequate macroeconomic conditions," and "efficient administrator of the public budget."[19] According to this logic, the neoliberal state should reduce its field of action, focusing on assigning public resources only to areas strategic for encouraging private investment.

In order to carry out the neoliberal package, Pérez had to distance himself from his election promises and the AD party machine, relying increasingly on his ministers, a team of technocrats known as the IESA boys. Technical institutes such as the Institute of Higher Management Studies (IESA) and the Center for the Dissemination of Economic Knowledge (CEDICE) and business groups such as the Grupo Roraima were sites for the diagnosis of the economic crisis and the articulation and dissemination of neoliberal economics. Over a decade of changing political leadership, the pared-down state apparatus, driven by a technocratic agenda and oriented toward global markets, came to have an irreducible presence independent of the ideological stripes of those in power.

Social policy under Pérez's neoliberal framework was also reoriented from its emphasis on providing equity, universal access to social welfare, and redistribution toward the privatization of social services and compensatory programs designed to mediate the effects of structural adjustment reforms. As Norbis Mujica Chirinos has argued, social policy came to be guided by the criteria and values of the market—economic efficiency, individualism, and competition.[20] Pérez's social policy was encapsulated in the program Plan de Enfrentamiento de Pobreza (Plan for Confronting Poverty, PEP), which included a mother-infant nourishment program, school nutrition programs, youth training and employment, day care centers, programs of assistance in popular economy, a project of urban improvement in the barrios, and a program of local social investment, among others.[21] Under a second phase of social policy, Pérez implemented the Mega Proyecto Social (Mega Social Project), in 1992. The Mega Proyecto Social complemented the PEP, providing investment in areas such as water, infrastructure, education, health, housing, social security, and environment. But while the funding for the program was initially projected at Bs 123,000 million, it was reduced to a credit of Bs 57,300 million, to be financed from assets sold off through privatization.[22] The responsibility for social services was increasingly delegated to NGOs and civil society groups, without the corresponding resources. The VIII Plan states, "It is imperative to improve the management of basic public services and incorporate civil society into the instrumental tasks of social policy and culture."[23] The program of day care centers was outsourced to 850 NGOs financed by the state and reached only 9 percent of Venezuelan children.[24] In a time of limited public resources, the burden for subsistence and welfare was shifted onto social sectors.

The government began to show signs of disintegration by late 1992, due to increasing discord between the AD and Pérez's technocratic cabinet, particularly over issues such as the minimum salary, as well as a coup attempt by Hugo Chávez on February 4 and a second coup attempt on November 27. Rafael Caldera was elected in 1993 on an openly anti-neoliberal and social Christian program, as part of a coalition of parties known as Convergencia Nacional. For his first year and a half in office, Caldera employed a hybrid mix of neoliberal and anti-neoliberal policies. As Julia Buxton outlines, Caldera's initial economic policy, known as the Sosa Plan, combined spending cuts with increases in taxation, and it had some success in closing the fiscal gap. But Caldera also had to deal with a banking sector crisis, which led to massive capital flight. Caldera fell back on neoliberal strategies of exchange controls, currency devaluation, and spending cuts in order to deal with the crisis. By the end of 1994, inflation had increased to 70.8 percent, unemployment had risen to 8.5 percent, poverty continued to rise, and public infrastructure was plagued by blackouts and shortages.[25]

Under Caldera, the PEP was replaced by a new social program, the Plan de Solidaridad Social (Plan of Social Solidarity), launched in 1994. The plan attempted to combat poverty through constructing a healthy economy that would reduce unemployment and increase salaries. This was followed by the Plan de Recuperación y Estabilización Económica (Plan for Recuperation and Economic Stabilization, PERE), where social programs were listed under a section for strategic social action. Caldera revived the neoliberal package in April 1996 in consultation with the IMF, as a program of macroeconomic stabilization known as Agenda Venezuela, although no formal agreement was signed with the IMF. As part of this program, the Caldera administration privatized the steel company, attempted to auction off the aluminum industry, and deepened the partial privatization of the oil company.[26] The Agenda Venezuela also contained a social component of fourteen programs, some carried over from earlier plans, such as mother-infant nourishment, school nutrition, youth training and employment, and day care centers. It was fairly similar to plans such as the PEP, with the exception that it utilized more direct subsidies in order to confront extreme poverty.[27]

But these social programs had little effect in mediating the impact of structural adjustment. Compensatory programs were short term and targeted small sectors of the population. By 1997, greater foreign investment and a rise in oil prices allowed for greater economic growth, but social indicators did not improve. By this time the official rate of unemployment was 12 percent, inflation had reached 103 percent, and real incomes had fallen by 70.9 percent since 1984.[28] The effectiveness of programs such as day care centers depended less on the state and more on the capacity of NGOs, which had increased to between 2,500 and 2,600 community-based organizations, private development groups, and private agencies.[29]

The shift away from protectionist to neoliberal orders produced new processes of class formation across Latin America. Alejandro Portes and Kelly Hoffman point to the appearance of a transnational elite class that included managers, executives, and elite workers.[30] Similarly, in Venezuela there was a shift in the power base of domestic elites, as some groups that flourished under the protectionist state declined and others adapted to the new conditions of liberalization by diversifying and moving to export-production. For example, in the automobile parts sector, the Sivensa Group shifted over half of its production to export, thus retaining its leading position within the industry. Others like Grupo Polar expanded by investing in domestic industries.[31] The retreat of the state from redistributive functions such as progressive taxation, controls, and regulation led to a concentration of power and resources in this transnational elite.

At the same time, a large and impoverished informal proletariat emerged which consists of the urban poor and former public-sector employees and factory workers.[32] Official statistics report that the informal sector in Venezuela grew from 34.5 percent of the labor force in 1980 to 53 percent in 1999, although these figures likely underreport the true number.[33] During the same period, unemployment went from 6.6 to 15.4 percent of the urban labor force.[34] As a result, many Venezuelans were unemployed or underemployed with no job security. Large numbers of urban poor, as well as the downwardly mobile middle classes, increasingly turned to street vending as a way of supporting themselves and their families following layoffs or after difficulty securing formal sector employment.[35] Some vendors left formal sector employment because they preferred the freedom of self-employment. Some even managed to accumulate enough capital to own and operate several stalls, where they employ workers to sell their merchandise. But for the most part, vendors are self-employed individuals who are vulnerable to loan sharks for purchase of their stalls and equipment, and they barely scrape a living day to day. And while these informal sector occupations have arisen in the absence of the state, vendors are still subject to policing and harassment by virtue of their permanent illegality, as well as problems of crime and insecurity.

Poverty had always been a major social problem in Venezuela, even under the social welfare state, but during the 1980s and 1990s it increased substantially. In 1978, 10 percent of the population lived in poverty and 2 percent lived in extreme poverty.[36] Between 1984 and 1995, those living below the poverty line went from 36 to 66 percent, and those in extreme poverty tripled from 11 to 36 percent.[37] By 1998, 81 percent lived below the poverty line and those living in extreme poverty had risen to 48 percent. In December 1997, there were 3 million homes in poverty and more than 1.6 million homes in situations of extreme poverty. Even during moments of economic growth, poverty continued to rise, defying the notion that the benefits of economic growth would trickle down to poorer classes.

The increase in poverty was related to a number of factors including the large scale loss of employment, higher prices and reduced purchasing power due to inflation, and reduced government spending on social programs. Purchasing power of the minimum wage was reduced by more than two-thirds between 1978 and 1994. There were major cuts in social spending, including cuts of over 40 percent in education, 70 percent in housing, and 37 percent in health. A downwardly mobile middle class gradually took over the public health care and education system, which was less accessible to the poor because of the registration fees for schools and costs of treatment supplies at hospitals.[38] Unemployment, inflation, and cuts in social spending impacted most strongly the poorest 40 percent of the population, whose income share fell from 19.1 percent in 1981 to 14.7 percent in 1997, while the wealthiest increased their share of income from 21.8 to 32.8 percent.[39] The effects of this unequal redistribution of income can be seen in processes of growing urban segregation and social polarization.

WAR ON THE URBAN POOR:
FROM A BENEFACTOR TO A REPRESSIVE STATE

Structural changes in Venezuelan society during the 1990s dramatically transformed the nature of urban life and the relationship of the barrios to the state. During the period of ISI, the barrios provided industrial labor for factories, public-sector personnel, and domestic labor for the middle and upper classes. In turn, the state intervened in the barrios through a system of clientilist redistribution of goods and services.[40] As Elizabeth Leeds identified in Brazil, the relationship between the shantytowns and the outside polity "was a symbiotic one, with each side extracting some good or service from the other."[41] But given the shift away from formal employment to informal employment, declining jobs in the public sector, and the reduction in redistributive social spending, the shantytowns came to constitute what Javier Auyero calls "a space of survival for those excluded from the rest of society."[42] The severing of the symbiotic relationship between the barrios and the outside world resulted in a growth of elaborate strategies of survival and parallel economies, and a state that became more repressive even as it failed to provide basic security for barrio residents.

The declining employment opportunities for barrio residents gave rise to a range of informal and sometimes illegal survival economies, one of the most lucrative among young barrio men being drug dealing. For an account of these survival economies, some suggestive evidence can be obtained from looking at popular culture forms such as rap music. It must be noted that rap lyrics are not a transparent account of working-class experience, as the lyrics are mediated by record labels and the commodification of the "ghetto" as it is marketed to middle-class audiences. But it is still the case that rap music is produced by and resonates strongly with barrio youth, who identify the lyrics with their own experiences. In their song "Malandrea negro" (Black Delinquency), the Venezuelan rap group Guerrilla Seca say that it is the poverty, hunger, and desperation of the barrios that leads to drug dealing for some as a means of survival. Trying to find meaningful work for unskilled black youth is practically impossible: "I go on desperately, looking for work is a joke." Even for those who want to find work in the formal economy there are few opportunities: "I look for legal cash, but destiny is changing me." If one needs money and there are no legal opportunities, then the turn to crime and the informal, underground economy is the only path, according to the rapper, especially when one has children to support. Similarly in the chronicle of street life "Historia nuestra" (Our History), the rapper Budu from Vagos y Maleantes relates that he began dealing drugs, "empecé en el jibareo," at the age of seventeen. While the parents of the rapper dreamed of his being an engineer, he dreamed of being a criminal.

The drug trade provided one form of economic subsistence for all those involved in the production, manufacture, and sale of drugs. According to Eithne Quinn, who has studied representations of the drug trade in American gangsta rap, the informal economy of the drug trade reflects a capitalist ethos of "the meteoric rise of the fledgling entrepreneur; the rejection of traditional notions of communal responsibility in an age of individualism; the 'ruthless' startup business organization; and the marketing and distribution of a 'dangerous' product."[43] In the song "Puro lacreo" (True Delinquent), the rapper Colombia from Guerrilla Seca describes a drug business. The dealers are managers who own and oversee the entire business and are intimately familiar with the production process. As compared with the degradation of wage labor or service work, the dealers themselves direct their business. The dealers are concerned with many aspects of a startup business. There is much demand, "everyone wants cocaine and rocks," but they need to establish a good name for themselves in the barrio and protect themselves against crackdowns by the police. As long as they have control over their zone and are street smart about how they do business, no one will mess with them. The song ends with guns being fired into the air, emphasizing that in the end it is violence and the cartel's monopoly over the means of violence in the barrio that maintain their control over trade.

Another example of a lucrative informal-sector activity that doubled as what Auyero calls a "surrogate social security system" was the Maria Lionza cult, a popular spirit possession cult that focuses on healing.[44] In addition to employment and income generated by the healing ceremonies, the sale of cult-related products distributed through street merchants was a mode of informal economy.[45] Given the lack of public services for barrio residents during the 1990s, the Maria Lionza cult came to constitute an alternative form of health care. Indeed, the "clinics" of the cult mimicked allopathic clinics, where patients are given a number and asked to sit in a waiting room. They then go into consulting rooms where they meet with the *materias*, the mediums who oversee the rituals. Patients are given "prescriptions," or pieces of paper with suggested cures, usually involving ways to remove a spell that has been cast on the person and is creating his or her ill health. Materias conduct spiritual "operations" which do not involve actual surgery but imitate the procedures and instruments of regular surgery. In the absence of health care services, the clinics of the cult came to serve as a surrogate form of consultation for barrio residents. One of the most popular clinics known as the Centro Madre Erika in Petare received close to 20,000 patients per week during the 1990s.[46] In addition to spiritual services, the center invited medical doctors to speak on topics such as teenage pregnancy and infant health, substituting for the services that an absent state no longer provided.

At the same time as the neoliberal state retreated from its integrationist roles as service provider and public sector employer, it reentered as a repressive force, maintaining the shantytowns in a state of permanent crisis and illegality. The liberal state had been involved in repressive interventions into the barrios since the early period of democratic rule when a guerrilla movement arose to contest the conditions of "pacted" or elite democracy. But in the late 1980s, combat between guerrillas and the police was replaced by tensions between gang leaders and urban security forces. As drugs began to circulate in the popular neighborhoods in large quantities during the 1980s, some former guerrillas left behind militant politics and began to enter the drug trade. According to Juan Contreras from the parish 23 de Enero, several leftist activists who had experience in doing expropriations of territory, using arms, and planning military operations began to use these techniques to their own benefit, setting up small drug cartels in the barrios and staking claim over their territories. At this time, the state formed various paramilitary units designed for urban combat. In 1994, they created urban squads known as the *Angeles Guardianes* (Guardian Angels), based on civil security forces in use at the end of the 1970s in the United States.[47] Another unit for urban control set up during the 1990s was the *Cascos Blancos* (White Helmets).[48] In public discourse the phrase "Plomo contra el Hampa" or "War against Delinquency" became common and has justified the use of severe punishments for acts of juvenile crime.[49]

Public security services became more repressive at the same time as they became more corrupt and underresourced. In the last few decades there has been an increase in crime and a decline in protective security for the poorer sections of the population who live in barrios. Ana María Sanjuán comments that in 1999 the homicide rate in Venezuela had risen 20 percent from the previous year.[50] This number was greater in Caracas, where the number of homicides sometimes reached the hundred mark on weekends. Official statistics for the year 2000 reported a total of 7,779 homicides in Venezuela.[51] An overwhelming number of these homicides take place in the barrios, and a personalized system of punishment and retribution has evolved to make up for the absence of state security forces enforcing the law on behalf of poorer citizens.

The absence of state protection for citizens was all too apparent to me through an incident that happened during my fieldwork. During a research trip in January 2005, all the money was stolen from my bank accounts, following my use of my credit card at an automatic teller machine in a neighborhood known as Las Mayas. My card was duplicated after I used it and all my bank accounts were wiped out over a period of two weeks. A friend took me to the police station in the middle-class neighborhood of Chacao, hoping that we could get attention for our problem. When we arrived at the station, I noticed that it was fully staffed, with several police officers in new-looking uniforms who were pleasant and courteous to the people waiting for help with their complaints.[52] When I reached the counter and explained what had happened, they said that I would need to go to the police station in El Valle, since the crime was under the jurisdiction of that station. The difference between the police station in Chacao and El Valle was striking. The station in El Valle had large numbers of people waiting to be attended to and only one police officer on duty, who disappeared inside his office for long periods of time. When I went to the counter and explained what had happened I was told that I would need to wait.

As I took my seat among the plastic orange chairs in the waiting area, I began to converse with the people around me. The woman on my left told me that her brother had been killed and she was trying to file a report so that his killer could be apprehended. On my right, a tired-looking woman said that her ex-husband was physically harassing her and she was trying to get a protection order against him. They had both come in several times, waiting for four or five hours at a time without having their complaints attended to.

When it was finally my turn to be attended to, several hours later, I was able to see at close hand the scarcity of resources for the barrio police stations. The attending officer asked me to go outside and find a place to make copies of my bankcard and other important documents, and while I was at it, he asked if I could photocopy a few forms for the station as well, since there was no functioning copier at the station. He typed up my report on an ancient typewriter that broke down at least twice. He entered my data into a word processor, and then printing out the data took another hour on an old dot matrix printer that skewed the text. Finally, the officer led me to another room and pressed my fingers onto an inkpad, but there was no ink, and he could not take my fingerprints. By this stage both the officer and I were shaking our heads in disbelief. It was clear to me that the police are overburdened and underresourced when it comes to citizen protection in the barrios.

The result of this underresourcing has been widespread corruption among the police, who abuse their position in order to extract personal benefits. Freddy Mendoza, a community activist, related to me that it was frequent for police to arrest residents of the barrio, particularly youth, and then release them for a certain amount of money. Freddy also told the story of a town clerk who had reached his position through deals with the political party COPEI in the 1990s. The clerk, known as "pica pollo" because he sold chicken, used to gamble until two or three o'clock in the morning, and when he lost all his money he would go to the police module and extort money from detainees so he could continue gambling. If they paid him, then he would release them. Paying bribes to police has become an accepted practice. Budu related to me an incident with the police:

> Once I was smoking a marijuana cigarette. I was in the doorway of my house and the police arrived—nearly six of them—and they caught me because me and my friend didn't realize in time. I had the marijuana. They saw me, and they said, "We're going to take you." I said, "OK, but don't handcuff me because I'm a public figure and I don't want people to see me like a kid." They asked, "How much do you have there?" "I have twenty thousand bolívares." "OK, give it to us." And they took my twenty thousand bolívares and gave me back my cigarette . . . There were eight of them and between the eight they shared the twenty thousand bolívares.

Twenty thousand bolívares is the equivalent of about $US9.50, and shared between eight police officers amounts to a little over 2,500 bolívares ($US1.20) per person. But corruption ranges from this kind of petty extortion and bribing to larger, regular payments by drug dealers, which can substitute nicely for the paltry salaries paid by the state.

As the state underwent changes during the period of the 1990s, it retreated from its role as a benefactor providing public services such as health, education, and security, and reentered the lives of barrio residents as a repressive state. Barrio residents were left to fend for themselves and often created elaborate strategies of survival that included illegal activities such as drug dealing and crime. When Chávez came to power in 1998, he promised to bring back the benefactor state and reverse processes of exclusion and segregation. The next sections of this chapter examine the changing nature of social policies under Chávez and the shift to a post-neoliberal state.

THE RECONFIGURATION OF THE STATE
UNDER CHÁVEZ, 1998–2007

Hugo Chávez was elected in the December 1998 general elections mainly because of his proposals to transition Venezuela away from the neoliberal model. In contrast to the neoliberal state shaped under Pérez and Caldera, Chávez conceived of a developmental, benefactor state that would act as a "promoter of private economic activity, regulator of economic agents, stimulator of the accumulation of physical and human capital."[53] The state would directly administrate policy and guarantee social justice and security, while involving social sectors in the construction of a participatory democracy.[54] Soon after taking office, Chávez initiated the process of rewriting the constitution as a method of reforming the state. Many of those elected to the constituent assembly had been human rights advocates under previous governments, and they incorporated a broad concept of human rights as both civil rights and social rights of public health, education, and welfare. The new constitution was completed over the next few months and approved by referendum in December 1999.

However, despite his anti-neoliberal rhetoric and legislation, during his first period of office from 1998 to 2001, Chávez followed many of his predecessors' policies. Initially, there was a strong emphasis on short-term macroeconomic policies of fiscal discipline and monetary control, practically identical to that pursued under the Agenda Venezuela. In July 1999, the Chávez government announced the ratification of nine of the fourteen social programs of Agenda Venezuela. In his Plan Bolívar announced in 2000, Chávez proposed short-term civic-military interventions to address the most urgent social problems.[55] There was also a move to centralize social programs within large state ministries.[56] Chávez's early period was marked by a contradictory orientation that combined macroeconomic adjustment policies with compensatory social programs, in contrast to the model of development he had proposed.

During this period, the Chávez administration collaborated with the World Bank, which continued its social programs in Venezuela. Shifts were taking place within leading development institutions themselves, away from the more aggressive structural adjustment policies toward "inclusive" poverty reduction and good governance goals. As David Craig and Doug Porter argue, by the end of the 1990s, the millenarian vision of global market integration was under siege. Development failure and zero net growth brought into question neoliberalism's trust in free markets and self regulation. The United Nation Development Program (UNDP) proposed a set of Millennium Development Goals (MDGs) in 2000, which included the eradication of extreme poverty, universal primary education, and the reduction of child mortality, among other goals. The idea was that economic growth resulting from neoliberal market integration would not on its own reduce poverty, and there would need to be a focused moral commitment from poor countries and their citizens to address social problems.[57] In

December 2002, the World Bank proposed the Interim Country Assistance Strategy (ICAS) designed to help Venezuela meet the MDGs by 2015. This included a $60.7 million Caracas Slum Upgrading Project with the state institution FUNDACOMUN. The WB also committed funds to public health services, urban transport, and finance.

However, starting in 2001, the Chávez government was ready to make a break with its predecessors' social policies, including its ties to the WB and international agencies. In November 2001, the Chávez administration passed a package of forty-nine laws which included the Organic Hydrocarbons Law to establish majority government ownership of all oil-related mixed companies, and the Lands Law, which made idle land subject to expropriation.[58] After 2002, the growing independence of the Chávez administration was due to its increased control over the state-owned oil company PDVSA and was also a consequence of the spectacular rise in oil prices, from US$24.13 per barrel in December 2002 to $84.63 in December 2007, which made more funds available to state coffers. As Thad Dunning argues, "Venezuela is again a rentier state in the midst of an oil boom."[59] In July 2002, the government proposed the Plan Estratégico Social 2001–2007 (Strategic Social Plan, PES), which had three sub-objectives: "the universalization of social rights, the reduction of the inequality of wealth, income and quality of life, and the appropriation of the public realm as a collective good."[60] At the center of this new social policy were the missions, a comprehensive series of publicly funded and administered poverty alleviation programs.

Two of the main goals of the missions were introducing universal education and health care. This was initially done by bypassing the established institutions and setting up programs in the barrios through a parallel set of institutions. The key educational missions included the adult literacy and elementary education programs Mission Robinson I and II; work-study program Mission Ribas; and a university program, Mission Sucre. Unemployed and informal sectors were incorporated into these programs in large numbers as both instructors and students, helping to partly alleviate poverty by providing them with small stipends for their involvement. In mid-2003, Chávez introduced the Barrio Adentro (Inside the Barrio) program of local health clinics, staffed by Cuban doctors, in 320 of Venezuela's 335 municipalities.[61] By mid-2005, he had added another two programs, Barrio Adentro II and III for additional medical services. In March 2005, there were over 5,000 Comités de Salud (Health Committees), which were created to supervise and help out with the Barrio Adentro program.[62]

In addition to educational and health programs, Chávez encouraged barrio residents to create a range of committees and cooperative organizations. In an executive decree in 2002, Chávez established the basis for Comités de Tierra Urbana (Urban Land Committees, CTU), in order to rationalize land tenancy through surveys, distribution of land deeds, and development of property belonging to the community.[63] Since most dwellings in the barrios were constructed through a process of massive squatting as people moved to Caracas from the countryside, few homeowners possess deeds or titles to their land. In March 2005, there were more than 4,000 Urban Land Committees in the urban capitals of Venezuela, which had distributed about 170,000 property titles.[64] The Chávez government also set up Casas Alimentarias (soup kitchens), where needy children and single mothers from the barrios receive one free meal a day. In 2004, 4,052 Casas Alimentarias were established in Venezuela.[65] Mission Mercal was a series of subsidized supermarkets also designed to improve nutrition.

By around 2005 it is possible to identify a shift in the nature of the Venezuelan state to a post-neoliberal state. Julia Buxton argues that the development agenda of the Chávez government places an emphasis on sustainable economic growth based in technological innovation, macroeconomic policy management, and basic social services provision. Fiscal and monetary policies are compatible with social policies. There is a disproportionate focus on the poor and a redistribution of assets and land. All these factors differentiate the agenda of the Chávez government from the targeted poverty reduction approach associated with MDGs, which still retain a jaundiced view of the state, focus on private-sector and trade-led growth, measure development by economic and not social indicators, and lack any emphasis on land redistribution.[66] In the post-2002 order, neoliberalism was no longer the dominant policy.

CONCLUSION: CHÁVEZ AND THE URBAN POOR

Under Chávez, the links between state and society were reconfigured, as the state once more took on the role of benefactor and protector, particularly to the urban poor. Economists have shown various improvements in social indicators since Chávez has been in office. Responding to negative assessments by Francisco Rodríguez and Daniel Ortega, who conclude on the basis of the Venezuelan Households survey that the illiteracy campaigns have been an expensive failure,[67] David Rosnick and Mark Weisbrot contend that the Household Survey is an inadequate measurement tool for illiteracy, since it has only one question concerning illiteracy and thereby does not capture the great variety of change that may be taking place.[68] In a further rebuttal of Rodriguez's consequent assertions,[69] Weisbrot shows that social spending increased from 8.2 percent of GDP in 1998 to 15.9 percent in 2006, and that since 2003 the poverty rate has been cut in half and the unemployment rate has been cut by more than half.[70] Weisbrot's figures may not capture the true scope of changes taking place, as they do not account for factors such as the siphoning off of stipends that may never reach intended beneficiaries; hoarding and pilfering of goods; and underemployment, which may be the case with some who are employed in the missions but remain without a livable wage. Nevertheless, it is still the case that provision of social services has led to improvements in people's lives in ways that are also apparent through ethnographic observation, whether it is health clinics in the highest reaches of the barrios where previously people died from preventable diseases; nutritious daily meals available for children from poor families; or high school dropouts continuing their schooling during evenings in the work-study program. Chávez has won a considerable degree of sympathy from the urban poor for his social policies, which was reflected in his consecutive successes in the recall referendum and 2007 elections.

The rate of violence since 2002 has also showed considerable decline. Figures from the Centro de Estudios para la Paz at the Central University of Venezuela show that in the popular parish of Antemano the rate of homicides went from 110 per 100,000 inhabitants in 2002 to 76 in 2006. In Petare the rate was reduced during the same period from 101 to 72, and the overall rate in Caracas was reduced from 51 to 37.[71] It is likely that the improvement in social indicators—creating jobs, reducing poverty, and access to education—is breaking up the vicious cycle of crime and violence. However, the problem of violence is at the same time an obstacle to putting in place some of these programs, as community organizers find themselves subject to threats and random violence. Throughout the remainder of this book, I continue to explore how social movements grapple with the issue of violence and to examine the community-based solutions to violence that they propose.

Chávez's support among the urban poor owes not only to his social programs and transfer of material goods but also to his image as an antiestablishment figure. As Yolanda Salas argues, Chávéz denounces the traditional political system and the given institutional order, appealing to the masses as his allies and interlocutors. The "Chávez myth" was strengthened by Chávez's biographical connections with the llanera region as symbolic of national identity; his expressed admiration for his great-grandfather Maisanta, a general who revolted against the military leader Juan Vicente Gomez; and his coups of February and November 1992 that challenged the existing political order.[72] The renovation of the old republic and the birth of the new are based in the ideology and cult of Bolivarianismo.

Chávez draws on and elaborates the popular Bolivarian cult as it has been formulated in spaces of exclusion. The independence hero Simón Bolívar has traditionally been portrayed in official representations as part of a cult of order, patriotism, and progress.[73] By contrast, in the rural communities of Barlovento and Oriente studied by Salas, Bolívar was reimagined in various guises as a statuesque African slave brought to the coasts of Barlovento, a saint descended from the heavens accompanied by his followers, and a common man who died poor and was betrayed by his friends.[74] From these collective popular histories emerges a Bolívar who is sanctified and mythified by those classes who feel outside the spheres of power.[75] Chávez's constant references to Bolívar and other heroes from the past are a reflection of these images preserved in popular historical memory. Chávez changed the name of the Republic of Venezuela to the Bolivarian Republic of Venezuela; the official Day of Discovery was renamed the Day of Indigenous Resistance; and the symbolic remains of the indigenous chief Guaicaipuro were moved to the national pantheon. As Salas argues, through these actions "popular consciousness has won an important space of political power."[76] Bolivarianism draws popular resonance from its appropriation of deeply rooted collective memory, legends, and histories.

On a more personal level, Chávez gives voice to the marginalized, their hopes, collective memory, and resentment. Chavismo derives much of its discursive appeal from its language of protest at political exclusion. It is associated with a newfound sense of hope, retribution for social injustices, and dignity for the urban poor. Chavismo has found strength by tapping into the deep reservoir of daily humiliation and anger felt by people of the lower classes. It is Chávez's ability to speak to the urban poor, to show that he understands their feelings of exclusion, that endears him to them. In the next chapter, I explore an individual biography that narrates one barrio resident's experiences of exclusion and daily humiliation, and I show how these experiences have found a voice and a vehicle of expression in Chavismo.

Chávez encouraged the voicing of a range of heretical and cathartic emotions in the public sphere, especially during the 2002 coup and the 2004 recall referendum, when his language of the people versus the oligarchs, and the patriots versus the *escualidos* (squalid ones), could benefit him politically. But in the post-2004 order as Chávez sought to consolidate a new state orthodoxy, he was concerned to rein in and channel these chaotic and potentially destabilizing collective emotions. A range of intermediaries has been involved in this task of political incorporation. Chavista political parties made a greater effort to penetrate and manipulate mass organizations in order to impose a leadership hierarchy and party line over these movements. María Pilar García Guadilla has noted the attempts by the Movimiento Quinta Republica (MVR) to intervene politically in the CTUs and Communal Councils, utilizing them in order to build electoral support in a similar manner to the AD and COPEI during the 1960s and 1970s. An example of this was the local elections in August 2005, when political parties mobilized community-based organizations in support of pro-Chávez candidates.[77] Cultural institutions have sponsored local cultural initiatives as a way of reconsolidating a patronage system. Some community-based organizations have also acted as brokers and mediators between the state and urban movements, using their authority at the grass roots to channel discontent and promote state directives.

But alongside renewed corporatist linkages between state and society, neoliberal logics have persisted in certain demarcated areas. Under Chávez, there has been an attempt to divide up the national territory into what Aihwa Ong calls "zones of graduated sovereignty," where "developmental decisions favor the fragmentation of the national space into various non-contiguous zones, and promote the differential regulation of populations who can be connected to or disconnected from global circuits of capital."[78] Social policy after 2002 focused on creating a protected zone where the welfare apparatus could be cushioned off from the demands and rationalities of global markets. Funds are channeled directly from PDVSA to the various missions. PDVSA manages a yearly fund of some $US2,000 million from oil revenue, and this is all channeled into social programs.[79] This considerable reserve fund, even if linked to a volatile and depleting natural resource, has allowed the state to disconnect social welfare provision from global circuits of capital.

The majority of social welfare organizations, mostly those formed under Chávez such as health committees, land committees, communal councils, and technical commissions of water, operate within this noncontiguous zone, and therefore they are protected from the demands and requirements of international markets. But other zones continue to be articulated to foreign and private capital, to different degrees, including culture and communications, mining and hydrocarbons, and the manufacturing sector. These zones are subject to market calculations, as they are tied more directly to global circuits of capital. In part II of this book I show that it is in these zones that the contradictions of the post-neoliberal state under Chávez are most apparent. It is also the groupings of cultural protest, community radio, and barrio assemblies, with their roots in the long-term social movements explored in chapter 1, which confront these instrumental liberal and neoliberal logics and are best placed to contest them.

I spent many months trying to find time with my housemate Yajaira Hernández to record her life history and competing unsuccessfully with the telephone, visitors, her nieces and nephews, her busy work life, and her daily chores. Finally, one day I invited her for lunch to the restaurant Cafe Arabica, in the middle-class suburb of Altamira, and I asked her if we could try to do the interview there. She agreed. But when we came up out of the metro at the Altamira stop and walked toward the restaurant, where I had met with colleagues and foreign visitors in the past, I wondered if it was a mistake. People were looking at us, especially as we entered the restaurant. With her black skin, Yajaira was more likely to have been a domestic worker in the house of one of these patrons, rather than a patron herself. When we sat down at a table, she told me that in all her years growing up in Caracas she had never come to a restaurant in Altamira before. After we finished eating, I asked her if she still felt comfortable to do the interview and she said it was fine, so I pulled out my microphone and began recording. Then people really began staring. "They think I must be some famous African American personality, like Alice Walker. Because why would anyone want to interview a poor, black person from the barrios?" Yajaira asked, jokingly.

The incident was revealing to me on many levels. It illustrated the structural coordinates of segregation, racism, and class that shape the lives of black women such as Yajaira. It showed me a difference between the United States, where class mobility had allowed some black women to carve out a space for themselves through artistic or intellectual production, and Venezuela, where black women were not recognized on this level. Yajaira's response also revealed the characteristic ways in which she responded to and resisted this kind of subordination. She employed humor to broach a difficult and painful subject, that of race. In her testimony that I recorded that day, all these features surface and resurface. In this chapter, I present Yajaira's life history, combining material from her testimony and also the many stories that she told me over the time that I lived in her house and came to know her. I also make reference to interviews and stories related by others who I came to know over the course of my research, as I see Yajaira's story as a part of a web of intertwined histories.

Factors of debt crisis, structural adjustment policies, and violence produced a specific matrix of changes in the Venezuelan political system, as explored in the previous chapter, but they do not convey how people experienced and understood those changes. The sociologist Javier Auyero has argued that while structural factors are important determinants of historical events, they only begin to tell us what the events are about and how people live the events. Rather, he is interested in the "biographical and relational ways in which their protagonists make sense of them."[1] In the case of Yajaira, we see that her involvement in the political events of the 1990s and opening years of the new century is related to personal experiences of racism and humiliation in her society. As she told her story in the restaurant, she was expressing a newfound sense of defiance, backed up by the sense of dignity gained through political involvement. Yajaira's narrative also reveals how her community-based activism stems from a need to protect and care for others, based in her everyday experiences and roles in her extended family as a caregiver and provider. I present her story here; the translations are my own. Yajaira's life story can give us insight into the ways that the intersectionality of race, gender, and class shapes the involvement of barrio residents in urban social movements.

YAJAIRA'S STORY

> I was raised in San Agustín del Sur, in Barrio Marin . . . We are two women and five men and we were raised in the barrio. Like many mothers in Venezuela, my mother became a single mother. She raised her children practically by herself because my father was with us at the beginning but later he separated himself from the family, and he had an alcohol problem also. This decomposed the nuclear family a little, and we were raised by my mother. I think that despite being illiterate, my mama knew to give us the best. She raised us with good values so that we could make the best of our lives, she encouraged all of us to study, she also taught us what was work,

about responsibility in the home. I may have been a little radical at that time in the sense that this is a machista society and the woman is accustomed to the notion that she should take care of everything and serve the man, this is probably how she was raised. But I was different to her because I didn't understand why I always had to be serving my brothers all the time. Just because they are men, therefore we had to iron their clothes. I reached a point when I said, "Hold on, it's not like this, they also have to wash and iron their clothes, they have to assume equal responsibilities to us."

Perhaps the younger ones were more protected because I was the oldest of the girls, so when my mama went out to work, I stayed at home looking after my brothers. My sister Zulay and my brothers Jaime and Franklin are younger than me, and Henry, Richard, and Victor are older. So with the younger ones I was like their mother at the time, while my mama worked. She began ironing in clothes factories, and she worked as a cook in restaurants also, but she was a *planchadora* [clothes ironer]. She made us look in the newspapers for employment. It was almost always fixed work, but it made her very tired and she didn't spend much time with us. So she started to look for other options that didn't demand so many hours of work and paid better, in addition to struggling for her social security so that we would have medical assistance.

It was our duty to bathe the kids and prepare the meals, but we also created disasters in the house. I always remember that when we knew the time she'd be getting back, generally around 5.30 in the evening, and we'd be playing in the house, throwing water all over and dirtying everything, and at 4.30 in the evening we would all tidy up and clean up everything in the house, because we would never be outside in the street, only in the house. When we reached adolescence there was a marked delinquency in the barrios, but in the midst of all this we didn't deviate. My brothers would have problems of liquor and cigarettes, but they're not delinquents. In the barrio, there were many who praised us, but others said that we were pretentious: "These *negritos* who want to put on airs," because we weren't in the streets making trouble. We, the women, were always very conservative and reserved, and there were people in the barrio who didn't like this. Others praised us and said, "But they are students, in spite of being *negritos*," because you used to hear those kinds of things being said. These are the things you realize . . .

What happened is that I am too hyperkinetic, or rather, curious. I like to keep learning new things. I don't know up till what point, maybe it's not that good because if you want to know too many things all at once, at times you don't do anything. If something attracted my attention I wanted to get involved in that, I had some limitations, but my whole life I always liked sport. In primary school I began to get involved in athletics and in high school I participated in basketball, football, "kickingball," volleyball. Later at university I began to get involved again in athletics and I continued with basketball, and I competed in championships. But ultimately I developed my abilities in marathons. Sport makes me feel good. . . . sporting activity gives me spirits and strength for everything.

Experiences of Work in the Formal and Informal Economy

Well, some of us could go on overcoming bit by bit with an academic education, but unfortunately some other brothers stayed out and didn't want to keep studying, they preferred to work . . . It is more difficult [for men] above all because of the racial problem. Because to be from a barrio and black, this is like a crime. It's the same as being a delinquent. You're not treated like a person who has studied and worked, even though you may have worked, even as a sweeper. But these experiences teach you, they've been happening for a long time, perhaps in a subliminal manner, and the one who carries the burden feels it. Maybe the others wouldn't realize it, but when you are the one who has the problem, you remember all these details.

I was sixteen or seventeen years old when I finished high school. I studied humanities, because I didn't want to know anything about the "three marias," which are mathematics, physics, and chemistry. Even though I like math somewhat, but this is why I didn't choose sciences. I identified with what I was learning, although there were so many things I wanted to study. I began to study administration, but left the course halfway. I began to work from age sixteen. I started in a polling company and from there I was called for a job in the population census, with OCEI, the Central Office of Information. I lived in San Agustín and so I began to bring in money to support my family.

In reality, I started working and doing sports, and I lost direction with my professional career. There were also critical financial situations at home and I dedicated myself to working.

At one time, when I used to read the newspapers looking for employment, I would come across ads that said, "Looking for a young woman to do public relations work," or "to do secretarial work." They would list the requirements as basic high school education, typing skills, good telephone skills, and I would be reading down the list, saying to myself, yes, I have this, I have this. Then at the end it would sometimes say, "with light skin." "Dammit!" I would say as I read down the list, "I have all the other features, just not the light skin" [laughs]. "I can do all the other things, I just don't have the right skin color for the job" [laughing]. I found one job as a salesperson going door to door selling household goods, but people would get scared when they saw a black person coming to the door, and they'd lock their doors and wait until I went away [laughs].

I found a job making hamburgers in a fast food chain and then I was working in a store selling casserole dishes and pots. After seven months of working there, the ownership changed hands and a young man took over the store. One day he came in and told us that we needed to pull together and contribute to the store by going out into the streets and promoting the business, distributing leaflets. I told him that I was contracted to work in the store, not to distribute his propaganda in the street. He said that this was a collective effort, we all needed to contribute and set an example. "What does he mean," I thought, "collective" and "contribute to the collective"? He's the one making all the money. I told him if anyone should set an example it should be him, why is he not out distributing his propaganda? The guy went red in the face, he must have been a *gallego* [Spanish origin], because he was really white. But he did go out and start distributing his propaganda. Later one of the other women who worked there told me I was going to get fired, and I did. He paid me my termination wages and let me go. I went straight to the Ministry of Work to check that I was paid and terminated according to the standards, and I was. But imagine, he fired me for standing up for my rights. I was contracted for work in the store and I had the right to refuse to do other work.

Later I got a place at the UCV, and I enrolled in sociology because it was one of the disciplines with less demand; at that time this was the strategy to enroll in public universities. One had to find degrees with less demand for enrollment and later if you wanted you could change your career. So I enrolled, I put my options in the CNU [Consejo Nacional de Universidades] national exam, which is the exam to select degrees. I put my first option as sociology and the second as administration and accounting and I was selected for sociology. But then I began to identify with this degree because it seemed that in the middle of it I was developing. So I stayed, I didn't change degrees, and I finished the degree but I got stuck on the thesis, and later I found other options for work and so I dedicated myself to the work.

While at university, I was working but the money was not sufficient and so I began to look for other options. The situation at home was quite critical because my brothers were unemployed and only two of us were working and my mama became sick, and even before this my papa came back home sick and we accepted him back and began to look after him. These were two intense years. My papa had a stroke and lost consciousness, understanding, and a part of his body was paralyzed. So we had to look after him, his medicines, his diet, and we didn't have enough money for the priority needs of the house. My brothers worked but by contract and later they stopped working. They had years with no fixed work. And when they found work where there was an opportunity to stay on, it was too much labor and it didn't pay well. And they resisted this by doing whatever they wanted rather than working for peanuts in some company.

I dedicated myself to work in education and on the weekends I worked in La Guaira with a friend, selling books for a workshop on human development and personal development and we always sold things related to the workshop. I liked the work, even though I had to get up really early because we had to be there before 6 a.m. and the people arrived at 8 a.m., and we the street vendors had to have everything prepared before the people who were participating in the workshop would arrive . . . So I went on Friday nights to my friend's house with all of my equipment, my suitcase. I liked this work, because it was relaxing, and I also liked to read these books on personal growth. I could detach myself from the problems at home and this served as an escape. I know that there are people who are skeptical of this "personal growth" and "self-esteem." Maybe you are also skeptical, but in my case it has helped me and sharing with those in situations more critical than me, one begins to see things in a different light . . . I know that I'm wrong at times, but I always look for solutions to my problems, I've always been persevering. I feel that I've tried to be a fighter and not be stuck and pitying myself.

Protector of the Disenfranchised

From as long as I can remember, Caracas has had divisions according to whether you live in an urbanización or in a barrio, and generally the barrios are called the Red Zones—"dangerous, don't go there." So many people who live in urbanizaciones think that in the barrios everything is bad, there's nothing good, it's all delinquency and drugs. But one who has lived in the barrio knows it's not like that: there are struggling, hard-working people, people who have overcome and have become major public personalities. What I don't agree with is when people leave the barrio, achieve some position in society, and later denigrate the barrio. At least in my case, if someday I have some power I'll never forget where I came from. In San Agustín the drunk on the corner is also my friend, like the *malandro*, the drug addict. Many times one comes across youth and adults in the world of drugs and alcohol and you feel like they look out for you more than others who are not in that world. I don't put up barriers with them, even though they are social misfits, not delinquents because it's not like that. Maybe that's how we were taught to see them at one time, but we can't catalogue them as delinquents. There are social misfits who one knows since childhood and with whom we coexist also.

In our home, Zulay and I picked up kids who were out there in the street without studying and we offered them classes for a minimum fee. We were adolescents and we knew the value of supervised study. We offered our services in the house and people brought their kids and we helped them do their homework, and that also helped us economically. We began to look after so many children, but some later became involved in serious problems of delinquency and have since died. This gives us pain and you want to do many things to avoid this. But given the situation itself and without the help of the people who should be attacking this problem, the little work that one does is not sufficient. The work of ants that one does in the community also needs economic resources to maintain it, because the resources are not even for a salary, but rather to invest in the work.

At one point, there were some children in the barrio who were orphans. Their mother died, she was my sister's godmother. She died and left three kids: one three years old, the other eight and the other eleven years of age. We knew them, there was an affiliation, a link. When their mother died, you would see them alone in the street, sometimes they came to our house looking for food. They wandered around out there, although they had their maternal family, but it was a broken family, one of the aunts lived with her children off the sale of drugs. One would see the children in the streets at midnight begging for food, all dirty, and it would break my heart. My sister, and my mama also. My mama was very protective and she was searching for justice, she wanted to help.

Many people who needed help came to our house they slept at our place, and we'd give them a plate of food. Darwin, this one child, began to stay in our house, and at times I observed that he was getting involved in this work of a *mula* [mule], they would give him drugs to transport from one place to another, it was a delicate situation. One day I decided I wanted to help him. I spoke to the others at home to see if he could stay and there was no problem. He was nine years old and had never enrolled in school and for his age that was a problem. I spoke to a child psychologist, we enrolled him in school and in the school he was involved in supervised work, and in sports activities of baseball. He was very restless and he was inclined towards wandering the streets and getting involved in fights, but we kept motivating him and he learnt to read, he passed through to the next grade. The child advanced and passed to the third grade, but things became more complicated at home with my mama's health . . . So one day I went to the District Attorney's office, submitted a complaint, and located the father.

The father lived outside of Caracas and I thought it was better for the three to be together and outside of this environment, because otherwise they would become the future delinquents of the barrio.

The father and I met. It was like a soap opera. I found him and we met in one place and the father started crying and telling me about his problems with his ex-wife's family. It didn't convince me much but he was Darwin's father and he had the right to reclaim his children, but I arranged it via the District Attorney's office to make him acknowledge his responsibility. He hadn't seen the children in a long time and one day we met with the children . . .

We took them all to a park, and the father appeared with a little girl that he had and when they met they hugged and cried, it was like a soap opera. All of them with those big tears, it broke your heart to see the drama of the meeting of the father with his three children, because there had been problems with the mother's family who threatened him if he looked for his children. There I realized that the boys needed their father. So we let Darwin finish his course. I had become used to the child like his own mother, but I understood the situation and decided to return him to his father who took him away. It's been a while since I've heard from them. They went to Barlovento, although I heard that it seems they aren't doing well and the father didn't take responsibility. I detached myself because we had many problems at home.

I also began to get involved in the barrio in organizing cultural activities for children, there were people who motivated me, one was Juan Sanoja from Barrio Mamón of San Agustín. I was working with a Cine Club, which is a cultural organization that is in charge of projecting films and doing cinema forums there in el Mamón. They did it in the street on a wall in 35 mm. Generally, the films were selected to give something positive to the formation of these kids. Outside of this, we organized *batidas*, where you go out in a *comparsa* [festival group] with clowns, drums, and samba, covering various sectors and taking them over with special events and games for the kids, traditional games of perinola, yo-yo, metras, títeras, so they would identify with them. These are traditional games that they shouldn't lose by thinking only about sophisticated games that our transnational companies are marketing. We did mask-making workshops for carnival, similar to the Diablos Danzantes de Yare; at times we asked for support from people in the cultural institutions, so they could help us in the work.

There I came to know friends such as Ricardo Guerrero, Ricardito, who at that time was a clown and they called him Payaso Pom Pom. Ricardo is a little person, and he got involved in this work for children and had a lot of love for them. He went around with another friend who died, he used to live in el Valle, and they called him Payaso Mosquito. They were both people who had an important work of consciousness-raising, of reclaiming our rights, and very involved in politics, committed to the political situation. I myself was never involved from the point of view of political struggle and identification with political parties. My work was to feel and to do and to see the things that were lacking and make my small contribution. In this way, I began to grow, mature, seeing other things and you begin to then search for a certain political inclination. You know that because of what you have lived, what you hear and see, even to where your life and direction is, that is, your roots, your formation and upbringing, and so you know more or less what line you'll follow in the future.

I couldn't identify with those people who we would question quite a lot in those times because of the things they did, who didn't do things because they were really going to resolve anything, but to make themselves feel good in their positions, in their parties, and that's it. And to throw crumbs to the people so they could show they were helping. It wasn't really a conscious work to truly bring change, to change what was not functioning. Now that I think about it, it was all deception. They did things, maybe even some good things, but they did things that were not in the interests of the well-being of poor people.

I met Johnny in 1997, Chávez had not yet won. I was working in La Guaira and I was part of a community organization that I'm still part of in San Agustín called EFORDRI—Escuelas de Formación Deportiva Recreativa Integral [Schools for Integral Recreational Sporting Formation]. Our center of action was sport and recreation. This was the hook to attract children and youth, but the idea was that we wanted to socialize them in an integral manner, with principles, values, and creating responsibilities. We began with children both in school and not in school, street children. We found them and involved them in our activities, to channel their enrollment in school. And we felt the need to work with people with disabilities, above all people with mental disabilities, with mental and motor retardation. I proposed such a work group, I had been working in this area since I had a godson with a problem of retardation, a niece of mine was born with certain retardation. I always had friends with some disability, many for accidents and others for congenital deformations. And it turns out that in San Agustín we did a lot for adolescents, as they had no options.

So we began with a foundation, that in reality was founded by Carlos Palacios and he brought me in. The work was all improvisation, we didn't have any kind of experience with this. And a group from there, Janet [the mother of her godson] and Sofia, the mother of my niece Yajairita, began to sound out the situation and we realized that in the parish there are a large number of youth with this disability. I was the one who designed the poll; we worked with various community organizations and we began to go to different sectors and people told us where the people with retardation were. We discovered that in every sector there were three or four people with some disability. We still had to cover a lot of areas, and I think that now that number would have increased, above all the number of people in wheelchairs because of the violence they live in the barrios.

There are many boys in wheelchairs because of firearms. One of the things that changed my life was when one of my brothers, the youngest, was shot at and is now in a wheelchair. You spend your life working in this and suddenly life gives you a challenge, that suddenly it happens to a member of your own family. There was an exchange of fire and he was one of the ones who was injured, he caught a bullet. There was a group of crazy kids in a car, he was in their path. I was all motivated with my work in the community, and this drained me emotionally. I also had to assume the work of caring for him, but if I have always dedicated myself to helping the community, if it's my family, with even more reason. In this sense, I've always been clear. They are my family and I help them. I've shared special moments as well as bad moments that I don't want to remember, but this forms a part of our life and existence.

Men are at greater risk in the streets, above all in the barrio. They are most vulnerable to getting into problematic situations, and are most watched by the police forces. The police are not stopping women to ask for their identification or beat them up, but always men when they are doing their "operations." In the current political *proceso* such aggressive treatment from the security forces has reduced a little towards youth of the barrios. The Metropolitana, who always had a reputation of being criminals themselves, at times create greater problems, maybe because of political differences, and they use this to assault people in the communities. And, well, when this happened to my brother, having known Johnny, having lived with him, this also made me see the situation of my brother as not so dramatic, because I had in mind the example of Johnny, who is a very valiant and ambitious person, who has broken down many barriers. I suppose that deep down they carry their pain inside, it must be hard for them to have a life and suddenly not be able to do certain things. For example, an athlete, a sportsman, who has dedicated their life to running and suddenly is in a wheelchair. This marks a person. We have to follow examples like Johnny and not be defeated by limitations.

I value human beings, I have always tried to find something in each person that is of value, they can do things, they can struggle, people have their value as human beings, their spirit, their social condition. For many years I have seen this. People have to be valued for what they are, without seeing the economic part or the physical limitation. I have a friend Luis Eduardo, who is on crutches after an accident. They told him he'd never walk . . . but he's on crutches. He is another example to follow, he's an inspiration. People see in his disability a limitation, but he himself doesn't see it that way, this is what I've learnt. I don't say, "Oh, poor thing," nothing like that, he's a person like any other. I always try to value people.

I am the protector of the disenfranchised: for people who don't receive protection from all points of view, I'm there to help them, support them, and protect them. One should not be in this life to suffer, but rather to feel good, because one knows that we are only passing through here, and it's important while here that people feel pleased and that there are marvelous things. You may not have good conditions of life, according to our Western culture, but there are the small things to make you feel good in this life. Above all I'm speaking from the point of view of the emotional and the spiritual, that are often devalued. I generally think that the most beautiful thing that one can have as a human being is to enjoy life with those around you, with the people, to do things that are insignificant to you but valuable to others. I won't become a millionaire with this, although many times I need money, but these are things that fulfill you as a human being and person and they make you live with happiness.

In the case of my family, my sister Zulay and I have been the sustenance of our maternal home, with our brothers and nephews, we've been both mama and papa without ever having children of our own. My sister and I have been the mother of my nephews, and we have been charged with supporting them, orienting them. I don't know if someday I'll have a child of my own to raise, only destiny will tell.

I think everything that has happened in this country is important, although I'm now taking a rest from community work, I think that all that is happening is super valuable, important, because people are becoming conscious and identifying with what is around them. Among so many things, what we see as small steps can serve to advance and achieve marvelous things. You see an effervescence of the heart, you see people more committed and emotional, because community participation was more scarce before this political proceso. There was organization and participation, but it was more limited. It's not like now where you see entire families participating and society in general. People are more conscious because a person has arrived who is motivating them, because the President [Chávez] transmits much hope, because he has located himself among the great majorities, people with scarce resources, and he talks to them and motivates them. He tries to value the people and give them incentive to do things, create awareness, so that people know to value what they have.

I remember that my mama used to say: "*Conchale*, I love this President [Chávez] because he has been a fighter who comes from below and knows what it is to struggle and become someone in life." She identified with him and she was in hospital at the time. I don't know if what was happening in the country at this moment [April 2002 coup] also had repercussions among some patients who were in the Critical Care unit . . . because this day was very convulsive and the doctors were celebrating without giving importance to the patients, and during April 12 and 13 they did not attend the patients. I noted that their treatment of patients depended on whether they were identified [with Chávez] or not.

My mama had her health complications, but she became worse after the situation of these days when she suffered a stroke in half of her body and they didn't attend to her like they should have because the doctors were more concerned about what was happening in the country. We submitted a complaint, we wrote a letter, we went to the Public Defender's office because this was a case of medical negligence. But what happened is that here doctors always think they are owners of everyone's health, they've lost their work ethic, and they don't properly attend to the patients of the Critical Care units. Because of political differences, they also limit their attention to patients.

After our complaint, the Public Defender went to the hospital and the doctors grudgingly began to attend to patients. The doctors said that my mama was fine and she could leave the hospital, but they sent her sick to her house and she became worse. We took her to a clinic because we have insurance, but they said the policy was expired and we had to take her back to that same hospital . . . In these moments you feel very desperate because you don't have the resources to cover necessities like this and you feel like everything is out of your hands.

LIFE STORIES AND POLITICAL ACTIVISM:
READING YAJAIRA'S NARRATIVE

I had witnessed Yajaira go through some of the struggles and triumphs, the sadness and hope that she describes; her narrative felt tangible to me. I was awakened by the call from the hospital at three o'clock one morning. As I lay in bed, I heard her washing her face, dressing, and then the door click behind her on her way to the hospital, where her ten-year-old nephew was in a coma after accidentally taking some of his father's medication. Another night, she answered the door to a street child from San Agustín who was in a delusional state after taking some drugs, and she took him in and sat talking to him gently. On Saturday afternoons as she sat with piles of books and papers, trying to finish her long-abandoned thesis, the house would fill with an array of relatives, friends, and neighbors, and she quietly put aside her work to attend to the visitors, laugh at their stories, and serve them whatever food she had in the house. Her patience and generosity made me consider my own inquietude and intolerance. Truly listening to other people is hard work. Writing their lives for the consumption of Western audiences is even more complex. I agree with Ruth Behar that the feminist project of translating across borders requires one to negotiate languages, dissonances, and relations of power.[2] Aware that I may not do Yajaira justice here, and mindful of the fraught exercise of cultural translation, in the following pages I attempt to interpret her story.

The historian Daniel James has said that if we are to begin to understand the complexity of the stories that people tell us, we need to look at the symbols and constructs contained within them, in order to fully appreciate their deeper meanings.[3] In telling her life story as a coherent narrative that day in Café Arabica, Yajaira considered the evolution of herself as a person. She begins her narrative by establishing her rebelliousness and curiosity, features not traditionally associated with women but central to her unfolding story of community activism.[4] She rebels against the machista conceptions of her society as represented in her mother's division of chores among her and her siblings. Her curiosity in the world finds expression at an early age with her involvement in sports but will also find expression later in other areas such as activism. These early events help confirm Yajaira's rejection of traditional gender roles and stereotypes, in the home and on the track, as a marathon runner. These tropes recur throughout her narrative, setting the stage for her entry into the political sphere.

Yajaira takes care to distinguish her upbringing as one of "formación," or socialization with values of self-respect and hard work. Even while creating disasters at home, Yajaira and her siblings stayed away from the corrupting influence of the street. On the one hand, the narrative reflects notions of social mobility and respectability available to some degree during the early 1970s when oil rents made possible a higher degree of social welfare for barrio residents. Yajaira is critical of the dominant construct of the *negro pretensioso* (pretentious black) which was used to discipline those who transgress racial and class boundaries. On the other hand, she also lived through a period of rapidly increasing violence, when large numbers of barrio youth who entered lives of delinquency ended up dead. Keeping young men away from the streets becomes a battle for their mothers and sisters. By emphasizing their distance from the culture of the streets, Yajaira protected her brothers, as she now protects her nephews, from the often fatal consequences of "deviation."

Yajaira's experiences on the formal and informal market are clearly differentiated from the experiences of the males in her family. For black men, it is difficult to find work because they are negatively stereotyped as delinquents and slackers. Yajaira's brothers tend to be employed in mostly casual, unskilled jobs; but rather than deal with the humiliations of the labor market they come back to the streets and the underground economy. This is similar to what Philippe Bourgois describes in the case of young men in East Harlem, who "find themselves propelled headlong into an explosive confrontation between their sense of cultural dignity versus the humiliating interpersonal subordination of service work."[5] But as Yajaira's narrative illustrates, it is often women as mothers and sisters who must compensate for the deficient incomes of male family members. She and her sister Zulay are the ones who "carry the burden" in both an economic sense as providers and an emotional sense as caregivers, even for an absent father who returns to his family only when he is old and sick.

The experiences of black women on the labor market are also shaped by race, albeit in different ways from males. Yajaira refers to the job advertisements that would list "white skin" as a required quality. A Venezuelan colleague said to me that this is highly unlikely, since Venezuela had certain antidiscrimination laws that would have prevented such blatantly racist hiring policies. But even if these ads never existed, Yajaira is clearly recalling the ways in which skin color was perceived by employers. Even today, for positions of secretaries and public relations workers, employers generally prioritize those who fit dominant notions of "good presence," a construct based on the racist belief that blackness is ugly. Young women also clash with authority figures in the workplace, as Yajaira relates in her experiences with her manager. Her story has a distinctly racialized interpretation, she as the black worker and her employer as the white male. But as compared with her brother's masculine pride and toughness, Yajaira laughs at herself and her employers. When she relates the story of the ads that require women with white skin, she makes fun of the situation. She expresses mock excitement that she has all the skills required, and then feigns disappointment when she comes to the last required "skill" that she does not and never will have. Her story about her confrontation with her manager in the casserole store is akin to what James calls a "carnivalesque inversion of status and deflation of pretensions" in authority conflict stories.[6] When Yajaira confronts the self-important manager, she depicts him as "red in the face" and humiliated. Her use of the derogatory term *gallego* is also a way of lampooning the manager. Although her actions get her fired, Yajaira has the moral high ground as she was standing up for her rights as a worker.

Given these kinds of labor market exclusions, Yajaira prefers to work in the informal market, for the freedom that it gives her. Like many of those I came across in the barrios, she was constantly engaged in some form of informal employment as a way of substituting or supplementing the declining value of her wages as a primary school aide. When I was living with Johnny and Yajaira, they would buy DVDs on the black market and send them to Johnny's cousin in his hometown of Yaracuy, who would sell them on the street and share the proceeds with Johnny and Yajaira. I would go to the black market with Yajaira, a large underground area in the Plaza Diego Ibarra, by the Torres de Silencio. There were many booths selling DVD movies, as well as blank CDs, DVDs, and all the equipment needed to make pirated copies. The most popular DVDs seemed to be hard core pornography, known colloquially as "carne con papas" (meat with potatoes). Yajaira would buy a hundred or so DVDs and then would return home to sort through the films, test that they worked, and then label them. At night, she and Johnny would select a few of the films to watch before sending them to Yaracuy; this was one of the small "perks" of the job. But Yajaira seemed uncomfortable with the work; she says she never saw herself as returning to "la turka negra," as the occupation is known colloquially, but that she has no choice.

"*Conchale*, there are so many necessities, bills to pay, and with the small salary they pay us—sometimes we don't even get paid—how are we supposed to get by?" she said. Johnny and Yajaira are always coming up with different schemes, like buying a small bus and servicing a new route to the mountains, or opening a *posada* or hostel in Yaracuy, but as Yajaira said to me, these are all bigger dreams. "In reality, it's just about making it from one day to the next. Imagine, us trying to sell films on the side of the road to save up for an air ticket to Miami or even Margarita [laughs]. This is just to get by day to day, that's it."

Yajaira's life history is one of caring for and protecting others, from her younger siblings to her father and mother, street orphans, children of the barrios, her nieces and nephews, children with mental retardation, her own husband in a wheelchair, and then her brother in a wheelchair. I wonder what it is that drives her to give so much of herself to others and how this feeling may be linked to the kinds of community action in which she engages. For Yajaira, caring for and protecting others helps to "fulfill you as a human being." In a society where she is denigrated for being poor and from a barrio and where she faces racism and humiliation in the workplace, being needed by others gives her a sense of personal fulfillment. This sense of fulfillment is akin to what Auyero notes in the case of Laura, a picketer in the uprisings in Argentinean southern oil towns in 1996: she is on the road "to do what gives her a sense of worthiness: to protect people. Her life (and now the protest) is all about that: finding and providing protection."[7] Likewise, for Yajaira, it is her capacity for caring, protecting, and valuing people for who they are, as well as her lived experience—"what you have lived, what you hear and see"—that frames her political activism, in contrast to the politicians who only want to "make themselves feel good in their positions." These women take their daily experiences of care giving and protecting others into the political realm, as the basis of their political activism.

MATERNAL ROLES, WOMEN'S PARTICIPATION, AND HUGO CHÁVEZ

The aspect of nurturance and maternal caring specifically arises in women's accounts about their participation under the government of Hugo Chávez. Susana Rodríguez, a leftist militant for over twenty years in the parish 23 de Enero, noted, "Women are always at the forefront and I think this has to do with maternity, with the necessity to look after and protect. To look after the fatherland, to look after the barrio, to look after friends, to look after the husband, to look after the president. It is a feeling that is generated among us women." In Susana's narrative, women's maternal role extends from family and community to their protection and defense of the president. Her framing needs to be understood in relation to constructions of women as nurturers and carers in Bolivarian ideology.[8] Like the Sandinista maternal ideal of Madres Sufridas in Nicaragua,[9] notions of revolutionary motherhood are also used in Venezuela to appeal to barrio women, a construction that both reinforces traditional roles and creates the groundwork for new possible roles and identities to emerge.

Various scholars have found that women use discourses of nurturance and their maternal role to frame their participation and construct a sense of collective identity.[10] But as Lynn Stephen argues, rather than understanding women's participation in terms of essentialized or uniform identities of motherhood, we need to look at the internal contradictions and differences being negotiated among women.[11] While for Yajaira and Susana, their maternal approach toward politics is embedded in long histories of community activism, for other women, it is Chávez who has made them feel needed. Carmen Teresa Barrios, from the sector Carretera Negra of the parish La Vega, talked about her politicization during the coup against Chávez in April 2002. When the opposition took over the presidential palace on April 11, there was little information available through the media about what took place. But as people heard what had happened, large numbers of them, predominantly women from the barrios, took to the streets to protest and demand the return of Chávez. Carmen Teresa recalls these days and she sees Chávez as awakening her qualities of nurturance:

> I am forty-something years old, and never in my life have I cared about what was happening in my country, and I'm saying my country, but also my Carretera where I live . . . It's like I am fulfilled. This work fulfills me. I want to be involved in everything, I want to participate in everything, I really feel that someone needs me and I can do it . . . That's why I say, it was Chávez who awoke the woman. He gave us importance, value . . . I studied, but I never felt interested to participate or do other things, to care about people other than myself . . . It was this voice that told us we could do it, that if we are united we can achieve something. I was one of those people who never thought about taking to the streets, like I did on April 11th, when they overthrew our president. I said, "My God, is this what you feel when you fight for what is yours?" I went all the way to Maracay in a car, I took a flag and I said to the others, "My God, what am I doing?" I didn't recognize myself . . . This was all asleep within me and because of this man, his calling, his way of being, or I don't know what, I got involved in this thing . . . And then I wanted to face the president

himself, and tell him how things should be, you may want to do it this way, but I don't agree. We should do it in this other way in order to achieve what we aim to do. That's why I tell you, it was an awakening, a calling, and he made us women go out into the streets, he made us realize that as women we can also struggle, we can do it and be involved.

Carmen Teresa's narrative contains several layers. On the one hand, there is a story of an awakening of almost biblical proportions, there is a "calling," and women have responded to this calling of the president. Chávez often appeals to a highly religious population with his rhetoric of an evangelical preacher, invoking love and redemption; his millenarian notion of a new start after the evils of the past; and his campaign posters featuring portraits similar to evangelical depictions of Christ.[12] Carmen Teresa's narrative reflects this kind of popular religious discourse that is appropriated by Chavismo. Carmen Teresa further expresses the importance that poor women feel as a result of Chávez's emphasis on the protagonism of the poorer classes. On the other hand, there is an awareness that Carmen Teresa knows best her "Carretera," as she refers to her barrio, and if she does not agree with the president, she can tell him the right way to do things. This latter aspect disrupts our ability to read the narrative as a populist manipulation of women's agency, as Carmen Teresa is expressing an initiative to decide what is best for her community rather than waiting for orders from above.

I observed this same dynamic with Yajaira; while watching a televised speech by Chávez on television she engaged in affectionate banter and maternal reproach with his figure on the screen. The speech was from Chávez's swearing-in ceremony at the Teatro Teresa Carreño, soon after he was reelected in December 2006. Yajaira was carrying out her evening chores, scrubbing some pots in the sink, preparing meat for Johnny's dinner, making juice, and struggling with the temperamental washing machine. She had turned up the volume on the small television set in the living room, and she would come in and out of the room, listening to the speech and offering her own comments to the screen. She talked with Chávez throughout his speech, discussing certain points with him, criticizing him, and laughing at his small diversions, jokes, and songs. At one point Chávez began to talk about corruption, saying that men who beat their wives are also corrupt. "I want to come out and ask the men to respect women," said Chávez. Hearing this discussion, Yajaira came out from the kitchen and paused in front of the screen, making emphatic sounds of agreement, nodding and repeating Chávez's words.

At one point toward the end of the three-hour speech, a few people began leaving the hall. Chávez reprimanded them, "Please, we haven't finished here . . . Look, we haven't finished. Discipline, I ask for discipline, I ask for discipline." Coming out of the kitchen, Yajaira wiped her hands on her dishcloth, exclaiming affectionately, "Ay, Chávez, you're too much! These people come from so far to see you, and now they have to get buses and find transportation to get home," she chided. "They have to go to their families." She looked over at me. "Just because Chávez has no family, his wife divorced him, his children are grown up, he can talk this way." While Chávez frames women's participation in terms of their family and maternal roles, Yajaira uses this same construct of the family to criticize his over-zealous and masculine concept of revolutionary "discipline." For Chávez, freed from his own family responsibilities, Yajaira feels that there are limits to his ability to understand the necessary domestic responsibilities of people, particularly women.

Chávez went on to elaborate his notion of revolutionary discipline, likening it to a Christian ideal of sacrifice. "If we want to be leaders of popular power, we have to give the example, friend, of force, of dedication to study, to work. For you there shouldn't be Saturdays or Sundays, nor Easter, nor Carnival, or anything . . . the leader should be capable of being like Christ going to the cross, that is, going to sacrifice and not one day, but every day of their life." In response, Yajaira continued to exclaim out loud to the screen. "Ay, Chávez!" she sighed. "Now you're saying we won't have our Sundays, our Christmas, our *parrandas* [Christmas celebrations], our vacations? No, no, this is too much!" For ordinary people like Yajaira, whose sense of community is rooted in shared Sunday meals, Christmas festivities, and vacations home to Barlovento or Yaracuy, the ideal of the disembodied militant is divorced from their realities.

Yajaira's commentary and dialogue with the screen was an expression of the unique individual relation many barrio women feel that they have with *el comandante*. He is someone who listens to their stories, and he is mind-ful of their concerns, but he is also a human being who makes mistakes and is in need of their guidance and protection. This kind of maternal protec-

tive relationship is not limited to barrio women or even Chávez supporters. A Venezuelan colleague was visiting New York with her cousin, an
older, middle-class woman who is a strong advocate of the opposition. As
we talked in the spacious Upper East Side apartment of another relative,
the cousin said that she felt sorry for Chávez because he is being taken
advantage of by those around him. "They are corrupt and he has a vision
for changing society, but he can't do it," she lamented, "because of the
inefficiency and corruption of those around him, *pobrecito*." She looked
wistfully out the large glass windows. When my colleague, amused by this
response, challenged her, she responded defiantly, "I am an anti-Chavista,
don't get me wrong, I just feel sorry for him." Even women who are not
politically aligned with Chávez and express their disdain for his policies
may still sometimes express maternal feelings of protection toward him as
an individual.

TERAPIA DE LA RISA (LAUGHTER THERAPY)

Yajaira's biography illustrates the ways in which individual life stories intersect with political processes: how people's trajectories are shaped by the
social worlds they come from and the collective histories they are part of,
but also how the details of their lives may inform the ways they take up
agency in those worlds. One final observation about her narrative concerns
the role of humor, and the ways in which Yajaira uses parody, joking, and
laughter to deal with some of the most troubling episodes of her life,
including racial discrimination in employment, the difficulties of making
ends meet, and the violence of everyday life. When I first met Yajaira, she
told me about a workshop she had once attended on *terapia de la risa*, or
laughter therapy, but she said she didn't need to learn how to do this
because it is what she does everyday. From then on, whenever we made
jokes or laughed, we would refer to it as terapia de la risa. In her study of
everyday life in the favelas of Rio de Janeiro, Donna Goldstein similarly finds
that humor was an important site of meaning making among the urban
poor: "Humor is a vehicle for expressing sentiments that are difficult to
communicate publicly or that point to areas of discontent in social life."[13]
This humor plays an important role in social movements. As Edgar "El
Gordo" said, "We are the kind of people who make fun of sadness, of hunger,
of whatever. This happiness has been a fundamental tool of resistance. Here
we are hungry and we make up jokes about it, someone in the family dies

and inside we are crying but we go out and throw a party." Laughing and making jokes is related to a popular spirit of survival and resistance.

Often when Yajaira and I discussed issues of race, she would make jokes. One of Yajaira's favorite songs is "La Negra Lorenza" by the original Grupo Madera. When Johnny would ask if dinner was ready, she would tease him with a line from the song, "Black woman, slave of all, I am no-one's slave." She would dance around the house, singing, "I am the Negra Lorenza. I have rebellion of my hair," the latter line a reference to the Afros of the Madera members, signifying resistance to white standards of beauty. We had many conversations about hair, and Yajaira admitted that unlike the Negra Lorenza she went every week to have her hair straightened at the hair salon:

> Maybe when my hair's wet it looks okay, but once the wind gets into it, it becomes a huge mess. If I walk down the street here in the barrio with my hair like a bird's nest, or if I go to work with a big Afro, people will start talking. They'll say to each other, "What's happened to Ya-jaira? Yajaira's gone mad." Tina Turner can walk down the street with wild hair and be glamorous, but if I do it, people will say I've gone mad.

By joking about Tina Turner, Yajaira points out the racial norms that define "normality" and "respectability" and make her feel compelled to straighten her hair. Even Johnny teases her before she straightens her hair, saying that she looks like a *bruja* (witch) and she should go to the hair salon. "The ways we shape and style hair," argues Kobena Mercer, "may be seen as both individual expressions of the self and as embodiments of society's norms, conventions and expectations."[14] Racist notions of "good hair" (*pelo bueno*) as straight and European versus "bad hair" (*pelo malo*) as "woolly" or "tough" are strongly embedded in Venezuelan society. But as Mercer points out, hair straightening is not simply an imitation of white hair; hair styling is itself a site for negotiating questions of identity, power, and agency.

It was on this very topic of hair straightening that I bonded with Yajaira's nieces and sisters, as we would talk in detail about the various methods and techniques for hair straightening. I myself used a ceramic iron or hairdryer to straighten my naturally wavy and curly hair. One of the times I left it wavy, Johnny called me a bruja, and after that I preferred to straighten it. Yajaira's sister Zulay and her fifteen-year-old niece Genesis used a regular iron to straighten each other's hair. We talked about hair texture, how the iron would take out the moisture, which meant you could go longer without washing it. Genesis would sometimes leave her hair in tight, springy curls. We talked about how men like Johnny preferred women with straight hair, and we discussed whether we styled our hair on the basis of what men wanted or how we ourselves desired it. Discussions about hair, and joking about hair, provided the basis for a deeper engagement with issues of race, intimate relationships, and how women negotiate those relationships.

Johnny and Yajaira also make fun of Johnny's disability and the disabilities of their friends and colleagues, up to a point. They would always correct others who referred to them as "disabled people." I once heard Yajaira explaining to a community activist, "We don't call them disabled people, because this assumes that being disabled explains everything about them, and not just one facet of their life. We call them 'people with disabilities.'" But beyond this, there was no sense of political correctness, everything was up for parody. Yajaira would say, "Johnny will give you a kick, well, one of these days when his legs work," and she would break up into uproarious laughter. Another day, she invited me to sit on their bed with them, and she said, "Just move aside all the rubbish," referring to Johnny's legs. Whenever we were out and we saw other people in wheelchairs, Yajaira referred to them as "Johnny's colleagues." This joking extended to Ricardito, a friend who is a little person. When showing me new home renovations, Johnny explained that they had specially built wide kitchen shelves "as extra space for Ricardito to sleep when he stays over." This joking was a form of defiance to the ridicule directed at people with disabilities; by making fun of Johnny's disability, Johnny and Yajaira removed the power of the dominant culture to label and belittle him. When Johnny worked for a community organization of people with disabilities, he would refer to them as "los patulecos, los mochos" (the armless, the mutilated). As Goldstein describes, people reclaim these derogatory terms as a way of taking control of their meaning.[15]

Every time I asked Yajaira to sit down with me and do an interview about her life history, she joked that I just wanted all the sordid details of her life because I wanted to write a steamy, sexy novel based on her life story. When she came to the end of the interview in the cafe in Altamira that day, after several hours of honest and often difficult material for her to relate, she finished up by saying, "There is it, there's your bestseller!"

II   EVERYDAY LIFE AND POLITICS

4 | Culture, Identity, and Urban Movements

Contemporary urban social movements have been shaped by experiences of over four decades of community-based organizing in the urban barrios, shifting relationships with a liberal and neoliberal state, and the struggles and triumphs of individual people. These contemporary movements, particularly as they have been reconfigured in a Chávez era, are the subject of part II of this book. I explore the ways that urban social movements draw on the inclusionary discourse of Chávez to contest long-standing structures of exclusion while at the same time grappling with the contradictions of the post-neoliberal state.

This chapter looks at the forms of cultural identity being deployed by urban social movements. Barrio residents in the urban centers of Caracas represent a large diversity of migrant groups from Europe, the Caribbean, and Colombia, as well as Andean, coastal, and Amazonic regions within Venezuela. In order to create a basis for building cultural community, social movement protagonists imagine new identities that can unite these diverse sectors. In contrast to dominant notions of a mixed-race nation, residents emphasize black and indigenous identity, with origins in Africa, slavery, and colonization. Theories of cultural identity have tended to present identity as strategic, invented, and contingent, rather than derived from ancestry or roots, as barrio residents often describe it. Some theorists ascribe to Eric Hobsbawm's and Terence Ranger's notion of "invented tradition," where identity is based on certain selected and institutionalized elements of the past.[1] Others, such as David Laitin, see identity as limited by given typologies, but also instrumental—constructed and reconstructed to serve individual purposes and take advantage of opportunities.[2] In contrast to these views of identity as invented or opportunistic, my own understanding follows the alternative approach set out by Stuart Hall, which sees identity as always positioned: "identities are the names we give to the different ways we are positioned by, and position ourselves within, the narratives of the past."[3] As Tania Murray Li elaborates it, identities are the product of a complex process of struggle and dialogue that draws on "historically sedimented practices" and "repertoires of meaning."[4] Barrio residents position themselves within fields of power and history, thereby connecting with others in broader social movements.

Popular fiestas and murals have been important vehicles in post-neoliberal imaginings of urban space and cultural identity, particularly given new geographies of exclusion. In barrios across Caracas, residents began to organize popular fiestas of San Juan and Cruz de Mayo as new sites of political agency. By 2005, fiestas were being celebrated in over forty barrios and sectors of the twenty-two parishes of Caracas. After decades of social dislocation, growing crime, and the militarization of the shantytowns, residents have used cultural forms as a means of taking back public spaces from the private sector and the police. San Juaneros, mural collectives, and devotees of the Cruz de Mayo claim the streets, walls, and plazas of the barrio as the domain of collective life and social interaction.

In the contemporary period, cultural identity has provided an idiom for the expression of class and racial cleavages in an emerging battleground between multiple competing tendencies in Venezuelan society. Opposition groups, consisting of business organizations and trade unions, as well as middle-class citizens' organizations and lobby groups, have declared themselves at the head of a universal civil society that resists the encroachments of the state, as embodied in the Chávez government. From the early years of Chávez's presidency, barrio residents were excluded from this notion of civil society and were represented in the media as lumpen (*lumpen*), hordes (*hordas*), and thugs (*malandraje*). In the religious celebrations of Cruz de Mayo and San Juan, murals of indigenous chiefs and the masked Bolívar, fiesta organizers and muralists created alternative repertoires of representation, positioning themselves against middle-class civil society. In forging alternative cultural representations, barrio residents make frequent reference to the official discourse of Chavismo. They identify icons such as San Juan with the figure of Chávez as a way of bolstering the legitimacy of their cultural movements. But as fiesta organizers begin to develop links with state institutions and official sectors of Chavismo, they clash with the technocratic principles of cultural management embedded in these institutions.

Culture itself has emerged as a crucial site of struggle within everyday wars of position. The field of culture has received greater public funding through oil revenues and local government in a Chávez era, but it also remains articulated to private investment and global circuits of capital. These contradictory tendencies are manifested in cultural institutions, which seek to incorporate cultural producers into a state-building agenda but are at the same time guided by neoliberal rationalities that emphasize the utility of culture in ameliorating social conditions and generating revenue. While cultural institutions view culture as both a means of political integration and a strategy for building social capital, barrio residents speak to the spiritual value of culture and culture as a way of being. The conflict between arts administrators and barrio residents is expressive of the contradiction at the heart of the hybrid post-neoliberal state. As the fiestas have adapted from being covert activities subject to policing under the opposition mayor Alfredo Peña to cultural festivities promoted by the Chávez government, organizers have been confronted with these new logics. By contrast, murals have been less incorporated into the utilitarian objectives of arts administrators, and they retain a greater connection with the everyday life of the barrio.

NARRATIVES OF CIVIL SOCIETY IN CHÁVEZ'S VENEZUELA

As state-society relations have undergone a series of transformations in recent decades, the term "civil society" has entered public discourse in an unprecedented way. Jean and John Comaroff compare the contemporary reemergence of the idea of civil society with its popularity during the second half of the eighteenth century, when society also faced dramatic transformations in the organization of production, labor, and the market; shifts in the connections between economy and polity; and challenges to the ontological core of humanity.[5] The eighteenth-century formulation of civil society proposed a measure of control over autocratic government, which should be exercised by an empowered citizenry. In its neoliberal guise, argue the Comaroffs, civil society has come to stand for society against the state; it is often synonymous with private enterprise or the market and is invested in an abstract community as the agent of collective action.[6] Similarly in Venezuela, neoliberal discourse equated the concept of civil society and civic freedom with freedom of the market or "private initiative."[7] Once Chávez came to power on an anti-neoliberal platform, self-proclaimed civil society groups denounced the interventionist action of the state in the economy as a threat to democracy. But unlike other postcolonies, where civil society was also a polyvalent construct capable of supporting various kinds of popular mobilizations, in Venezuela it became an exclusionary category, reserved for the middle and upper classes.

The concept of civil society in Venezuela was historically associated with the middle- and upper-class neighborhood movements of the 1980s discussed in chapter 1. The 1990s witnessed an explosion of NGOs and citizens associations which broadly identified as civil society. Following the Caracazo, there was the emergence of human rights groups such as the Comisión de los Familiares de las Víctimas del 27 de Febrero (Commission of the Relatives of the Victims of February 27, COFAVIC), and others that grouped together NGOs working on the same issues, such as the Coordinadora de ONG de Atención al Niño (Coordinator of NGOs Serving Children, CONGANI). In 1993, the National Encounter of Civil Society brought together 1,500 associations, and by the mid-1990s there were some 10,000 civil society associations in the country.[8] As explored in chapter 2, part of the reason why self-help groups and NGOs rapidly expanded during the 1990s was to fill the gap left by the withdrawal of state services. In this inclusionary version of civil society, NGO professionals, social organizers, and international development and financial agencies all sought to strengthen civil society as the basis of economic growth and sustainability.[9]

After Chávez was elected in 1998, civil society began to take on a more oppositional character; middle-class sectors allied with business groups and political parties self-identified as civil society confronting the Chávez-led state. This middle-class opposition coalesced into a new grouping known as the Asambleas de Ciudadanos (Citizen Assemblies, AC) that emerged from earlier associations of the neighborhood movements, but rather than rejecting political parties like their predecessors, they sought to build alliances with parties of the opposition. The AC worked closely with the Coordinadora Democrática (Democratic Coordinator), a body that united opposition political parties, and business organizations such as Fedecámaras and the official trade union group, Confederación de Trabajadores de Venezuela (Confederation of Venezuelan Workers, CTV), who actively opposed Chávez.[10] For a time, the Chávez government tried to wrest the language of civil society away from the opposition. It incorporated the category of civil society into the constitution and tried to promote various state-sponsored groupings such as the Círculos Bolivarianos (Bolivarian Circles) or the Red Social No Hay Marcha Atrás (There Is No Retreat Social Network) as the face of the new Bolivarian civil society.[11] However, these experiments were short-lived, and the concept of civil society had little resonance among barrio-based sectors and organizations. This situation differed markedly from other parts of Latin America where civil society was closely linked to issues of social rights and land redistribution. For instance, revolutionary groups in Mexico such as the Zapatista indigenous rebels issued a call for the formation of a new civil society;[12] civil society was seen as a multifaceted concept with possibilities to support this kind of radical politics.

The private media in Venezuela actively identified the concept of civil society with those sectors in opposition to the Chávez government. In the daily newspaper *El Nacional*, Pedro Carmona, president of Fedecámaras and leader of the 2002 coup, was asked the following question: "Will Fedecámaras continue coordinating the forces of civil society, for example the CTV?"[13] This question reveals a conception of civil society as consisting of various sectors under the leadership of the business sector and civil society is equated with corporatist entities such as the official trade union. In another article, civil society is defined broadly as "religious civil organizations, political parties, and universities" and in another it is strongly identified with the private media.[14]

At the same time, groups associated with the Chávez government are excluded from civil society because of their overtly political character. The journalist Romero Barboza differentiates civil society from what he refers to as political society, which is "constituted by organizations with political ends, oriented towards the attainment of political power to implement policy."[15] For instance, the Círculos Bolivarianos, as groups associated with the government, are not seen as civil society because of their *political* orientation. The sociologist Roberto Briceño León asserts that "the Bolivarian Circles are not civil society, but rather a political organization, the arm of a political party where to be involved you have to share their political orientation. They are more of a political party than an organization of society."[16] According to this narrative, civil society should be concerned only with influencing policy and acting as a pressure group,[17] but not assuming political power. Civil society protagonists assumed a clear boundary between state and society, thereby disqualifying those groups that maintained linkages with the government and misrepresenting their own connections with the political sphere, which included political organizations such as opposition parties. As Elias Iturrieta notes, this usage of civil society had a deeper ideological agenda, referring to "a special class of Venezuelans" who were not Chavista militants or unionists and not residents of the barrios.[18]

Many Venezuela scholars and social commentators have addressed the ways in which the civil society concept came to be an exclusionary discourse with specific class and race associations.[19] In his study of media representation at the time of the coup against Chávez in April 2002, Luis Duno Gottberg argues that the press and television in Venezuela played an important role in constructing some subjects as "organized political subjects" and others as "dangerous masses."[20] Juan Antonio Hernández locates these kinds of representations within a broader media orientation that can be seen in all the private media, including radio stations such as Unión radio and television channels such as Globovisión and Venevisión.[21] The marginalized majority, particularly those who support Chávez, are consistently denigrated as scum (*chusma*) and mobs (*turba*).

Political leaders with African, mestizo, and indigenous features are openly ridiculed in the private media. In an illustration that appeared in *El Universal* (March 3, 2002), Chávez is depicted as a monkey, evoking the most banal and crude stereotypes about people of African descent (see figure 1).[22] Chávez's full lips and broad nose are accentuated in the cartoon and he is shown in his regalia of the presidential uniform but with the body of a monkey. In each of the three representations he jumps, screeches, and covers his eyes and ears, associating his supposedly juvenile political conduct with his racial background. This kind of debasing stereotype has been used repeatedly in the media to refer to Chávez, and to his nonwhite ministers. For instance, in figure 2, from the supplement *El Camaleón* of the daily *El Nacional*, the newly elected black Minister of Education, Aristóbulo Istúriz, is also compared to a monkey. After the 2002 coup when Pedro Carmona was briefly installed in power, Istúriz was said to have taken refuge in a cage in the local zoo.[23] These kinds of derogatory statements imply that nonwhite peoples are unfit to govern the country, reflecting racist views held by large sections of the middle-class opposition.

Parodies of mythic indigenous chiefs in the private media reveal the emergence of a new set of racist stereotypes about popular sectors. While

1 Chávez portrayed in illustration from *El Universal*, March 3, 2002.

El nuevo Ministro al lado de su nuevo Administrador .
(Aristóbulo es el de la derecha).

2 Illustration from the supplement *El Camaleón* of *El Nacional*, 11 January, 2002. Translation: "The new Minister next to his new Administrator (Aristóbulo is the one on the right)."

during previous periods the cults of Maria Lionza and the indigenous chiefs, and images of San Juan were seen as shared icons that bound together Venezuelans of different class and racial backgrounds, in the contemporary period of rupture in the social order, these icons are re-imagined in negative terms. One piece published in *El Camaleón* on January 11, 2002, titled "Founding of the Bolivarian Circles in the Community of the Tabayara Indians," reports the visits of Chávez to the imaginary Tabayara community. In one visit to the Cacique Konsoda, a parody of an indigenous chief, the chief supposedly speaks with the president for an hour and a half, but since the president does not speak indigenous languages he is unable to understand anything. The report concludes: "That is the problem with these *indios*, nobody understands anything they say." In the parody of another chief immortalized in the sculpture by Eloy Palacios, the Indian of Paradise, Chávez tells the people that they need to build a paradise where all Indians can have the same privileges as the black Aristóbulo. The so-called report continues in this fashion, ridiculing the bolivarian circles as comprising indigenous people who are ignorant and incomprehensible. The shared jokes reveal the racist exclusions upon which "civil society," as constructed in the mass media, is based. They also demonstrate the resurgent anxieties of middle-class and opposition sectors, similar to what Philip Deloria notes in the case of iconography of American Indians in the postindependence period: "The mythic chief signified real-life savages who threatened the nation, a hostile class that had taken democratic politics too far, and a privileged elite reluctant to share its power."[24]

Racially motivated distinctions have their origins in Venezuela at the moment of colonization. During the nineteenth century, the white creole aristocracy developed stereotypes of blacks as stupid, lazy, ugly, sensual, and dirty in order to restrict their mobility and maintain them in a state of servitude.[25] As Cristina Rojas argues in the context of colonial Colombia, the discourse of civilization, materialized in certain privileged economic, religious, and educational practices, as well as habits, dress customs, and a mestiza civilization, was the model to be followed by the elite, while black and indigenous practices were seen as vices to be eradicated.[26] The struggle for civil society in Venezuela shows marks of similar associations with middle- and upper-class European habits, practices, and models, while denigrating black and indigenous cultures.

These negative stereotypes have always been a part of exclusionary discourses expressed by dominant classes in Venezuela. But dating back to the catastrophic currency devaluation of "Black Friday" in February 1983, and continuing with the rise of Chávez and the coup of 2002, racist stereotypes have formed part of a more concerted effort to disqualify lower classes from political participation and effectively to deny them citizenship.[27] In a broader global context, this racist and exclusionary language is related to an intensified moment of neoliberalism structured by the war on terror that has redrawn the boundaries of civilization and barbarism. After September 11, elite classes had a further justification for racist myths in favor of a separation between the "civilized" middle and upper classes and the "barbaric" masses.[28] The label of "terrorist" or "barbarian" took on new global political meanings.

The exclusionary appropriation of civil society by elite groups revealed the new visions of civilization at the heart of the neoliberal project itself: as the nationalist bonds that unified diverse social classes during an earlier period of national-populism disintegrate, society needs to find new means of ordering, regulating, and segregating the masses from emerging elite classes. The concept of civil society, with its ideological associations of "civility" and "civilization," becomes a means for justifying social exclusion and legitimating new elite classes associated with social and economic restructuring under a neoliberal order.[29] The exclusionary notion of civil society has various race, class, and gender associations that mark out certain social groups and classes as unfit for participation in the public sphere. Elite groups draw on discourses such as civil society to reframe oppositions such as civilized-savage, interior-exterior, and nation-Other. The mythic chief, who once provided a source of common national heritage, was now symbolic of a social fabric torn apart by savages.

Given the appropriation of the civil society concept by elite groups in Venezuela, barrio-based organizations and community groups have tended to self-exclude from identifying with it. At a barrio assembly in 23 de Enero in July 2004, a professor from the Central University of Venezuela (Universidad Central de Venezuela, UCV) was addressing the audience and he asked rhetorically, "Where is civil society?" One community organizer in the audience stood up and answered, "Chacao pa' alla" (from Chacao onward), indicating the east of the city, mainly inhabited by middle- and upper-class residents. His comment was greeted with laughter and spontaneous applause by the audience. The exclusionary appropriation of civil society by middle-class sectors and the media has resulted in a break with this concept. Instead, urban social movements use religious fiestas, iconography, and heroes from the past in order to reinvent marginality, blackness, and indigeneity as oppositional identities.

The turn to identity politics in Venezuela has gained impetus from multicultural reforms enacted under Chávez. Charles Hale defines identity politics as "collective sensibilities and actions that come from a particular location within society, in direct defiance of universal categories that tend to subsume, erase, or suppress this particularity. *Location*, in this sense, implies a distinctive social memory, consciousness, and practice, as well as place within the social structure."[30] According to Hale, and others such as Nancy Postero, the rise of identity politics in parts of Central America and the Andes was related to a series of reforms that they term "neoliberal multiculturalism," where governments passed legal reforms to recognize the cultural particularity of racial and ethnic groups such as indigenous peoples, while at the same time driving a wedge between cultural rights of these groups and their control over resources.[31] As indigenous actors in places like Bolivia embraced the language of the reforms and contested the exclusions inherent in them, they forged new modes of citizenship and engagement.[32] In Venezuela, where there was a shorter period of neoliberal ascendancy, multicultural reforms were not passed until after Chávez was elected, in the context of a broader anti-neoliberal agenda. The constitution of 2000 recognized Venezuela as a "multiethnic, pluricultural, and multilingual" society. Although the constitution failed to make overt provisions for the inclusion of Afro-Venezuelans within this description, despite appeals from the Afro-American Foundation and the Union of Black Women,[33] it does include sections that recognize the cultural rights of indigenous peoples, linking these with their collective rights to the land and natural resources of the territories they occupy. Urban barrio residents drew on this language of the constitution to stake their claims over public space and to demand access to resources and inclusion.

"WHO CAN STOP THE DRUMS OF SAN AGUSTÍN?":
LOCAL FIESTAS IN THE FORMATION OF CULTURAL COMMUNITY

Popular festivals are a form of cultural expression through which barrio residents reappropriate public space, emphasize their commonality, and imagine their social and historical origins as the basis for urban popular movements. The main festivals celebrated in the barrios are the Velorio de la Cruz de Mayo in May, Fiesta de San Juan in June, Diablos Danzantes in May and June, and the Fiesta de San Pedro in June. Since these fiestas originate in rural areas and are linked to the agricultural cycle, they mainly cluster around the rainy season, which lasts from May through August.[34] Other religious fiestas include San Benito, Santa Barbara, San Antonio, and more recently Santa Ifigenia. Urban communities separated from their rural roots appropriate popular traditions as a way of expressing the realities and experiences of urban life, while identifying their origins in a rural past, slavery, and the African diaspora.[35] In the contemporary period, this cultural identity is linked with popular protagonism, and it is the idiom through which communities assert their collective rights over resources and public space.

The fiesta of San Juan, celebrated in the events of Cruz de Mayo and San Juan, is one of the most popular of the fiestas among urban residents in Caracas. San Juan, like the other festivals, can be traced back to the period of colonization. As David Guss recounts, St John's Day, a church festival celebrated six months before Christmas, was the only day of the year when slaves were permitted to gather freely, dance, and play drums.[36] Most scholars have seen the fiesta of San Juan as speaking to both power and resistance. On the one hand, religious fiestas in Venezuela were strongly shaped by interactions with the colonizer. The creation of coherent religious systems like Santería in Cuba and Candomblé in Brazil was not possible in Venezuela due to the strict censuring of African and indigenous practices, the imposition of Christianity, and the heterogeneity of Venezuela's slave population.[37] The arrival of slaves in Venezuela predated the arrival of Yoruba to the New World by a long period, which makes it less likely that San Juan was associated with the Yoruba god Shango, as in Brazil and Trinidad.[38] Saint John the Baptist was seen by the colonizers and the Catholic Church as the bringer of civilization who would redeem heathen souls.[39] The figure of San Juan that is worshipped today in religious festivals is blond haired and blue eyed, reflecting in part the denial of color associated with the myth of *mestizaje* (the mixing of races).[40] On the other hand, the popular cult of San Juan bears strong traces of black influence and existed as an alternative countercultural movement within colonial society. The slaves accepted the Catholic saint San Juan, but they incorporated ancestral drums and African spirits.[41] Various scholars of Africa and the African diaspora have theorized this reconstitution of African-derived cultures as "creolization," "syncretism," and more recently as "innovation."[42] While the cult of San Juan reveals the partial acceptance of Catholic belief systems of civilization and ideologies of mestizaje, it has also functioned as a powerful symbol of cultural resistance and transformation for marginalized communities.

The ambiguity of the cult is reflected in the shifting interpretations of San Juan as both the religious figure of San Juan Bautista (Saint John the Baptist) and the popular figure of San Juan Congo. Representations of San Juan Bautista adhere to discourses of morality and purification inherent in the Christian idea of baptism. Raúl Britto, from San Agustín, specifically referred to San Juan as the evangelical who preached the word of Christ and baptized people. Raúl says that San Juan Bautista was decapitated because of his defense of morality. San Juan had castigated one of the Romans by saying, "You are sinning, you are bad, you live with the wife of your brother." Raúl's descriptions are infused with conservative and traditional biblical notions of sin. Señora Priscilla from 23 de Enero, an older woman attending the San Agustín fiesta, also affirms that San Juan Bautista was a disciple of Christ and he was the one who baptized Christ.

The popular figure of San Juan Congo is distinct from the civilizing Catholic figure of San Juan Bautista. In the coastal regions and urban barrios, it is common to hear narratives of San Juan Congo as a figure associated with slave rebellion in the colonial period, as the saint who freed the slaves, or as himself a runaway slave. According to Guss, until 1870 the figure of San Juan Congo was supposed to have been black, with a phallus, a feature that was common with African figures.[43] Although this black figure has since been replaced by a white one, the participants in the fiestas continue to view San Juan as black and poor much like themselves. For Williams Ochoa, who founded the Grupo Autoctono in Barrio Carmen of La Vega, San Juan Congo is a garrulous drunk who likes to argue. While the figure of San Juan used in the fiestas is white, he is perceived as black. "The people don't see San Juan as white," said Williams. "The people say to him, 'Shit *negro*, you let me down,' and they start fights with him as if he were any old black, they don't treat him as white." These seemingly contradictory interpretations of San Juan point to the specific configurations of race in Venezuelan society, where, as Guss observes, blackness is often associated with a social condition of oppression and poverty.[44]

The cult of San Juan may be seen along the lines of what Roger Lancaster describes in Nicaragua, as part of a set of patron-client relationships. Throughout the year, people make requests to the saint and during the festival of Cruz de Mayo they then repay the saint for the wishes he has granted through the act of *promesas*, or carrying the statue of the saint around on their shoulders. The relationship of the people to San Juan reflects another set of relationships in the political sphere, where the president or political leaders are seen as patrons of the poor. Since coming to power, Chávez has received thousands of petitions, letters written by people to ask for his help in resolving a particular issue, so much so that a special department was set up to handle the letters. Like San Juan, Chávez is seen as a benefactor who will protect the interests of the poor. But as Lancaster notes, this kind of patron-client relationship with the saint depends on reciprocity: "One's loyalty is at least theoretically contingent on the saint's fulfillment of his obligations to the people, and the saint's authority ultimately rests on the execution of his role as benefactor of the poor."[45] People believe that they can negotiate and bargain with the saint, as Williams relates: "I can start a fight with the saint because he didn't fulfill my request. San Juan is my equal." As I have described in an earlier chapter, the language of patronage can be a means of ensuring accountability, while at the same time upholding a certain structure of paternalistic authority.

Of all the parishes, the celebration of San Juan in San Agustín has been most associated with black identity, since a large majority of the barrios' population migrated from the former-slave, coastal communities of the northeastern state of Miranda, popularly known as Barlovento. During the fiestas of May 2004, residents identified both with their rural origins and their African ancestry. Juan Palacios referred to himself as "Barloventeño," from San José de Río Chico: "I come from descendents of the African race and let's be clear, I am of the black race, my parents are Barloventeños, and supposedly this comes from the people of African race who are situated in the Barlovento region." Two women, Yolanda and Rosaria, said that the popular festivals come from Barlovento but are being reinterpreted by the people of the barrio: "These fiestas come from our ancestors who were slaves and we are retaking them because these are our roots and this belongs to us." The fiestas are a means by which the women construct lineages and ancestry that link contemporary marginality and poverty with the oppression experienced by earlier generations of rural blacks and slaves.

3 Altar at San Juan celebrations, Sector Las Casitas, La Vega, July 3, 2004. PHOTO BY THE AUTHOR.

In other parishes such as 23 de Enero and La Vega, migrants have come from a range of rural locations. In La Vega, there are residents from Barlovento, the coast of Aragua, Tamunangue from Barquisimeto, and the northwestern state of Yara. At the San Juan fiesta up in Las Casitas of La Vega, which I attended on July 3, 2004, there was one central altar with the statue of San Juan from Miranda, San Antonio from Lara, and Santa Barbara, from the Cuban religion of Santería, and also the African court of the María Lionza cult. Despite this diversity, the identification with blackness and slavery is still strong among residents in La Vega. Edgar "El Gordo" Pérez is one of the long-term leaders and residents in Las Casitas. True to his nickname, El Gordo ("fatty") is a large, brown-skinned man, with a jovial demeanor and the reputation of being an organic intellectual of the community. El Gordo locates himself as part of a long genealogy of Afro descendants: "I am the fourteenth generation of Domingo Riva. Domingo Riva was one of the first blacks, born in Barlovento, in Guatire . . . I feel super-privileged to be black." El Gordo's use of the term "black" reflects a shift in popular usage, away from a simple description of color and as a means of refashioning new collective identities. As Winthrop

Wright has noted, in Venezuela the terms "negro" and "africano" have traditionally been used to describe clearly black or African people, while lighter-skinned people were seen as part of the mestizo or pardo population.[46] El Gordo's complexion is brown and not black, and likewise, Williams is light skinned; both would probably be seen as mestizo, but instead they choose to identify as black. At the same time, El Gordo rejects the term "Afro-descendant," which he sees as highly intellectual and disconnected from the vernacular uses of "negro" as a term of endearment. He makes the following humorous observation: "For us, the word 'negro' has a connotation of affection, I'll say to my woman, 'negra, give me a kiss.' I can't say to her, 'Afro-descendant, give me a kiss.' " For El Gordo, the redefinition of blackness is still organically connected with vernacular usages.

El Gordo goes on to link racial heritage to political struggle: "Our struggle didn't begin with the current president . . . I feel part of a social historical current and I am a participant and I am in this country since my ancestors who came from Africa and today we continue the struggle for a free society." El Gordo, like Juan, Yolanda, and Rosaria, is engaged in a struggle to make and remake himself through historically continuous narratives. El Gordo acknowledges the importance of Chávez in helping to promote their struggles, but he also asserts the autonomy of these movements, which have a longer history and tradition. The invocation of history is more than an attempt to determine ancestry. It is an identification with a past of domination, and a desire to address historical legacies of marginality and inequality.

Festivals in the barrios are organized by *cofradías*, which are brotherhoods or units of organization that are charged with collecting money for events, soliciting donations, and researching the historical and religious significance of the events. Historically, cofradías are Spanish in origin, and they were established during the seventeenth and eighteenth centuries in certain churches and parishes for the organization of religious activities, raising funds, and providing food for ceremonies. The cofradías were administered by laypersons, and they were autonomous in both structure and finances from the church.[47] In rural areas such as Chuao, a northern coastal village that subsists on cacao production, the cofradías have maintained their historic role in organizing the fiestas of San Juan and Cruz de Mayo.[48] It is only more recently that these institutions have been recreated in the urban context. The collectives constitute a social basis to mobilize the diverse populations of the barrios and unify them around new interpretations of culture and tradition. Raúl described culture as something that needed to be preserved or rescued: "We formed the cofradía so that we don't lose our culture. It's so that our culture doesn't die like it's dying in many communities. We want to rescue our culture." But despite this reified language, for fiesta organizers, culture is not a static concept as in mainstream understandings of "folklore" or "tradition." It is rather a set of practices that link communities to their imagined past and the realities of their present; as Néstor García Canclini has argued, culture fulfills the functions of "reelaborating social structures and inventing new ones."[49]

In the barrios of Caracas, the cofradías are exclusively limited to males who are bound by oath. This differs significantly from the cofradías in rural areas such as Chuao, where the majority of cofradía members are women. In Chuao, the Sociedad de San Juan (Society of San Juan) is essentially a woman's organization, and the few men who join play secondary roles.[50] Women in the barrios are strongly present in the fiestas as planners, dancers, and historic figures of the community. Yet in the translation to the urban context, machismo and heterosexism have predominated over the matriarchal structures of rural life. In an urban context where men have greater access to resources and the time to devote to religious activities, they have taken over the leadership positions and redefined the ethos of the cofradía to privilege heterosexual men. "In the cofradía," said Williams, "men have to be men, they don't accept homosexuals." The kind of masculinity promoted in the urban cofradía excludes those who are not considered to fulfill heterosexual ideals.

There is a hierarchy and specifically defined role for individuals within the cofradía. In the cofradía of San Juan in La Vega, Williams is the custodian of the saint. He explains that, "There is a first, second and third captain; the donkey of the saint, who carries the saint; the custodian, in charge of educating new recruits, the paying of promises, and internal commitment to the oath, explaining the meanings of the festival, and staying true to tradition." The captains must ensure that the fiesta goes according to plan, that resources are available, and the saint is dressed. In some ways, the tight organization of the cofradías reflects the sense of a community under siege, who must organize in order to protect themselves. But this sense of siege and adherence to traditional forms of hierarchy gives rise to other forms of exclusion, such as gender exclusion. As Daniel Goldstein notes of

Bolivia, "The fiesta, intended to challenge the unjust exclusion of the marginal barrio from membership in the city and the nation, has itself developed its own forms of belonging and exclusion."[51]

Prior to the 1980s, there were no public celebrations of the popular fiestas in the barrios. Barrio residents returned to their native place in order to celebrate the fiestas, and a few celebrated privately behind closed doors in their homes. Ricardo Hernandez, a fiesta organizer in the parish of Catia, says that during this time people were reluctant to openly practice their religious traditions for fear that they would be ridiculed. But in the 1970s, musical groups and movements such as Madera, Convenezuela, and Un Solo Pueblo, as well as individuals like Ricardo and Williams, began to travel across the country carrying out research on traditional musical forms and fiestas.[52] Ricardo recounts that he would consult with a local informant in the barrio, say someone from San José de Guaribe, who could explain the origins of a particular musical form and give him contacts in his hometown. Upon arriving in the rural area, Ricardo would speak with many people, relying on their oral testimonies and his own observations in his investigations. In La Vega, Williams would speak with the *abuelos* (elders) of the barrio and travel to the rural areas where these abuelos were born to observe the week-long festivities. The investigations were done in what Williams referred to as a very "rudimentary manner," observing the cultural festivities, making recordings where possible, and taking notes. Then, back in the urban context, they organized demonstrations of their investigations, gradually forming a small school to teach music, dance, and knowledge of local traditions. In 1974, Williams founded the Grupo Autoctono, which combined music and dance instruction with artisanship and cookery. In these activities they were assisted by the abuelos. For Williams more so than Ricardo, the investigations were connected to a rediscovery of African heritage. "We realized that there were a lot of black people participating in the religious fiestas and these fiestas came from Afro-communities," says Williams. "It occurred to us that this was an 'Afro' culture that had been silenced." As compared with earlier understandings of folklore as the shared heritage of a mixed-race society, Williams presents the fiestas as the particular lineage of black Venezuelans.

In the urban context, the festivals of Cruz de Mayo and San Juan have been historically linked to the parish San Agustín. In the 1960s, Cruz de Mayo was kept alive by a rural migrant, Felix María Mata, and his wife,

Dolores Brito. After they passed away, the tradition died along with them. But in 1982, Jesus "Totoño" Blanco and two other friends revived the fiesta of Cruz de Mayo and in 1989 the parish celebrated San Juan for the first time. In La Vega, Williams and El Gordo began celebrating San Juan in Barrio Carmen and Las Casitas in the late 1990s. During the first decade of the new century, these fiestas spread across urban sectors of Caracas, due to the growth in local organizing networks, state sponsorship, and with the promotional activities of local community media.

CELEBRATING SAN JUAN IN THE PARISH OF SAN AGUSTÍN

During the month of May, residents of San Agustín celebrate the Cruz de Mayo, or the Cross of May. On May 31 a celebration marks the ending of the Cruz de Mayo and the beginning of the San Juan festivals. In 2004 I attended this celebration, known as the Velorio of the Cruz de Mayo, in San Agustín. I arrived with my friends Johnny and Yajaira in San Agustín at 11 p.m. at the historic square, El Afinque de Marín, where the fiesta was to take place. Johnny drove up into the square and we were greeted by Yajaira's many friends and family from Barrio Marín. The altar was decked out with brightly colored flags and crosses. The mural of the original members of the historic musical group from San Agustín, Grupo Madera, was illuminated by soft lights. The laughter and chatter of the black youth with their hip-hop gear, corn rows, and dreadlocks gave the scene a sense of urban contemporary reality. Devotees of the cross stood at the altars singing songs to the mounted crosses, while the youth passed around bottles of beer and malta.

Anticipation and excitement were in the air, and at the same time a certain sense of apprehension. A large shiny white jeep of the Metropolitan police, known as the Metropolitana, circled the Afinque repeatedly. Yajaira explained to me that the Metropolitana had a history of intimidating barrio residents during festivals, but that it had become more serious in recent years, since the opposition-identified city mayor, Alfredo Peña, had been in power. At least twice in the past year the Metropolitana had showed up at festivals and fired shots into the air to scare people. This evening the people were addressed by community leaders who said they had word that the Metropolitana might show up again and try to intimidate the crowd but that people should not panic, as the police just wanted to demonstrate their power and authority to break up the fiesta. That evening there were

4 Devotees at Cruz de Mayo celebrations, Barrio Marín, San Agustín, May 31, 2004.
PHOTO BY THE AUTHOR.

no incidents with the police, other than their continual surveillance. Local leaders realized the importance of standing up to the police, as a sign of community strength and power. Through the popular fiestas, residents are defending public spaces as spaces of collective life, against the police who have turned these spaces into war zones.

Just before midnight, I went with a group of barrio residents looking for the figure of San Juan, which was hidden in one of the houses of the barrio. Nobody is told in advance where San Juan will be hidden; only the organizers and the house owner know. We walked up and down the old cobblestone streets and past the elongated, colonial style houses of Barrio Marín in a procession led by a large white and red flag until we came to the house, and when we entered we saw the statue of San Juan, dressed in a gold cape and hat and bearing a cross. After singing several songs to San Juan around an altar, the procession made its way back to the Afinque. There was a brief mock struggle as the Cruz de Mayo devotees resisted the entry of San Juan. But they gave way, and then people carried the San Juan statue on a platform above their heads, making *promesas*, expressing their appreciation to San Juan for a favor they have asked of him. Following this,

5 Arteaga distributing aguardiente to participants in the San Juan procession, San Agustín, June 24, 2004. PHOTO BY THE AUTHOR.

the batá, fulía, and culo e' puyo drums were brought out, and people stood in a tight circle as young men played the drumming style of *sangueo*. As they played, people began to form circles of dancers. Around four o'clock in the morning they began the *perra*, an intense fast style of dance and drumming, common to the region of Curiepe. The importance of the drums and the overt sexuality of the dances mark out the ritual as distinct from the Andean festivals of the south.

The San Juan fiesta in San Agustín is celebrated on June 24 with a day-long procession through the barrio, singing, dancing, and drumming. The fiesta was already in full swing when I attended it in 2004. Men, women, and children led the procession down the main street of San Agustín, waving brightly colored flags that are said to purify the road ahead of them. Two young men, Alexander Arteaga and Raúl Britto, moved through the crowd offering people *aguardiente*, a liquor made from sugarcane, from bottles slung around their necks. In rural areas, the procession tradition-ally passes by the church so that San Juan can be blessed by the priest.

"Here we have an issue," Raúl told me. "When we go to the church the priests don't want to bless San Juan. Every year this happens."

Alexander added, "And today we had a mass because for months we've been requesting a mass for the saint, and we wanted to know why the priest didn't want to bless the saint."

"Why doesn't the church see this fiesta as part of the church?" I asked them.

"They say that this isn't part of the church but I've been to the church at times and they talk about San Juan," replied Raúl. "They say that this isn't a religious issue and that's why they can't bless San Juan. But it is a religious issue, it's the religion that we have."

"The priests have refused many times to do the mass for San Juan, in the Church of Fátima and of Nazaret," added Alexander.

Raúl continued, "But San Juan has to be blessed by the priest, by God, because we go purifying the path, and we don't want problems with anyone. Anyway, San Juan was a man of the church, he was a baptist. We had to bring him [the San Juan statue] to the church and say, 'Please, give this damned guy some holy water, 'cause we're missing out on the party.' The priest thought it was a joke and it's not. This is a religion for us, that we love and respect. Why do they always reject us when we're working so hard? . . . Just because we're in the Central that is Caracas, the heart of Caracas, why do they reject us? The president says, "Nobody outdoes me" [*A mí no me mueve nadie*] and that's San Juan now. The police also want to dominate us, but they are very mistaken. Who thinks that they can stop the drums of San Agustín here?"

Alexander and Raúl appeal to the church for inclusion, mentioning the status of San Juan within the Catholic hierarchy and desiring the purification that comes with the blessing of the church. In the rural setting, the church is more likely to accept and incorporate the fiesta of San Juan into its mass, but in the urban context this relationship is more contested. Along with the constant policing of the urban fiestas, these fiestas are also culturally rejected and excluded from dominant frames of religiosity. In contrast to the fiestas of San Juan in the eastern village of Curiepe, marketed and promoted as a folkloric celebration of national identity,[53] the urban fiestas are denigrated by dominant classes as disorderly and potentially disruptive. Raúl draws on the associations of San Juan Bautista as "a man of the church, a baptist," as a way of asserting the legitimacy of their religion. He also compares San Juan to Chávez in his determination to withstand the repeated onslaughts of the opposition. Just like Chávez,

San Juan and "the drums of San Agustín" are symbols of their resistance and struggle in the face of discrimination and misunderstanding from the broader society.

The plan was to take San Juan up to the *cerro* (hillside shanties), and after people from the ranchos had joined the group they would return to the Afinque for dancing and drumming in the evening. Alexander said, "San Juan will go up to the cerro, up into the hills, we will take over the cerro . . . And we will keep purifying paths: the police won't stop us as we go up and then come back down." When the procession reached La Charneca, we stopped and the singing and dancing continued in large groups. At one point, there were several young men from the army, dressed in fatigues and dancing and singing along with the other members of the group. It was clear that these young men themselves come from the barrio, and their presence was accepted by the barrio residents. But the police, while also often young men from the barrios, have a different institutional relationship with barrio residents and would not dare attend a popular fiesta dressed in uniform. Particularly today, given Chávez's military insignia and his origins in a radical sector of the army, people from the barrios are more likely to welcome members of the army into their celebrations, rather than the police, who have a history of intervening in the barrios and harassing residents.

Again, the fear that the police would stop the procession was palpable, and in fact the march was stopped, but not by the police. As the procession came down from the cerro it confronted a shootout between rival gangs, which resulted in the death of a young gang member. A large crowd gathered around the body of the young dead man and the dancing and singing stopped, as the police came to cordon off the area and an ambulance carried away the body. Later that evening in the Afinque there were no celebrations as on May 31 but rather an air of gloom and despondency, as people shared alcohol and reflected on the sad events of the afternoon.

The popular fiestas are part of a broader resignification of public space, and fiesta organizers and participants are forced to confront the realities of gang violence and police harassment. When Williams Ochoa and other community leaders in Barrio Carmen of La Vega began the celebrations of San Juan in 2001, they saw the celebrations as a way of reclaiming public space for the residents of the community, who were living at a time of heightened violence due to the clashes between local gangs and the police.

6 Barrio residents, including young men from the army, sing traditional San Juan songs, San Agustín, June 24, 2004. PHOTO BY THE AUTHOR.

A year later, during a procession of the effigy of San Juan through Barrio Carmen, Williams's seventeen-year-old son, Williams Alexander, was killed while confronting a gang of youth who were trying to sabotage the procession. During the course of the procession, two or three gang members arrived and began harassing fiesta participants. Williams Alexander reprimanded the gang members three times. The members left, threatening to come back and shoot him; at the end of the procession they returned and shot him several times. Residents across the barrio went looking for the gang members, but they had escaped and one was later killed in a shootout with police. It was difficult and painful for Williams to lose his son this way. Through the tragedy of his son's death, Williams has struggled to understand the meaning of violence among youth. "While there is no employment, education or constructive activities; while they keep pulling down basketball courts; while there are no spaces of recreation for the kids; what we have is a bubbling pot of *malandros* [delinquents]," Williams reflected. "Violence is the only form of expression available to them in the face of so much anger, impotence." But he has faith that by making available another form of expression—that of the fiestas—they will choose instead to participate in the social justice struggles of the community. "My son died," he said. "But come what may, we will never stop the fiesta of San Juan and we won't forget the kids of the barrio, because it is for them that we are rescuing these traditions." Williams and other fiesta organizers seek community-based solutions to the problems of violence, which may mean painful sacrifices for them and their families.

CULTURAL PRODUCERS ENCOUNTER THE HYBRID STATE

Culture is an important means by which urban social movements express their collective identities, make claims over public space, and forge new kinds of protagonism—especially as they are excluded from a middle class–identified civil society. But while barrio-based cultural expressions were relatively disconnected from state institutions in the early years of Chávez's presidency, as Chavismo was consolidated in the post-2004 order, cultural producers were gradually drawn into the orbit of state cultural institutions and subjected to the instrumental logics of the hybrid state. These logics include both political incorporation as a tool for ideological cohesion and the market-based rationalities that have come to dominate the administration of culture. Both of these logics combine in the cultural legislation and programs of the Chávez government, rendering culture a highly contested site in a post-neoliberal era.

Historically, state sponsorship of culture in Latin America meant that the culture industries were controlled and sometimes subsidized by the state. In Argentina, Brazil, and Mexico during the 1920s and 1930s, cultural forms such as samba, carnival, murals, and tango were nationalized in an attempt to unify the population during the stage of import substitution industrialization.[54] In Venezuela, state promotion of popular culture as part of a national culture came later, beginning with a brief period of democratic rule from 1945–48 and followed by the era of national-populist democratic rule from the late 1950s through to the 1980s. Under the auspices of the Folklore Service headed by Rómulo Gallegos, Juan Liscano choreographed a five-day "folklore" performance in Caracas in 1946 with groups from around the country. Through this and subsequent performances, the image of San Juan became the center of a new national identity and was publicized to the country as a whole.[55] During the 1970s, the oil boom facilitated a distribution of wealth to the cultural sector. As Guss argues, the government began to play an increasingly important role in cultural renewal, as it formulated the first comprehensive cultural plan and created the Consejo Nacional de la Cultura (National Council of Culture, CONAC), which coordinated cultural activities and the arts across the nation.[56] In 1971, the Afro-Venezuelan coastal village of Curiepe was named "National Folklore Village." State patronage also became tied to a clientilist system, as drummers in Curiepe received nominal payments from the political party in power.[57] Amid nationalizations of the iron and oil industries in 1975, state sponsorship of culture helped to bolster a fervent nationalism and contributed to a system of patronage.

During the 1980s, culture was increasingly commercialized, but corporations still focused their efforts on promoting national identity in order to sell products. As Venezuela was hit by the debt crisis, the significant reduction in state funding for cultural programs was supplemented by corporations such as the Cigarrera Bigott. Cigarrera Bigott was a Venezuelan tobacco company with a national reputation that was purchased by the transnational cartel British American Tobacco in 1922. In his comprehensive analysis of the company, Guss relates that British American Tobacco remains one of the world's largest cigarette manufacturers and Britain's third largest industrial enterprise. In 1963, British American set up the Fundación Bigott (Bigott Foundation), primarily as a philanthropic association designed to aid workers to finance their homes. During the nationalist years of the 1970s, as foreign-owned companies began to undergo nationalization, Bigott had sought to associate itself with the sphere of national culture by sponsoring cultural initiatives and workshops.[58]

This plan proved fruitful in 1981, when the government of Luis Herrera Campíns outlawed all tobacco and alcohol advertising on television and radio. As Guss recounts, the Fundación Bigott began to invest more heavily in the field of popular culture as a way of promoting itself without advertising cigarettes.[59] Two of the main aspects of this campaign were cultural workshops and television programs. The popular culture workshops were part of an ambitious nationwide program for the teaching of local forms of Venezuelan music and dance. Groups that emerged from these cultural workshops were important forces in projects of cultural renewal in the barrios. But it was a delicate balance for radical cultural groups to accept support from a corporation and for Bigott to work with leftist groups, and as Guss says, this balance only worked if each group thought they were using the other.[60] Ricardo Hernandez himself justified it this way: "In some ways Bigott served our interests, actually we utilized it, because it allowed us to meet people from isolated regions that later we ourselves began to visit, we began to gain their confidence, and then apply their techniques in the urban communities." Bigott also produced a television series on popular culture in the mid-to-late 1980s that included over 140 programs. In place of mentioning its brand, the programs displayed the company's logo with the name of Fundación Bigott.[61] In addition, Bigott developed the magazine *Revista Bigott* through its publications program, a rural radio series in tobacco-growing states, and grants for culture-related activities. Through these programs, the tobacco corporation redefined popular culture and itself, as symbolic of national values and identity.[62] In some ways, corporations had taken over the state's role in patronizing national-popular culture and disseminating vernacular forms.

An important shift took place during the 1990s, with the election of Carlos Andres Pérez and the neoliberal turn ushered in by his government. In this period, culture was resignified as a product or merchandise for consumption. As Yolanda Salas argues, "The *pueblo*, the subject and actor of the popular, is substituted by the product that should be advertised via the mass media."[63] The "popular" was being transformed into the "consumer." At this time, other corporations were pursuing programs in popular culture, introducing competition for Bigott. The field included the Fundación para la Cultura Urbana (Foundation for Urban Culture), affiliated with the Grupo de Empresas Econoinvest; the Centro Cultural Corp Banca, funded by the private bank Corp Banca; Fundación Pampero, a program of Pampero Rum; and the Fundación Polar, founded by the beer company Polar.[64] In a neoliberal climate of greater openness to foreign investors, private foundations were less interested in promoting national identity as a way to market themselves and were more direct about publicizing their products. The new director of Bigott, Antonio López Ortega, told Guss in an interview that after 1991 "the foundation decided to completely abandon its old course and start coming out in public and begin speaking really clearly about our programs, our achievements, and the various objectives we've accomplished."[65] Bigott became more frank in its language of publicity, integrating its cultural activities into a promotional campaign.

But the transition that took place was more than the resignification of culture as a commodity; as George Yúdice argues, in a neoliberal era the field of culture itself becomes regulated by an economic rationality based on utility. Instrumentalized art and culture are actively recruited by states and foundations to improve social conditions, support civic participation, or spur economic growth.[66] Along these lines, Pérez's VIII Plan of the Nation proposed to deal with poverty and create economic efficiency through deepening cultural development, as promoted by international foundations such as UNESCO and the World Bank. Under a section headed "The New Strategy of Cultural Change," the plan lists the nature and contributions of culture in development, including "culture as a factor and means of development," "harmonization of growth with social wellbeing," "culture as a distinctive end of economic growth," and "culture as a right and public service."[67] Another policy released a few months later as the Plan of Sociocultural Participation proposed to "develop a culture with strategic value, that is, one which permits a more positive insertion into social life and the field of labor."[68] As compared to culture as an end in itself, culture was increasingly seen in instrumental terms as a means for promoting development and economic growth and ameliorating social problems. As state expenditures in the arts were reduced, private foundations like Bigott were given an expanded role in meeting these goals.

After Chávez was elected in 1998, cultural producers encountered conflicting rationalities that included both the use of culture for political gain and integration—especially as state financing of the arts was revitalized—and a utilitarian approach to culture as a resource in which to invest. Fiesta organizers, cultural producers, and residents countered these logics of the hybrid state with alternative views of culture as a way of being and as linked to their everyday lives and religious cosmologies.

Chávez implemented new policies for arts funding. The Proyecto de Ley Orgánica de la Cultura (Project of the Organic Law of Culture, PLOC), jointly designed by the Ministry of Education, Culture, and Sport and CONAC in 2000, established the approach of the Chávez government as contrary to dominant neoliberal models by increasing state patronage of culture, and it highlighted the importance of the state in protecting and preserving cultural patrimony.[69] The Chávez government has channeled oil revenues into the sponsorship of culture, making greater funds available to municipal governments. Local level councils such as Fundarte, the Foundation for Culture and the Arts of the Mayor of the Libertador Municipality, have played an increasingly important role in the funding and stimulation of cultural forms such as the urban fiestas.

The increase in state sponsorship for fiestas was visible between the 2004 and 2005 celebrations. During the San Juan festivities in San Agustín in June 2005, Raúl and the other members of the cofradía were outfitted in identical yellow t-shirts which read, "San Juan—San Agustín." Although the t-shirts did not advertise the sponsor, they had been given by the Chavista city mayor, Juan Barreto. Fundarte had also contributed some resources toward the organization of the fiesta. The difference was notable from the previous year when opposition mayor Peña had been in power and the fiestas had more of an oppositional and subversive nature. But despite accepting state support and wearing the t-shirts, barrio residents spoke about wanting to maintain the fiestas as religious events and not tools for partisan intervention. Raúl articulated some of the ambivalences arising with state support:

> Fundarte is with the proceso. It has always existed and has helped us, but at times we don't want to politicize our culture and Fundarte is another institution of the government. Now we ourselves are the government, the people is the government, it is no longer Fundarte, or Freddy Bernal or Chávez, it is the people . . . We don't receive money from the state. And we don't want the state to suddenly come and tell us they're gonna give us millions of bolívares. No, this is culture, it is a religious issue, not political. We want the community to be united.

Raúl strategically places himself both inside and outside the state as he negotiates the contradictions of state funding. He draws on the official slogan, "El estado somos todos" (We are all the state). After many years of organizing the fiestas with scarce resources, Raúl welcomes the access to state resources made possible under Chávez. Yet he also wants to maintain the autonomy of culture from politicization, meaning intervention by partisan interests that could introduce divisions. Against a notion of culture as a tool for political integration, Raúl affirms its spiritual and religious dimensions.

These ambiguities of state funding for fiestas were also apparent at the National Meeting of Black Saints, directed by Williams Ochoa in June 2005. The mayor's office gave money to bring in groups from around the country for processions and seminars in Barrio Carmen of La Vega, as well as for a large concert in the Plaza O'Leary, where various groups gave short presentations to the crowd. The event at Plaza O'Leary was reminiscent of Liscano's staged events, with the fiesta as a spectacle for consumption.

This staging of fiestas was reintroducing the idea of the artist as performer, of having a separate stage, and of paying the artist. As Freddy Mendoza, the community leader in La Vega, observed, in the local fiestas, "Drummers are not seen as artists, they are part of the community who produce music . . . the artist is not distinct from the community." The performers and the audience at the O'Leary concert felt uncomfortable with the format, and some groups called for getting rid of the stage, saying that this is a religious ritual, not a public concert. Finally, in the last performance by the San Juaneros from Caracas, audience members climbed onto the stage and everyone joined in the singing, disrupting the pedagogy of the event as spectacle. Then the tambores were brought out into the crowd, and the audience broke up into small circles with people dancing and drumming.

The staged event reinforced a static and reified notion of cultural practices that contrasted with the more fluid understanding of culture among barrio communities. Another illustration of this was the continued use of the concept of "folklore" by state administrators and foundations. The cultural institution for the promotion of traditional cultures was called Foundation of Ethnomusicology and Folklore (FUNDEF).[70] Guss recounts that Bigott also had a notion of folklore as a detachable object, as evidenced by its later policies of "de-folklorization," or the repackaging of culture for the middle and upper classes, and the view of folklore as a commodity, prevalent in the 1990s and beyond.[71] Williams, among others, was critical of the notion of folklore: "For a long time we called our culture folklore, but we eliminated the term because it identified us first with our language and later with our way of being. It seemed to us that folklore was a cold term and the people in the countryside, for instance with respect to the *bailes de tambor* [dances of the drums], they didn't call this folklore, they called it *bailes de tambor*." Williams points out that the categories and framing of traditional cultures in terms of language groups is arbitrary and not reflective of the ways in which people themselves conceive of their cultural practices.

Increased state funding under Chávez promoted the idea of culture as a tool for national cohesion and political integration. But at the same time, the field of culture continued to be oriented toward foreign and private investment. According to Title V of PLOC, "With the goal of incorporating private investment as a substantial source of financing, it [the law] establishes a regime of fiscal incentives in agreement with the principles, criteria and procedural norms envisioned in Chapter II." Early on in the Chávez administration, relationships were established between cultural institutions and corporations. In October 1999, the Ministry of Education, Culture, and Sport signed an agreement with the Fundación Bigott, offering technical assistance to specialist instructors working in the areas of traditional dance and music. Over 1,200 instructors were funded to travel across the country holding culture workshops. Each workshop cost Bs 1 to 1.5 million.[72] In 2000, the director of Bigott, López Ortega, was appointed to the Ministry of Education, Culture, and Sport. Bigott, along with the Central Bank of Venezuela, the Fundación Polar, and the Corporación Andina de Fomento (CAF) lobbied for the formulation and approval of the Law of Mecenazgo to provide fiscal incentives for private companies to invest in the arts. López Ortega argued his case in terms of the financial benefits of encouraging private investment: "The Law of Mecenazgo in Brazil, approved in 1993, has converted Brazilian culture industries into the second largest product for export in Mercosur."[73] These corporations pushed for the development of culture as an export industry and for its conversion into a profitable activity in Venezuela.

The Chávez administration defended its alliances with the tobacco company in the promotion of culture. Yolanda Salas, an anthropologist who was the director of FUNDEF from 1998 to 2001, relates that during her time in this position she encountered an attitude of complacence among high cultural officials in the Ministry of Education, Culture and Sport toward the contradictions represented by the dominant involvement of Bigott in cultural programs and the "strategic alliances" between the state and this transnational corporation. In her dealings with cultural officials, Salas encountered "silence before my proposals, defense of the excellent quality of the activities of the Bigott Foundation and, in addition, arguments that defended the importance of the income received by the state from the collection of taxes on the sale of cigarettes." In Salas's experience, state officials mimicked the promotional discourse of the company about its success in cultural affairs and excellence of production, ignoring the implications for public health of addiction and illness caused by smoking.[74] Early on, private capital was assured a stable environment to continue investing in culture.

The orientation of the arts toward private investment has encouraged the prevalence of market-based calculations within state-sponsored programs. The utilitarian approach to culture as a service or product with the end of enhancing growth and development is clearly outlined in PLOC. Article 133 of the law declares, "The state, by way of the Cultural System of Culture, will promote the creation of Cultural Agencies, with the goal of increasing the offering of cultural goods and services and to promote economic growth." As Yúdice argues, the utilitarian idea of culture as a resource entails its management. Technicians are subordinated to administrators, and artists are required to manage the social. Arts administrators as "managerial professionals" become intermediaries between funding sources and artists or communities.[75] This technocratic management of culture by arts administrators can be observed in the policies and practices of cultural institutions under Chávez.

Under the Plan of Cultural Funding, the Chávez government created new administrative bodies to determine the allocation of resources for culture, the distribution of the population, the degree of importance of certain cultural traditions, and the areas that should be promoted.[76] Although the idea is to democratize the sphere of culture, it continues to be managed and regulated by technocratic principles. In 2006, Fundarte had begun implementing a program known as "Joint Programming, Operative Plan of Diagnostic Revision." I was present at a meeting at Fundarte on February 9 at which arts administrators came up with a list of their priorities for the organization of cultural activities in the barrios. These priorities included a census of possible facilitators in the barrios, raising the profile of these select facilitators, and building a local investigation team to study cultural practices, such as the fiestas. Like Li argues in the context of World Bank development programs in Indonesia, informal practices and relationships have to be rendered technical to prepare for an intervention. Experts had to identify groups and enroll social forces, and then these groups could be funded, counted, legitimated, and replicated.[77] As cultural practices and communities were rendered technical, they were also prioritized according to instrumental ends.

As they discussed how to proceed, some arts administrators at Fundarte argued that local leaders of the community should be able to come up with their own proposals and present proposals to Fundarte for funding, since the people in the communities know their own necessities best. But others took a more paternalistic approach; one administrator said that Fundarte should create proposals on behalf of all the community groups, based on

Fundarte's institutional diagnosis and line (*lineamiento*). "The fiestas in the communities are too general and undefined," she said. "They don't solve their necessities." This administrator's assessment of fiestas as "general" and "undefined" is another way of saying that they do not serve instrumental purposes, such as resolving the basic needs of residents. Rather, according to this discourse, there is a need for expert diagnosis from the arts administrators to analyze how fiestas could be mobilized to ameliorate social conditions. The discussion reveals the intersection between neoliberal-technocratic discourses and what Li identifies as the "will to improve" that is present in all development interventions. Arts administrators are self-styled experts who presume to know better than local leaders what is good for the community.

Another site where the technocratic management of culture was apparent was a workshop by an arts administrator at the Alameda Theater in San Agustín. The Alameda Theater was a privately owned abandoned theater that had been occupied and recuperated by fiesta organizers and residents of the parish as a Casa Cultural (Culture Center) in April 2004 (the experiences of the residents in organizing their cultural center will be more fully explored in chapter 6). Certain cultural institutions became involved in the Casa Cultural after the takeover and they sent arts administrators to the barrio to carry out workshops for the residents. While well intentioned and socially committed to their work, these administrators are beholden to instrumental notions of culture as a resource.

Through state-promoted activities and workshops in the Casa Cultural, arts administrators sought to promote the strategic notions of culture as showcased in PLOC. On July 25, 2004, a facilitator from the Cinemateca Nacional (National Film Library), Maria Borges, held a workshop in the Casa Cultural. Borges, a white, middle-class, professionally trained woman, was the coordinator of the Program of Associated Cinema Halls. The workshop was attended by twenty-five or thirty residents active in the Casa Cultural, men and women of all ages. Borges began by putting up a statement, "Strategic Actions for Cultural Change," which included the following:

—new cultural legislation
—regionalization, decentralization

—reordering of public cultural administration

—designing cultural policies adjusted to national and regional development plans

—organization of social and cultural networks

—creation of regional advisories of culture

—autonomous institutes and state foundations for regional and municipal processes of cultural development

—institutional qualitative evaluation and programming for assigning resources

—private participation in cultural development

As Borges spoke about the government priorities for culture, she referred to the residents as "beneficiaries" of resources rather than active participants. Borges's statement reflected the technocratic approach to cultural policy that has become standard under neoliberal administrations. There is a focus on decentralization, where cultural promotion is handed from the national state to regional and local governments. The notion is that culture is a resource that can be linked to "national and regional development," primarily through tourism and the development of social capital. The idea of "qualitative evaluation and programming for assigning resources" seeks to weigh the benefits and costs of a particular program in order to justify investment. Finally, the statement makes mention of private participation in cultural development in line with Title V of PLOC.

Cultural institutions such as the Cinemateca Nacional promote forms of neoliberal instrumentality, and they often clash with the goals and perspectives of residents. In the workshop, Borges asked the participants to break up into groups; each group had the task of defining what it saw as culture. The groups came up with the following:

Group 1: Culture is "the everyday" of the people. Culture is to carry out events on the social-political level.

Group 2: Values, created and obtained by the people from generation to generation.

Group 3: Culture is everything around us; it's what people do collectively in their community, and in a specific place.

Group 4: Culture is actions, teachings, and knowledge of the family, the sector, the city, and in oneself, a process that transforms.

7 Workshop in the Casa Cultural, July 25, 2004. PHOTO BY AUTHOR.

The definitions provided by the participants in the workshops gave an indication as to their understanding and relation to culture. Barrio residents saw culture as what they create in their everyday lives. For them, culture is not a universal category but a local process of sociopolitical change linked to the family, the sector, to "a specific place." By comparison, Borges interpreted their responses through an instrumental notion of culture as social capital or a resource. For the first group, she said, "What you are talking about here when you say '*realizar eventos*' is diffusion." Borges placed Group 1's response into a framework of cultural promotion. For Group 2, she said that "valores" refer to "our cultural patrimony, our local, regional, and national identity." Again, Borges imposed her framework onto the responses: local culture exists as a channel for the creation of a greater national culture. In reality, the participants had not mentioned national identity. Borges sought to reformulate and reinterpret the responses of the participants to fit the framework that she sought to impose.

Borges then entered into a discussion of what she referred to as "Strategic Lines," which she said were drawn from the National Plan of Culture embodied in PLOC. The diagram she showed the group consisted of Cultural Public Intervention → Body of Cultural Policy → Organizational Culture. Borges explained to the participants that they needed to raise their activities to the level of "Organizational Culture." What was ironic was that 278 members of the community had organized and achieved what no group had before, the takeover and running of the Casa Cultural Alameda. Borges's paternalistic approach was apparent in her pedagogy: she would pose questions to the participants and answer them herself. At one point she asked, "Why do we work in culture?" She followed this with a response, "Work in culture should have the objective of offering services to the community and allowing the community to consume its products." In addition to being "beneficiaries" of services, the residents are also repositioned as "consumers." Borges illustrated her argument with another diagram:

Inputs → Organization → Results: Achievement of Common Objective
Resources
Medium
(human, material)

Borges's diagram and explanation reflect a highly technocratic and instrumental approach to culture. Conceived in terms of an economically utilitarian model, people become "inputs" and "resources" whose labor must produce certain "results." This is part of a discourse of "social capital" employed by institutions such as the World Bank, where people are the "untapped human resources" of development planning.[78] As Borges had explained earlier, the results must be demonstrable in measurable terms in order to qualify for state patronage. The reaction of the workshop participants to Borges was one of general indifference and boredom. Some participants doodled, others stared blankly into space. As an outsider to the community, and clearly from a different class background, Borges had little credibility among the participants of the workshop.

As cultural producers begin to collaborate more with arts administrators, a new site of struggle is emerging over the nature and uses of culture. Instrumental approaches to culture as a tool for political integration on the one hand, and as a service or product designed to ameliorate social problems and promote economic growth on the other hand, have been seen as anathema to one another. But under the cultural legislation of the hybrid post-neoliberal state these strategies overlap and combine. While arts administrators look to the utility and political uses of culture, emphasizing reified and technocratic interpretations of cultural practices, fiesta organizers and residents offered alternative versions of culture as identified with a way of being, as a local category linked to sector and place, and as part of religious rituals and cosmologies.

POPULAR ICONOGRAPHY AND MURALS IN THE BARRIOS

Although culture is a zone that continues to be articulated to private capital under the post-neoliberal state, some cultural forms are less subject to cultural management and intervention, such as murals. While the fiestas are mostly concentrated in the rainy season, murals—created and observed year round—are a more quotidian part of barrio culture. Mural collectives have received grants and support from cultural and local government institutions for their projects, and some murals in the barrios have been government commissioned. But murals are less transportable to other contexts and hence not so commodifiable. Affixed to the walls and buildings of the barrios, murals are less easily drawn into strategies of tourism or cultural promotion. These factors may give muralists greater opportunity to build alternative and collective modes of sociability.

Like San Juan, popular elaborations of Simón Bolívar, the cult of indigenous chiefs, and mythical figures such as Negro Primero and Maria Lionza have also played a role in shaping new cultural imaginaries and identities. In one mural by the La Piedrita collective in 23 de Enero, Bolívar is represented as "encapuchado," or wearing a hood, that is painted with the color of the Venezuelan flag. The hood is a form of symbolic protest strongly associated with the student movements of the 1980s and 1990s. Next to the mural is a sign that reads, "Bolívar reclaims the hood in Latin America and the world." One of the members of La Piedrita, Nelson Santana, remarked, "If he lived today, Bolívar would have worn and reclaimed the hood. For our generation the hood was, and continues to be, a symbol of popular resistance. It is the same rebellious and contestatory Bolívar that history brings to us, but I wanted to present him actualized, modern, the face of the future."[79] Santana's discourse draws strongly on the Bolivarian narrative present in Chavismo, about calling on the past as a way of expressing the hope of the future.

Images from the cult of indigenous chiefs and black heroes such as Negro Primero have also been widely appropriated by muralists. The images themselves date back to the intellectuals and chroniclers of the early eighteenth century. The historical events of Spanish colonial invasion and conquest involved numerous battles between the colonizers and the native

8 Mural of Simón Bolívar in Sector La Piedrita, by muralist group La Piedrita, July
2004. PHOTO BY THE AUTHOR.

indigenous population and rebellious slaves during the course of the six-
teenth century. Based in the myths and legends of heroic black and indigenous fighters elaborated after these events, creole intellectuals and writers
of the eighteenth century created enduring literary representations, such
as José de Oviedo y Baños's *Historia de la conquista y población de la
provincia de Venezuela* (History of the Conquest and Population of the
Venezuela Province). These early texts played a fundamental role in establishing the borders between the inevitable authority and rights to governance of the creoles and the defeated culture of indigenous people and
blacks.[80] As in the case of American Indians, representations of a savage
and exterior Other assured the elites of their civilized nature and justified
the dispossession of real Indians.[81]

In the 1940s, the images of mythic heroes became widely disseminated
as the basis for national identity. Beginning with Antonio Reyes, and
his text, *Caciques aborígenes venezolanos* (Aboriginal Venezuelan Chiefs),
several writers, sculptors, and painters began to elaborate the mythical
images of the indigenous chiefs as symbols of a "mestiza Venezuela." Under the military rule of Pérez Jiménez in the 1950s and his doctrine of

the New National Ideal, these images became institutionalized through the use of Reyes's text in schools, official paraphernalia such as postage stamps, the construction of sculptures of the chiefs by Alejandro Colina to adorn plazas and murals in public areas, and the launching of a new line of hotels with the names of indigenous chiefs.[82] Political leaders used these homogenous and ahistorical representations as a way of projecting national unity and mestizo identity, hiding the existence of real Indians and blacks. Nationalist intellectuals such as Juan Liscano, Juan Pablo Sojo and Miguel Acosta Saignes criticized official representations and sought to create alternative representations based in archival research and historical sources. Meanwhile, in the cult of Maria Lionza and other local interpretations, urban sectors also developed interpretations of these symbols. Michael Taussig sees the elaboration of these figures by the urban poor as a means of reinvigorating state power, through supplying the concrete referents to official discourse.[83] But in the contemporary era, given the inability of national myths and symbols to unify a fractured polity, local interpretations have taken on a life of their own. Daisy Barreto's argument holds true, that "the chiefs of Reyes have contributed objectively to elaborating an imaginary world by which both elites and popular classes, each time with their own desires, identify in order to rethink their past, present, and future."[84] It is important to stay attuned to the multiple meanings of these figures, as symbols of subversion, legitimation, and challenge.

Contemporary local interpretations of the chiefs can be seen in a set of murals of indigenous chiefs in the zone of Monte Piedad Arriba of 23 de Enero, painted by one of the residents, Oscar Betancourt. Betancourt is brown skinned, with a youthful face and a bushy moustache, flecked with gray. Popularly known as "El Indio," he identifies himself as a descendant of indigenous people from the *llanos*, or southern plains, and a son of the organized community of 23 de Enero. This affirmation of multiple histories and ways of belonging is increasingly common as urban residents seek to frame their experiences in terms of rural and historical tropes. El Indio explained, "Via the murals we want to show our roots, our struggles, because this is where it began, the struggle for land during the Spanish invasion." As barrio residents negotiate identity in the urban environment, claims to "roots" and authenticity are increasingly connected with rights over resources. Residents appropriate black identity and remake them-

9 Oscar Betancourt, "El Indio." PHOTO BY THE AUTHOR.

selves as descendants of indigenous chiefs, as a means of vindicating their rights over "what was lost."

El Indio related to me the stories of the various chiefs, their indigenous modes of resistance and their bravery in battle. His narratives about the chiefs clearly draw on the histories given in texts such as Oviedo y Baños's *Historia de la conquista* and Reyes's *Caciques aborígenes venezolanos*. However, while the chiefs of Oviedo y Baños and Reyes are symbols of a defeated race, El Indio connects himself with contemporary indigenous people through invoking his own ethnic lineage. The first mural is of the chief Terepaima, who, El Indio says, captured animals by grabbing their heads with his bare hands, and in this manner he caught a Spaniard. In Oviedo y Baños's version of the story, the hero is the Spanish leader Francisco Fajardo, who brings Terepaima under his dominion:

> They came out to meet him bearing arrows to take his life, but Fajardo's strength of reasoning was so vehement and so natural was the dominion of his voice over the Indians, whether for hidden sympathy or the respect with which they venerated his mother, Doña

Isabel, that Fajardo himself went to talk with him in his arbaca language, to tell him whose son he was, which converted the anger of the chief [Terepaima] into meekness, treating him [Fajardo] with such friendship and gratitude that he accompanied him to the valley to leave him safely in the savanna of Guaracarima.[85]

In this passage, Fajardo is able to tame and coax the wild Indians into submission; he wins their loyalty through persuasion rather than force. El Indio draws on and elaborates the account of Terepaima given by Oviedo y Baños. But in El Indio's account, Terepaima is converted into the hero. As El Indio tells it, Terepaima forced the Spaniard to give him information and was told that the Spanish were going to invade the community of the chief Naiguatá in the Vargas state. Terepaima released the Spaniard and crossed the mountains of Guaraira Repano, today known as the Avila, until he reached Vargas and could speak with Naiguatá. In El Indio's account there is guile and cunning rather than meek submissiveness on the part of Terepaima. After Terepaima informed Naiguatá, his liver burst and blood came pouring out through his mouth. This is why, says El Indio, Terepaima is painted with his mouth open. El Indio seeks to counter the "emasculation" of indigenous chiefs in the narrative of Oviedo y Baños, over-emphasizing their masculine bravery and brute force.

El Indio identifies the chief Mara, represented in one of the murals, as a leader who fought to retain his land against the invaders in Maracaibo. Another of the murals is a portrait of the indigenous chief Chacao, who El Indio says was good at escaping the Spanish. In El Indio's account, the Spanish tried to kidnap three indigenous children bathing in a river, but Chacao rescued the children. He was shot three times by the Spanish but still managed to return to his community with the children. The chief Guacaipuro was able to unify all the indigenous chiefs and organize a joint struggle, terrorizing the Spanish, says El Indio. What El Indio refers to as a "joint struggle" is for Oviedo y Baños an "evil alliance."[86] El Indio says that at that time the indigenous people did not have guns or bullets; they had knowledge and they made knives from a plant called *vero*, which, depending on the phase of the moon and when it is cut, becomes hard like steel. They combined this with another poisonous plant to make lethal weapons. They then planned an attack on the enemy in the early morning, during which many Spanish surrendered. While El Indio relates the story of Guai-

10 Terepaima from the Gallery of Chiefs, Monte Piedad Arriba, 23 de Enero, mural by Oscar Betancourt, July 2004. PHOTO BY THE AUTHOR.

caipuro as a success for the indigenous chiefs, for Oviedo y Baños it is a misjudged win: "the barbarians judged that they had secured victory."[87] In the discourse of eighteenth-century creoles such as Oviedo y Baños, the chiefs are "barbarians" and "savages," exterior to civilized European society.

El Indio's depictions of the bravery and courage of the chiefs are closer to the representations by Reyes, writing in the mid-twentieth century. In the writings of Reyes, Guaicaipuro is a warrior who "fought for an ideal. An ideal of the fatherland, of defense of his native soil against the invader."[88] For Reyes, the chiefs are symbolic of national identity, not barbarism. Yet it is only by way of their complete defeat and disappearance as indigenous subjects that the chiefs can be reincorporated into the mestizo nation. Reyes celebrates the downfall of Guaicaipuro in his text: "He succumbed. He succumbed with glory. Faithful to the fighters forever. His death constituted the definitive defeat of indigenous defense."[89] Likewise, the death of the chief Tiuna signaled the disappearance of indigenous people: "His disappearance ended in the painful and resigned submission of the tribes that formed the peninsula of Caracas."[90] Intellectuals such as Reyes promoted the defeated chiefs as part of a common history of struggle and

11 Mara from the Gallery of Chiefs, Monte Piedad Arriba, 23 de Enero, mural by Oscar Betancourt, July 2004. PHOTO BY THE AUTHOR.

12 Guaicaipuro from the Gallery of Chiefs, Monte Piedad Arriba, 23 de Enero, mural by Oscar Betancourt, July 2004. PHOTO BY THE AUTHOR.

13 Chacao from the Gallery of Chiefs, Monte Piedad Arriba, 23 de Enero, mural by Oscar Betancourt, July 2004. PHOTO BY THE AUTHOR.

national defense, but real Indians were excluded from the life of the nation.[91] By contrast, El Indio declares himself a descendant of indigenous people who survived colonial invasion and continue to struggle today. El Indio draws on the ritualized accounts of Oviedo y Baños and Reyes to give a counternarrative that converts the barbarians into resistance fighters staking their natural rights over resources.

Although El Indio presents himself as part of a long line of indigenous fighters, his stories are not documents of a natural historical continuity with his indigenous past. As James Clifford suggests, "Metaphors of continuity and 'survival' do not account for complex historical processes of appropriation, compromise, subversion, masking, invention, and revival."[92] El Indio's stories are built from the pieces of popular legend that are passed down from generation to generation, eighteenth-century chronicles and official textbooks, and his present realities. Oral narrative is an important source of popular knowledge and El Indio says that some of the stories of the chiefs came from his grandfather. El Indio says that he has received much of his information from the chronicles of the historian Fray Bartolomé de las Casas. In school texts and popular tradition, Las Casas is often mythically elaborated as defender of the Indians, which is why El Indio identifies him as a source of information, but in reality Las Casas did not write the stories of the mythic chiefs. El Indio says that the impetus to pass on indigenous history and "know our roots" has also come from the discourse of President Chávez:

> In the proceso, one of the fundamental objectives of reclaiming the indigenous chiefs is to know our roots and to know that they gave their lives to defend this land. We have this in our genes and it has flowered, it was what was missing, but our leader revived it. In the proceso, the Gallery of the Chiefs is there, alongside the Gallery of the Heroines and the Gallery of the Liberators. Our leader gave us the interpretation that we need to know our roots, in order to understand where we are today, and why we are fighting, what objective do we seek.

Through his Gallery of Indigenous Chiefs, El Indio participates in the reinvention of tradition as posed by Chávez. His idea of coherent and stable roots belies the discontinuous and relational experiences of Afro-descendants and mestizos. However, in the details of his stories about the chiefs we see not merely an imitation of official discourse but a making and remaking of identity. A panoply of mythical figures from the past provide the language for articulating contemporary cleavage and inequality, a metaphor for survival that resonates with those excluded from civilized society.

In addition to recuperating Bolívar and the cult of indigenous chiefs, figures who have always occupied a central role in official narratives, barrio residents also seek to rescue and recreate marginal historical figures such as Negro Primero and Manuel Piar, who have mostly been invisible in official histories. Negro Miguel, also known as Negro Felipe, led the first slave revolt in Venezuela in December 1552. Slaves led by Negro Miguel established an alliance with indigenous people and successfully attacked principal strongholds of the Spanish, attempting to establish a zone free of European domination.[93] At times, the figure of Negro Miguel is conflated with the figure of Pedro Camejo or Negro Primero, a hero of Venezuelan independence.[94] The figure of Negro Primero has also been a part of popular consciousness through its presence in the cult of Maria Lionza. Maria Lionza is an indigenous deity and the central figure in a syncretic cult of saints that includes Negro Primero and Guaicaipuro. According to Yolanda Salas, beginning in the 1970s, there has been an Africanization of the cult, and through Negro Primero and other black spirits, devotees "speak of a suppressed and relegated blackness, that wants to tell its own history, although modeled according to its own expectations and in accordance with certain stereotypes of traditional circulation."[95] Other figures such as Manuel Piar are also part of this countertradition. Piar, an independence hero of humble and mixed-race origins, was killed by a firing squad on the eve of the Third Republic for pursuing a regionalist war strategy that went against the orders of Bolívar. In Bolivarian ideology, the shooting of Piar is justified to calm fears of disunity, racial transgression, and civil war that his presence evoked. But in popular oral traditions, Piar is vindicated and his memory is converted into a struggle against injustices committed.[96] Alongside the official cult of Bolívar exist parallel popular cults, whose figures and antiheroes constitute an alternative frame of reference.

Community leaders appeal to these figures from history, and to the historical process itself. Freddy Mendoza compared Chávez's Fifth Republic to the Third Republic of 1819, when Bolívar presided over a post-independence order. According to Freddy, the Third Republic was lost because Bolívar and the mantuanos could not conceive of governing along with the indigenous and black population. Today, says Freddy, the Fifth Republic will also be lost if the bureaucrats in Chávez's administration resist the inclusion of people from the barrios and indigenous groups. Freddy draws a parallel between the administrators of Bolívar's time and the administrators of today, and the continuing racism that popular sectors continue to face, even from a government that asserts it is committed to representing the people's interests. A repertoire of icons recreated from the margins of official history is the grounds upon which barrio residents elaborate their concerns, hopes, and desires in the present.

CONCLUSION: IDENTITY POLITICS IN A POST-NEOLIBERAL ERA

The appeal to cultural identity by urban movements in the contemporary era contrasts with earlier national-populist movements that sought to celebrate the mixed-race roots of the nation and subsume cultural difference into national identity. Under successive military governments in Venezuela between the 1930s and 1950s, intellectuals and popular classes collaborated to integrate local traditions and histories into a national culture. As Barreto argues, symbols of national unity had to be fabricated in order to overcome local ethnic particularities and integrate the rural masses that migrated to urban centers.[97] With the return to democracy in the 1960s in Venezuela, and a new national-populist politics, heroic figures, cults, and images were defined as the unique heritage of the popular classes.[98] But beginning in the 1980s, musical groups and community organizations in the barrios began to retake popular fiestas as an expression of black and popular identity. Muralists put forth alternative interpretations of independence hero Simón Bolívar and the cult of indigenous chiefs, retrieving figures such as Negro Primero and Manuel Piar from a historical tradition within which they were silenced. As part of the social movements that emerged, barrio groups drew on racially defined and historically invisible aspects of national cults.

The contemporary moment has seen the rise of barrio-based movements that link cultural identity to claims over public space, access to resources, recognition of land titles, and the right to participate in governance. The multicultural reforms enacted by the Chávez government recognizing ancestral land rights and resource control for historically marginalized groups, and Chávez's language of diversity and inclusion, have provided novel repertoires of contestation. Fiesta organizers described their activities as defending public space from the gangs and the police. Barrio residents made references to their "roots" and black and indigenous identity as a way of framing their demands in historical battles over land and resources. They invoked Chávez as a symbol of their rights to governance, while noting that their struggles predated him. The strategic uses of identity by barrio residents are different from identity politics in the United States. While in the United States, identity politics often involves organizing along racial and ethnic lines, defending one's own race or ethnic enclave, and competing with other enclaves for resources, in Latin America understandings of race have been more fluid, and notions of identity function more as a means of articulating a sense of shared marginality.

But as they sought to generate collective, emancipatory, and everyday visions of culture from within state-promoted cultural forms such as the popular fiestas or culture houses, urban movements came up against the contradictions of the post-neoliberal state. Along with a renewal of arts patronage, the state has attempted to use culture as a tool for political integration, and cultural institutions are also guided by neoliberal technocratic rationalities that emphasize culture as a resource. In contrast to these logics, fiesta organizers and residents emphasized the spiritual dimensions of their cultural activities, and culture as a way of being that is linked to a specific sector and place. Perhaps in the case of murals, groups may have more opportunity to build these alternatives in spaces that are a part of everyday life and less amenable to state management.

The situated nature of cultural identity for barrio residents also helped them to define their difference to a middle-class-identified civil society from which they were excluded. While in some contexts civil society has been paraded as a universal category—often masking economic interest and class privilege—in Venezuela it was revealed to be a class and racially specific concept marked by exclusion. The exclusion and self-exclusion of some marginalized sectors from Western-derived models such as civil society leads me to ask, following the Comaroffs,[99] what might Latin American forms of associational life look like? How can we understand what is outside of civil society, as it is narrowly constructed by elite classes in Venezuela? How might we broaden the concept of civil society to theorize a plural and diverse domain of social activity? My description of the San

Juan fiesta is an attempt to show the contours of one kind of counterpublic that is emerging in the barrios of Caracas.

Social scientists have tended to focus on political parties, trade unions, and organized civil society as the main sites of politics and representation. Many see the crisis of traditional political institutions as a crisis of democracy, without paying attention to the emergence of new forms of popular organization such as cultural fiestas, murals, community radio stations, and barrio assemblies that are reinvigorating a nascent public sphere. Given the paucity of academic frameworks for describing the institutions of popular politics, I have turned to ethnographic thick description to investigate them. Javier Sanjinés proposes that we look at marketplaces, festivities, and rituals to see how a vibrant Indian urban culture in Bolivia formed the environment for the emergence of an alternative public sphere.[100] The private media parodies the supposed incomprehensibility of the Other, and social science tends to dismiss forms of cultural life that are illegible to the researcher. But barrio groups are creating and sustaining novel forms of communication through languages of music, performance, and street art. Empirically grounded, ethnographic, and non-Eurocentric modes of research have a crucial role to play in shifting the discussion of agency to the horizontal and regenerative forms of association that are emerging in a post-neoliberal era.

HOST: Our great friend Nicolás Díaz is calling from the sector Santa Cruz. They have a cofradía for the organization of San Juan Bautista of Macarao, and they're inviting all of the community in general to participate in the *Encuentro de Tamboreros* (Meeting of the Drummers) that will happen tonight in the street Río de Santa Cruz, on Saturday July 2—today—at two in the afternoon. And they're telling us that the girls are making a *sancocho* there. And we'd like to give space on the air to Nicolás. Good day Nicolás!

NICOLAS DIAZ: How are you, my friends, from Radio Macarao, from the parish Macarao . . .

HOST: We're well and we want to say hi to all the people out there. We want to let you know that you're on air right now.

DIAZ: Of course, and the neighbors from the parish, all our colleagues, the community radio, and all within this alternative movement, in search of a process of change and transformation. Look, we're here. The proposal is for the people to come by, to the shopping center, between the basketball court and the plaza. Right now there's an important team making the *sancocho* . . . Joana, Materano, el Yoyo, Carmen Medina, Otilia. Here is the precious Guaya Márquez, Cecilia Salazar, Josefina Márquez, *la niña* Judith Vázquez, and Tiago. And of course, what we want is simply to give a kick-start to this activity, something that, within our community activities in the parish, is necessary.

—RADIO MACARAO, JULY 2, 2005

The residents of the Caracas parish of Macarao have been celebrating the popular fiesta of San Juan since 2002, and the local radio station has been an important tool in helping them to organize this fiesta. On a Saturday afternoon as residents take care of household chores, drop by to visit the neighbors, or prepare the evening meal, they tune in to their community radio station. They might stop by the plaza to see the drumming groups or join in the dancing and partake in the traditional *sancocho*, or soup. Fiesta organizer Nicolás Díaz is calling in to the radio program on his cell phone, drawing on innovations of cell phone technology and radio transmission to publicize his event. The mention of people's names, streets, and places indicate the highly localized nature of community-based media.

In the previous chapter, I explored how popular fiestas and street murals are a means for barrio residents to emphasize their commonality and imagine their social and historical origins in the creation of an urban cultural identity. Community media allows social movement actors to project this cultural identity on a larger scale, reinvigorate a popular democratic public sphere, and create alternative strategies and visions for change. Based in the everyday life and cultural activities of barrio residents, community media plays a crucial role in the emerging new spaces of associational life. These forums promote debate about issues in the barrio and they allow people to recuperate their ability to speak and be heard. Embodied and historically located subjects challenge the claims of a universalist civil society to speak for all. They use a language of particularity, of belonging to a specific barrio or sector, class, and racial or ethnic group. Low-power radio, along with community newspapers, assemblies, and television, provides a forum for those citizens who, as Jaqueline Urla says, "do not or will not speak the language of civil society."[1] As the concept of civil society is constructed as an exclusionary discourse in the private media, community media producers create their own alternatives.

Community radio, assemblies, and newspapers form a layered set of publics that have expanded dramatically since Chávez was elected to office. There are multiple media collectives affiliated with barrio organizations. There are those who are linked to tightly knit, cadre-based organizations, where a smaller leadership usually makes decisions. There are some who have acted as brokers between the government and barrio groups. There are other collectives with less formal structures, which operate through assemblies and collective decision making, at times leading to the emergence of informal cliques. Certain groups have sought to make strategic connections with state institutions in exchange for resources; others tend to rely more on self-financing. Through a series of interactions with state institutions, including the debates over the formulation of a law governing community media in 2002, the formation of a cooperative to disburse state funds in 2004, and the state's confiscation of a community radio transmitter in May 2005, the differences between groups emerged more clearly.

Communications—like culture—is a field directly exposed to the market logics of global capitalism, and community media producers experience the disjunctures between the anti-neoliberal rhetoric of the Chávez government and its need to meet the objectives imposed by foreign investors. As they sought authorization from state media bodies, radio collectives countered the requirements of statistical data, instrumental language of utility, and the technocratic analysis of the functionaries with appeals to local knowledge, oral narrative, and historical memory. They opposed the attempts by regulators to police the airwaves by denying unauthorized stations access to funding and confiscating their equipment. As a result of these conflicts, community media groupings moved into more clearly defined blocs that positioned them differentially in relation to the hybrid post-neoliberal state. While some groups formed alliances to contest the neoliberal rationalities and disciplinary techniques of certain state institutions, others played a role in enforcing the hand of media regulatory bodies.

COMMUNICATIONS TECHNOLOGY AND ASSOCIATIONAL LIFE

One of the distinctive characteristics of urban social movements in the contemporary era is their use of electronic media, including radio, television, and print. Several scholars have addressed the reasons for the centrality of communications technology to new forms of associational life. The availability of communications technologies such as cable and electronic audience feedback has led to political messages being constructed more through the mass media than through parties and interest associations.[2] Transnationalization is located primarily in the field of communications such as satellites and computer networks, which has meant that issues of nationality are also increasingly addressed in this field.[3] The massive growth of communications technology has also facilitated the entry of citizens into the public sphere, especially where political parties and unions have failed to address their needs.[4] But as some of these scholars acknowledge, the spaces available within the mass media are limited: although media culture is now much more a part of everyday political life, functions of deliberation, organization, and representation play a minor role.

Given the limited spaces available within the mass media for creative

14 Centro de Comunicación in Sector La Piedrita, 23 de Enero. PHOTO BY THE AUTHOR.

political action and deliberation, community activists and barrio residents have begun to utilize technological advances to produce their own alternative forms of communication. In the parish 23 de Enero of some 80,000 inhabitants, there are about 100 cybercafes. In a small sector of this neighborhood, Barrio Sucre, with a population of 5,000 people, there are 7 cybercafes. Most of these cybercafes have about 10 or more computers and they are always occupied. There are also centros de comunicación (communication centers), which emerged from the availability of flat rates for cell phones. Since it is expensive to call cell phones from home or another cell, and many people in the barrios do not have home telephone lines, street vendors set up booths where you can make calls. These centers are a vibrant part of the informal economy and communications technology. Text messages on cell phones have become an important part of local communication. *Motorizados*, or motorbike workers, who work as messengers and run errands through the congested streets of the barrios, constitute another informal network of communication in the city.[5] All of this technology has come to be utilized by social movements in Venezuela, and in particular by radio collectives.

15 Sector La Ceiba, San Agustín. PHOTO BY AUTHOR.

Radio has been one of the most important mediums of popular communication because of its privileged relation to popular culture. As Jesus Martín-Barbero argues, radio counterbalanced the unifying tendencies of television.[6] Radio has a way of capturing the popular world through music, sports, and colloquial expression; it is able to attract more varied publics; and it is able to facilitate new social identities not related to traditional party and union politics. The radio is a part of life for most households in the barrios of Caracas. It is generally on all day in the home, whether as the sole source of information and entertainment or as background noise. People will switch between government or private channels and local community stations. The hills and high locales of the barrios of Caracas—like the shantytowns and favelas of other Latin American cities—are a vantage point for community radio stations, which are able to reach larger territories due to the natural height of their antennas. For example, Radio Negro Primero in Barrio Sarría has only a 14-watt transmitter, but it is located close to El Ávila, a mountain spanning 2,600 meters, which serves as a transmitter.

Radio technology is basic and accessible as compared to print media and television. The community radio station Un Nuevo Día, located in a poor barrio in the hills above the old highway out of Caracas, began in the bedroom of one of the women residents. The residents put a borrowed mixer, a CD player, and a microphone on the woman's dresser. They transmitted through a small antenna. Invited guests would sit on the woman's bed and people would send in text messages via cell phones. This story is exemplary of many experiences of radio collectives globally.[7]

By contrast, community newspapers have had a much harder time sustaining themselves, due to a lack of resources and finding people to write reports. Gustavo Borges started a local newspaper in Barrio Sucre, *Sucre en Comunidad*. A long-time resident of Barrio Sucre, Gustavo only became involved in politics since Chávez came to power, and especially after the 2002 coup. He and his son initiated the newspaper in 2002 and they also maintain a website. Gustavo related that as community print media experienced an upsurge in 2004 to 2005, printing presses realized that they could make money from printing the newspapers and began raising their charges. For many community newspapers these prices became unaffordable, putting them out of business. But radio and print media are also integrated in various ways. Interviews on radio are sometimes transcribed and reprinted in newspapers, or newspapers have spaces on radio programs, for example, *Sucre in Comunidad*, which has a space on Monday and Friday mornings on Radio Comunitaria San Bernardino, or *El Tiempo de Caricuao*, which carries transcriptions of radio discussions about local history. Murals are also a popular alternative to newspapers and have been referred to as a form of "street journalism." Mural brigades in the barrios, such as La Piedrita in 23 de Enero, paint over old murals and replace them with new ones regularly, thereby creating a dynamic forum for street dialogue.

THE EMERGENCE OF COMMUNITY MEDIA IN VENEZUELA

A movement of community media began to emerge around 1992–93. The first community radio station was in the parish of Catia, and then community activists began to hold workshops in Caricuao and La Vega, creating Radio Perola and Radio Activa la Vega. These early radio stations were *radios parlantes*, or stations that broadcast through megaphones rather than antennas. Radio collectives then began using FM transmitters of 13 volts, and they operated as *radios clandestinos*, or clandestine radio stations. During the presidency of Rafael Caldera the stations suffered from state repression and Radio Perola was closed down twice. After Chávez was elected in 1998, community media activists began to raise issues of the right to communication. The surge in community media happened after 2002. While in 2002, there were 13 licensed community radio and television stations nationally, as of June 2007, there were 193. In addition to these 193 legally recognized and funded stations, there have emerged over 300 unsanctioned community stations. There are also around 100 community newspapers. These are created and operated by a range of local groups, in the Amazonian south of Venezuela, the Andean regions, the coastal north of the country, and the barrios in the major urban centers.

There are several reasons for this explosion of community media. One was the passage of new laws by the Chávez government in 2000 and 2002 which facilitated the legal recognition of clandestine radio and television stations. The Ley Orgánica de Telecomunicaciones (Organic Law of Tele-communications), passed in June 2000, promoted the right of community radio stations to exist. In January 2002, another law, Reglamento de Radio-difusión Sonora y Televisión Abierta comunitarias de Servicio Público, sin fines de lucro (Regulation of Open Community Public Service Radio and Television, Nonprofit), established the conditions under which authorization would be granted to community radio and television stations. Following these laws, the government made substantial sums of money available for authorized community media. In late 2004, five thousand million bolívares ($US2.3 million) was given to community radio and television stations in grants for purchasing equipment, and at the end of 2005, sixty-five of these stations had received new equipment.[8] The funding available to community stations created an incentive for people to create their own stations and to seek authorization. In 2008, the projected budget for state funding of community media through the Ministry of Popular Power for Telecommunications and Information (MPPTI) and the Ministry of Popular Power for Communication and Information (MINCI) was Bs F 9.3 million or $US4.3 million, allocated for equipment, technical assistance, state publicity spots, events, and workshops.[9] This funding was intended to promote community media as a vehicle for pluralism and participation, and also as a bulwark to the private media, which was launching regular attacks against the Chávez administration.

Another reason for the dramatic increase in community radio stations in this period was the desire of urban movements to have control over the means of communication, following the media blackout engineered by the opposition when Chávez was removed from office on April 11, 2002, in a coup. At that time, Napoleón Bravo, an opposition journalist, came on the air and falsely broadcast that Chávez had resigned. While the opposition was taking over the presidential palace, the private media replaced its regular news broadcast with cooking shows, soap operas, and cartoons. The public was deprived of access to information, as the state-owned television station, Channel 8, and several community radio and television stations were taken off the air. During this time, it was mainly the alternative print media that was able to get the message out about what was happening. According to Roberto, a worker at the Caracas Municipal Press, activists came to the press and labored to produce 100,000 copies of a bulletin informing people about the events. Radio Fe y Alegría had also continued transmitting during these days and began to make announcements about the coup. Through the bulletins, alternative radio, *radio bemba* (word of mouth), and the exchange of text messages through cell phones, people were able to pass on the news of the coup and come out onto the streets in massive demonstrations that would put Chávez back into power two days later.

Several people noted that the events of the coup were the incentive that led them to form their own radio station. Rafael Hernandez was one of the founders of the movement Macarao y su Gente that emerged during the late 1980s in the parish of Macarao. Although the movement dissolved in the mid-1990s, Rafael and some of the others formed a radio collective and began working to put their radio on the air. Rafael explained, "After Chávez took power, on April 13, we decided, look, we have to accelerate the process of installing our radio because this will go on and somehow we have to keep the people informed and we have to counter the mediatic campaign of the commercial media." The media collective in Macarao had been given some equipment from Fundarte in 2001, including a low-power transmitter, an antenna, microphones, and recording equipment, but they were unable to go on the air for lack of premises. When they heard the news of the coup on April 13, they took the equipment to Miraflores, intending to begin broadcasting from there along with other radio stations. But the popular mobilization was swift and Chávez was returned to power before they could set up their equipment. A week later, a resident of Macarao made available a small office space to the collective and on April 22 the first signal of the radio went out.

The combination of the new legislation, increased government funding available for the community radio and television stations, and the impetus among urban sectors to have access to their own media following the 2002 coup contributed to the growth in community and alternative media. Certain radio stations with a longer history and trajectory such as Radio Negro Primero and Radio Perola served as a nucleus for the multiplication of radio stations. A worker at Radio Negro Primero described how once the station received authorization, it duplicated its application for other groups: "The detailed project that we presented to the government to obtain authorization was copied by twenty different groups, they copied the same project and put their signature, they just changed the name of the barrio." Legal assistance, technology, and technical skill was passed from one radio collective to the next, allowing for the rapid creation of functioning radio stations. Media activists went from urban to rural areas, bringing equipment and demonstrating technical basics of radio transmission. The idea caught on and before long low-power radios mushroomed in cities and rural areas across Venezuela. Yet in the overall media landscape, community media still holds a relatively small percentage of the airwaves. Only 5 percent of the radio spectrum belongs to community radio stations, while 85 percent of airwaves is still in the hands of private capital and 10 percent is in the hands of the state.

Community media is distinguished from government and commercial media in several ways. For Gustavo, community media need to reflect the essence, struggle, and spirit of the barrio, with reports produced by people living in the barrio. Commercial media tends to be focused on the negative elements of barrio life—complaints about the lack of services, violence and crime, ranchos that collapse—without recognizing the positive aspects. Reporters from government-controlled media such as *Vea* are generally sent to the barrio when there is an official event, such as the inauguration of a new popular health clinic. According to Gustavo, "When they come, it's because there's going to be a big assembly, or an extraordinary event. But in the barrios there are extraordinary events every day. In a barrio where there's a high degree of delinquency, a high rate of drug addiction, of vagrancy, or where the kids have nothing to do, when a young girl decides to form a volleyball team on her own initiative and her own resources, this is an important act within the barrio." From the perspective of community media, the construction of "news," as either the sensational reporting of tragic events or the media spectacle created around official inaugurations, needs to be reconfigured to privilege the everyday events that take place in the lives of ordinary residents of the barrio. By inviting the residents themselves to do the reporting—the organizer of the volleyball team, the housewife who teaches a literacy class, or the sisters who started a health clinic in their spare room—Gustavo emphasizes the participatory nature of community media.

In some cases, participation is encouraged by the form of the media itself. The newspaper *Cayapo* in La Vega consists of several folded broadsheets joined together in unconventional ways. In order to read it, one first has to figure out how to open and then navigate the origami-like sheets. As Freddy Mendoza, one of the founders of the newspaper, says, "My culture has taught me that someone writes for me and I'm not allowed to write my own experience . . . This makes you mentally and intellectually weak, not disposed to creativity, so that's where our newspaper aims. We want to aim for people to get it, to go against the current, and that's embodied in the form that you read it, that people participate and interact with the newspaper." *Cayapo* is specifically designed to question the hegemony of established forms, in particular the notion of people as beneficiaries rather than active participants.

Community media is also distinct in that people reject the label of professional "journalists" and prefer to see themselves as "popular communicators." The authority or knowledge that comes from textbooks and communication degrees is less valuable than immersion in the community and knowledge of the barrio. Carlos Carles is one of the founders of Radio Perola in the parish of Caricuao. With his signature baseball cap, baggy clothing, and goofy grin, he looks like just another one of the *chamos*, or kids, at Radio Perola. "We try to demystify certain concepts people have about knowledge," said Carlos. "An old guy from the community who works with kids or organizes a soup kitchen has much more value to us than a cookie-cutter radio announcer with a melodious voice who doesn't tell us anything about what's happening in our community." Practical experience is also valued more than formal training. An interaction between an established journalist from the opposition and a popular communicator from a local community radio station illustrated this difference. The

16 Carlos Carles, Radio Perola, Caricuao. PHOTO BY THE AUTHOR.

established journalist asked the community radio activist, "I have done a course of five years to train as a journalist. What have you done?" The popular communicator replied, "We did a course of three days, 11, 12, and 13 of April." The days of the coup were a "baptism by fire" for community media activists; the activist establishes his credentials not in any school or course but in the growing collective awareness that took place during those days.

The field of community media is a heterogeneous one, with media producers establishing differential relations with the state. In the following sections, I look at the local orientation and social base of the media, the degree to which they facilitate deliberation and democratic decision making, their relationship to state funding, and access to technical knowledge as key factors shaping community media.

LOCALITY, PLACE-BASED CONSCIOUSNESS, AND IDENTITY

Community media activists draw on place, locality, and cultural identity in creating alternative languages of resistance and oppositional discourses to the private media. Arif Dirlik sees place and locality as signifiers for processes, rather than locations conceived in narrow geographical terms.

While some theorists have tended to use terms such as "local" and "place-based" interchangeably, in opposition to terms such as "global," Dirlik argues that the global and local are always producing each other, and that the reassertion of place may provide a means of critiquing the power asymmetries implicit in globalization.[10] This is precisely what is taking place in the case of community media in Venezuela, where the geographical specificity of community media has emerged in response to the homogenization of private media under processes of neoliberal reform. Similar to the United States, syndicated programming and market-researched playlists as a result of ownership consolidation in Venezuela led to less diversity, fewer viewpoints, and a devaluing of the regional and local.[11] By contrast, community media proponents have sought to ground their operations in the place of the barrio. Community media networks are based in local neighborhoods—for instance, Radio Perola in the community of Caricuao, Radio Macarao in the parish Macarao, Radio Al Son del 23 in the parish 23 de Enero, Catia TVe in the parish of Catedral, and Radio Negro Primero in Pinto Salinas. These stations are part of the social and cultural life of the barrio and are often sustained by the barrio. But retaining their local vision versus developing broader audiences is a key tension faced by community media.

The themes that the community media address are generally local in nature, concerning life in the barrio or the cultural life of the community. On radio and television there are talk shows, educational programs, cultural shows, sports segments, local history programs, children's shows, cooking shows, and a variety of music programs, including salsa, bolero, hip-hop, rock, and *llanero* (country) music. Community newspapers have editorial pieces and discussion sections, articles about sports teams and cultural events in the barrio, and pieces on local history, health, and politics.

The programming of community media is linked to cultural activities in the barrio, such as the fiestas. Radio stations are a prime means for organizing and advertising religious festivals such as San Juan and Cruz de Mayo. At the start of the chapter, I described the role of radio in promoting the San Juan fiesta in Macarao. Similarly, the radio program *Tambor y Costa* on Radio Comunitaria de la Vega helps to organize the Encuentro de los Santos Negros (Meeting of the Black Saints) as well as other fiestas in the parish. Francisco Pérez and Gilberto Sandoja from the station frequently travel to the coastal zones during the fiesta time and record the

17 Radio Rebelde, Catia. PHOTO BY THE AUTHOR.

18 Radio Macarao. PHOTO BY THE AUTHOR.

19 Musicians performing in the studio at Radio Macarao, July 2005. PHOTO BY THE AUTHOR.

festivities to play later on the show. Much in the same way that Williams Ochoa and others went to rural areas during the 1970s to investigate local traditions, media activists are researching fiestas and then broadcasting their recordings on the radio. In July 2003, *Sucre en Comunidad* reported on the celebration of Cruz de Mayo in the sector La Piedrita in 23 de Enero, with information about the history of the fiesta and the organizing committee. Catia TV regularly makes short documentaries about fiestas in different parishes.

Media activists promote and organize activities such as children's vacation plans, sports events, and musical activities, such as karaoke festivals. During the summer of 2005, Radio Perola activists Carlos Carles and his wife Ely Flores were busy organizing a children's community vacation camp in the Andean state of Mérida. Carlos announced on Tomando Perola that there was space for three hundred children and one hundred adolescents between twelve and fourteen years of age. Carlos and Ely were working with Radio Eco in Mérida as well as Radio Horizonte and Radio La Zulita to provide this opportunity for the children of the neighborhood. At the same time, Radio Macarao was organizing a karaoke festival in the street, by the metro station. The residents entered the competition and prizes were given by small businesses in the barrio. The radio station Al Son del 23 helped to facilitate dance classes, dollmaking workshops, and boxing lessons for members of the community, and it also organized a vacation plan for local children. Popular communicators are concerned to integrate local media with the life and culture of the residents.

The radio is used as a means of reflecting on the meaning of the geographical and everyday place of "the barrio." In 2005, four young women from the parish of Caricuao, from seventeen to twenty-one years of age, had an hour-long program on Radio Perola on Saturday mornings called *Poder Popular* (Public Power). The young women, Maria Cristina, Gladys, Clara, and Lilibet, divided *Poder Popular* into distinct segments. These included an invited guest to speak about a specific topic relevant to the community, a news segment, a roundtable discussion about a particular current event, and then a segment called "Community Realities." During this final segment, the women debated with each other, as well as with listeners who called in or sent text messages via their cell phones. When I visited, the young women were addressing the theme "Living in the Barrio."

Maria Cristina introduced the segment. "OK, it's 10:44 in the morning, we're entering the section 'Community Reality.' Today, we're commenting on the theme of community in the barrio, because we speak about the barrio and we live in a barrio, but we don't know what the word 'barrio' means. It's like that. So, look, when we try to find the meaning of the word 'barrio,' for all that we can find in the library, in dictionaries, sometimes we still don't understand because the meaning can only be found in being with the people, in the verbal, in the physical, with the people. And at times it's important to know how the barrios began."

Clara chimed in on the discussion: "Exactly, supposedly we all live in a community, we should help each other out, like we commented in the first program. I agree that a barrio is not only the place where you live, it is to share our daily existence with each other, because they are the people who are closest to you, those who really know the problems that exist in the community. A barrio is not simply a hillside of stairs, a barrio is the community, it's your house, you are close to it, you live there. So, why should you be ashamed that you live there? I live in a barrio, Santa Cruz de las Adjuntas. And the reality is not what they have told you earlier—that if you live in a barrio you don't have a future, that if you live in a barrio you are a nobody. It's not like that."

Maria Cristina contrasts the knowledge produced by written texts with the local and situated knowledge that is learned through daily life, which comes from "being with the people, in the verbal, in the physical." As the children of parents who have migrated from rural areas, these young women have grown up in the urban centers. They feel the stigma of being from the barrio, and at the same time this is where they seek meaning and identity. Gladys, one of the young women, says, "The barrio is a place and a way of life at the same time." Gladys's observation illustrates the notion of place as both location and process. The barrio is a physical space of narrow lanes and steep staircases, bodegas and open plazas, but it also encompasses a set of relations of power, kinship, and territory. Through their involvement in the radio, the young women are creating a place-based consciousness, connecting place to social identity. They are transforming stigmas of place and culture into positive signifiers of collectivity and community.

The interconnections between place, history, and identity are apparent in the names of radio stations. The station Radio Negro Primero takes its name from both the Barrio Negro Primero located in the parish and the mythical hero. According to media activist Madera, part of the project of community radio is claiming these local heroes who have been eclipsed by official history: "Everyone knows Bolívar, Francisco de Miranda, all the great leaders, but Negro Primero was a sergeant, a middle level cadre . . . We are revindicating those from below, those eighty percent who are segregated by official history, from *el negro* Sambo Andresote to Alí de España." Other stations also draw on the narratives of mythic chiefs and antiheroes as they describe their own projects. Angel from Radio Tiuna noted that the station takes the name of a mythical indigenous chief because "Tiuna is one of the chiefs from here, from Venezuela. When the Spanish arrived they fought with Tiuna, with Guaicaipuro, all of these chiefs who were here, who are native to this country." Carlos from Radio Perola incorporates the antiheroes of Venezuelan history into the popular figure of Bolívar. On the show *Tomando Perola* (Taking Perola), Carlos describes Bolívar: "Simón Bolívar was not Bolívar. Simón Bolívar was also Páez, he was also Zamora, he was also Boves, he was also Piar." Carlos refers to this mix of celebrated caudillos, radical populists, and antiheroes,

20 *Poder Popular* on Radio Perola, June 2005. PHOTO BY THE AUTHOR.

21 Radio Negro
Primero, Barrio Sarría.
PHOTO BY THE AUTHOR.

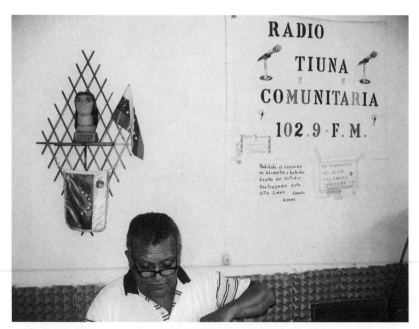

22 Radio Tiuna, Santa Rosalia. PHOTO BY THE AUTHOR.

some of whom were suppressed within official historical narratives, only to be appropriated and recirculated in popular oral traditions.

Community media producers make claims to indigenous and black identity as a way of positioning themselves in broader relations of class and marginality. Carlos identifies "el pueblo" as descendants of the indigenous chiefs: "We are the children of Guaicaipuro, those who screamed in the last moments of their lives, 'Come, Spaniards, and see how the last free man of this land dies.'" There are echoes of Reyes in these statements, as the death of Guaicaipuro signals the disappearance of indigenous subjects. But like El Indio in the previous chapter, Carlos presents himself as a descendant of the chiefs, in both a literal and a metaphorical sense. Indigenous people were not eliminated by the colonizer but continue to exist both in their descendants and in the living traditions of popular resistance. For Carlos, el pueblo is a descendant of the indigenous chiefs and an embodiment of their ongoing struggle against the colonizer: "We are children of indigenous resistance, Caribbean indigenous resistance. They almost wiped out our population, but we will not accept that the invader, the colonizer, can wipe out our dignity and our territory." Carlos invokes the specter of indigenous resistance, not as a past historical relic but as a means to

23 Madera, Radio Negro Primero, Barrio Sarría. PHOTO BY THE AUTHOR.

recreate a sense of collective action. More broadly what is taking place is a reframing of el pueblo from the virtuous foundations of the mixed-race nation to el pueblo as a marginalized, excluded majority who are seeking recognition and their rightful share in the country's wealth.

Popular communicators also elaborate and construct notions of blackness. Madera, a brown-skinned man in his late forties with a shaved head and a beard flecked with white, is a broadcaster on Radio Negro Primero. Neatly attired in a shirt with a collar and a pen in one pocket, he speaks slowly, carefully considering his words. Madera has a show on Radio Negro Primero, which he says is "for black men and women":

> OK, continuing here from 101.1 Radio Libre Negro Primero. Only for black women and men. If you're not black, please change the dial, that's how we say it. Because blackness is not a problem of the color of your skin, blackness is a problem of feeling, of commitment to others . . . That's why we do this program, only for black men and

women, to make visible what here they want to make invisible—that here there is no racial problem, that here there is no ethnic problem, more than racial, ethnic. So, we make it visible from Radio Negro Primero.

Madera's style is tongue-in-cheek; in making his program "only for black men and women," he is being provocative. Madera uses the radio as a tool to counter the invisibility of black people in society and his polemical style invites people to engage in debates about race. At the same time, he does not define blackness only on the basis of skin color or ancestry; he defines it as a "problem of feeling, of commitment to others." Madera gives the example of Ricardo Guerrero, a white drummer from the popular parish of La Pastora, who for Madera embodies this more spiritual notion of blackness. The expansive categories of blackness and indigeneity are often used to refer to a shared condition of marginality, or in this case solidarity with others.

There is little space for the discussion of cultural difference within the state-run media or the private media. Madera says that the question of race has been invisible, or taboo, within Venezuela society: "Nobody here talks about the Afro problem . . . I'll give you the example of our constitution, that talks of the plural and the multiethnic, it names the indigenous, and then the whites, but the black is just assumed." The airwaves may provide new spaces for rethinking blackness and black subjectivity. As Kathy Newman argues in her essay on black radio in the 1940s and 1950s in the United States, while blacks were left out from mainstream visual representations, black "sound" found a niche in music and radio.[12] Similarly, in Venezuela where racialized notions of good presence have led to the exclusion of blacks in television, there may be more opportunities in radio to assert a black presence through sound.

Local history programs on radio are one means of connecting expressions of cultural identity with narratives about place and linking these to political projects over the reorganization of space. The popular historian and history professor Freddy Hurtado from the parish of Caricuao has a local history radio show called *Programa Etnografía* (Ethnography Program), which he does on Radio Perola, Radio Macarao, and Radio Antímano, and he also writes articles in *El Tiempo de Caricuao*. Professor Hurtado says that while official history is constructed through the archives, popular history draws on the living archives: historical memory and oral histories of the residents. He is mostly concerned with excavating the history of the parishes Caricuao, Macarao, and Antímano and telling the stories of the indigenous Toromayma people who inhabited these parishes before they were invaded and settled by colonizers. On his program on Radio Perola in January 2006, Hurtado said that knowing local history is the basis of regional and then national history and that "local power is the first expression of popular power." In contrast to the official versions of indigenous resistance and surrender in accounts such as those by Oviedo y Baños and Reyes, Hurtado speaks of the conquest and sacking of the country and the massacre of the indigenous population, which he says needs to remain present in the memory of barrio residents and young people. During his two-hour programs, he interviews popular historians; he recounts stories of colonial conquest; he tells stories about locales such as the metro station and what happened in those locales in the past; he talks about the roots of popular music; and he mentions popular drinks, such as the *solesombra*, which, he says, used to cost one bolívar.

The construction of this place-based historical memory is part of the project to create a sense of community and a shared past and, moreover, to reclaim public spaces that have been privatized or abandoned in recent decades. As Hurtado mentions in his show on Radio Perola, the parish of Caricuao has no casa de la cultura (culture house), and the local sports center was privatized. Spaces that were previously centers of community life have gradually been sold to the private sector by local politicians or occupied by gangs, taking them out of the hands of the residents. As a result, public space has become more militarized, with an increased repressive police presence in the barrios. Part of the project of reclaiming these spaces entails not only confronting drug dealers or working with young people to give them employment and direction but demilitarizing the barrios, as Carlos says in his program *Tomando Perola*: "We don't have to militarize our barrios or our communities, rather, we have to fill them with happiness, with color, with collective experiences, and important experiences." Like the fiesta organizers, community media activists promote community-based models of violence prevention, as compared to a law enforcement model.[13] This is a crucial step toward opening spaces for increased participation and renewed cultural life.

Barrio-based media producers make appeals to the local—they address local themes and history and they seek to integrate their programming into the life of the barrio: the space of the local is vital in defining new forms of collectivity. Yet it is important to be aware of the ways in which local forms are themselves imbricated in and produced by broader global forces. Most community radio stations and newspapers have websites, where they maintain blogs, livestream their shows, and connect with audiences and publics outside their immediate vicinity. Like other locally based social movements which, as Arturo Escobar says, "borrow metropolitan discourses of identity,"[14] community media activists draw on transnational narratives. Also, as I will elaborate, media activists receive international support and participate in global exchanges and forums. But at the same time, the defense of place serves as an ongoing reminder of the power relations that shape the configurations of what Dirlik has called "glocality."[15] It is through a reassertion of place-based memory and consciousness that corporate and private claims can be contested.

Holding on to a place-based politics often comes into conflict with other tendencies, such as the desire of some stations to have a broader reach. The radio Al Son del 23, operated under the auspices of the militant organization Coordinadora Simón Bolívar (CSB) is a case in point. The station was inaugurated in January 2006 and it functions in the headquarters of the CSB in La Cañada, a community of popular housing projects, where the CSB was born. Ronald, one of the young men who works at the station as an operator, noted, "Now we would like to buy a satellite of 17 watts to cover one hundred percent of Caracas and part of Miranda. We are now covering almost all of Caracas, but we want to cover more, there's a part where the signal fails." The television station Catia TVe also aims for this kind of broad reach. They began with a transmitter of 30 watts that covered the parishes Sucre, Los Junquitos, 23 de Enero, and La Pastora. But they moved on to a high potency transmitter that attempted to cover the entire metropolitan region of Caracas, although in reality the coverage is much more uneven. Others, such as Radio Macarao, are critical of this move and are committed to retaining the local nature of their programming. According to Rafael, community radio relies on highly localized codes and language—names of places, people, and events that may have no relevance to someone in another sector or barrio. "If there is a party in Kennedy, why do the people in Negro Primero need to know about it?" posed Rafael. For stations such as Radio Macarao, a radical agenda is inseparable from a politics of place, which is more important than expanding their audience base and outreach.

SPACES OF DELIBERATION AND COLLECTIVE DECISION MAKING

Critical debate and deliberation play an important role in the functioning of community media. Community media has become a central means by which barrio activists engage in dialogue about the issues facing their community and formulate collective strategies. The Bolivian activist Oscar Olivera notes that as compared to the organized trade union movement or political party caucuses, deliberation has shifted in the contemporary era to the informal sector as the site of working-class politics: "Deliberation— which for us encompasses expressing opinion, debating, deciding, and putting into practice—now occurs in the new world of labor that the *modelo*, or neoliberalism, has created."[16] The local radio station is used by a range of groups to discuss ideas and promote their activities, including land and health committees and soup kitchens. The producers of radio shows are often members of these different committees and they report back on their progress and achievements. Although the missions and committees have often been designed and receive support from the Chávez government, the degree of democratic functioning depends on the integration of these programs into organizing structures such as community assemblies and radio.

Assemblies have been integral to the formation of several community newspapers, radios, or television stations. *Sucre en Comunidad* has its origins in a broadsheet known as *La Esquina Caliente* (The Hot Corner) that was created by participants of street assemblies who regularly convened in the Plaza Bolívar. Radio Rebelde in Catia emerged from an assembly called by community leaders. Assemblies continue to be important in the daily functioning of many community radio stations. The spaces of radio stations can also be converted into assembly and meeting halls. Radio Negro Primero has a large room from which it broadcasts; it is set up with chairs to facilitate debates and discussions with members of the barrio during the regular programming.

Community media networks vary in terms of their internal democracy, decision-making structures, and participation. The radio station Al Son del 23 adheres more to a style of centralized decision making. Juan Contreras, the president of the CSB, is the general director of the radio station and has the final decision about programming and content. One of the station operators described the process: "If someone approaches us and has a well-organized project, we will study it and then Juan Contreras as the general director takes the decision about whether or not to accept it." This style of decision making fits with the general style of the CSB as a cadre-based organization with a strongly directive leadership. Although there is space for discussion and debate in meetings and on the air, the parameters are often defined clearly by the directive.

Other stations such as Radio Negro Primero, Radio Perola, and Radio Macarao, function through a constant process of assemblies, meetings, and consultation. At Radio Negro Primero, the process of decision making is fairly diffuse and fluid. A committee consisting of all those who are active in the functioning of the radio meets twice a week, either early in the morning before people disperse to do their work for the day or in the evening when people are back in the station. There are special meetings of the committee to discuss the budget, reporting back on the previous year and projecting the budget for the year to come. If a serious problem arises, say between the radio station and the community or related to something that was said on the air, the committee reconvenes to discuss the issue and take a decision about what to do. Rather than a fixed structure, Radio Negro Primero reflects what one collective member Fernando Barret refers to as "a custom, a habit, a culture of convening assemblies to discuss things . . . our decisions are collective, talked about and discussed methodically." The flexible structure enables the station to respond quickly to events. For instance, when I was visiting the station one day, the activists were trying to decide whether to respond to the *buhoneros* (street vendors), who were demonstrating in Sabana Grande for relocation after their businesses were shut down by the Chavista mayor. The activists convened as an assembly in the morning and decided that the issue was an important one that was not being covered in the government press, and so they sent the director of the station to cover the events for the radio.

Radio Perola also has a fluid and flexible structure. Decision making is done through popular assembly, which is convened regularly by the coordinating team (*equipo de coordinación*). There are small assemblies consisting of fifteen to twenty people and larger assemblies of fifty to seventy. Carlos describes the process of decision making as a "permanent assembly," where "we reach agreements, we often say very critical things at times, but it is necessary in order to organize ourselves." They discuss their work plans, the division of tasks, the programming, and the everyday functioning of the station. Like Fernando, Carlos sees this process of decision making in assembly as a habit that is inculcated over time: "It is a practice, that nobody instructs nobody, nobody learns alone, human beings learn in collective and this process of collective learning is a process of liberation as well." The assemblies are not seen purely as decision-making forums but as spheres of dialogue that enable the participants to build a political analysis and strategy.

The efforts by some community radio stations to establish fluid mechanisms of deliberation, flexible processes that can respond quickly to events, and favoring a culture or habit of decision making through assembly has strengthened the internal democracy of those stations. However, at times the lack of a formalized structure can itself lead to the emergence of an informal de facto leadership. The absence of explicit and formally structured work teams may encourage the emergence of informal cliques and concentrate power in a few leaders of the organization. The general directors of the radio stations are male leaders or couples who have powers to give orientation and direction to the radio.[17] Many of these leaders have a daily or weekly show, like Juan Contreras's daily morning show, Carlos Carles's daily *Tomando Perola*, and Rafael Fernández's weekly *La Revista de la Mañana* that sets the agenda for the radio. It is assumed that these male leaders provide an ultimate guidance to the collective, an assumption that is part of the broader political culture of centralized leadership.

Radio Macarao has implemented a more organized structure than the other radios. The communicators meet together in teams, in order to evenly distribute the tasks of running the radio. A production team works on programming and seeks to fill empty spaces and ensure a balance between music, news programming, and community programs. At one point, this team decided that there were too many music programs and so they organized a weekend workshop to orient producers toward community programs, teaching them skills of interviewing and reporting. A technical team monitors the technical needs of the station; an administrative team oversees the functioning of the station; a publicity team looks for local advertising and sponsorship; an education team organizes workshops; and a cultural team arranges cultural events and forums. For example, the cultural team organized a public forum to discuss the evolution of

Macarao as a parish, its recent history, and what the people of the neighborhood want for the future of their parish. Every team has four or five people who are in charge of their area, and they report back to the broader assembly on their activities and decisions. The assembly consists of between eighty and ninety people who are actively involved in the functioning of the radio. It is the assembly that decides on the editorial lines of the radio, to the extent that such lines exist.

By participating in assemblies and work teams, residents learn skills of deliberation and collective decision making. This involves listening to others, respecting the opinion of others even when it differs from one's own, and learning to defer when one is outvoted by other members of the assembly. In principle, most radio stations adhere to the notion that communication should be free, which means giving access to a plurality of voices on the air. Radio Macarao allows all residents of the barrio, regardless of their political affiliation, to participate in the station. As Rafael recounted, there are people involved in the daily running of the station who signed against Chávez in the recall referendum or who do not identify with Chavismo. And there are people such as Rafael himself who support the current of change associated with Chávez but do not see themselves as Chavistas. This plurality is not the norm, and Radio Macarao has come under criticism for it and has been accused of being *escualidos*.[18] For Rafael, this is part of a struggle against unilateral modes of thinking: "There cannot be only one way of thinking, because this goes against the principles that I conform to as a communicator . . . Dialogue is confrontation, discussion, collective growth. If we're all in agreement, hey, it hardly makes sense, does it?" Listening, contentious argument, and respect are crucial aspects of collective decision making and community media production.

SELF-FINANCING, STATE FUNDING,
AND TECHNICAL KNOWLEDGE

Community media networks vary according to the localism of their work and the degree to which they facilitate deliberation and debate about the functioning of the station and issues affecting the community. Another factor differentiating community media is their access to state funding and their degree of integration in the informal economy of the neighborhood. Some community media draw on their political connections to gain authorization and resources, some have tried to sustain themselves through local community support, and others rely on a combination of state and local funding. Stations with larger transmitters and broader coverage are more likely to attract bigger advertising grants from state bodies, and in turn these greater funds increase the technical capacity of those stations. Meanwhile, stations focused on their local areas with basic technology and low-power transmitters have less need for large endowments from the state. The access to technical knowledge has also been an important factor in ensuring democratic control and local management of radio resources.

Questions of infrastructure, financing, and sale of airtime are crucial factors that influence the nature of community media. A handful of Caracas-based stations and newspapers receive all of their funding from state institutions and do not need to raise money from the community or through local businesses. The newspaper *El Tiempo de Caricuao* has been strongly affiliated with the Chávez government. Leonardo Heredia, one of the media activists with the newspaper, said that they began the newspaper after they met with Chávez and he suggested they create a community newspaper. Their first article was titled "Doing Politics in the Barrio" and was written by Chávez. The newspaper is affiliated with the Bolivarian Bloc of Alternative and Community Media (Bloque Bolivariano de Medios Alternativos y Comunitarios), a grouping of government-affiliated community media organizations.

In contrast to this state-affiliated community media, most barrio-based media seek some level of autonomy from the state. Critics of the opposition tend to see all community media as instruments of the Chávez government. An article published in the private daily, *El Universal*, on June 26, 2005, refers to the community radio stations as "radio-electronic media of the state," which are "employed for propaganda and political proselytism." The writer laments what he sees as the lack of quality and cultural homogeneity of the community stations, and their bias toward the Chávez government. But this kind of analysis misses the negotiations and often quite heated disagreements between government bodies and community activists, as well as the subtle interplay between struggles for autonomy and strategic alliances.

Media activists from Catia TVe and Al Son del 23 have successfully integrated themselves within official networks, using their political connections—often with former comrades now in official positions—to bargain for resources and visibility. The founders of Catia TVe and Al Son del

23 tell of how they approached Chávez personally with their projects and received support. While Chávez was visiting Catia, Blanca Eekhout was able to have a moment with Chávez to explain the idea of the community television station. Chávez intervened to speed up the authorization process, and Catia T Ve was legalized in May 2002.[19] The members of the CSB also sought a direct audience with Chávez as a way to promote their radio station. In 2002, Chávez came to record his weekly program *Alo Presidente* in a small hall near the Cristo Rey theater. One of the leaders of the CSB, Cristel Linares, approached the president at this event and gave him their proposal. Nearly three years later, for lack of a locale and available frequencies, the radio was still not functioning. Guadalupe Álvarez from the CSB came to see Chávez when he was presiding over the granting of land titles in Petare. She introduced herself as a leader of the CSB and said that 23 de Enero still had no community radio station. Eventually, the CSB took over the headquarters of the Metropolitan Police (PM) in their sector, a deteriorated building where activists and delinquent youth of the barrio were often hauled to be interrogated, detained, and sometimes tortured. With the tacit support of the Chavista mayor Juan Barreto, they took over the building and reclaimed it as their new headquarters, setting up the radio station there. According to Guadalupe, they received support from Chávez for the purchase of new computers and technical equipment for the radio. Activists from CSB and Catia T Ve appealed directly to Chávez as a way to promote their projects.

The CSB and Catia T Ve have strategically chosen to make themselves legible to the state in order to access resources. James Scott defines "legibility" as the ease of assimilation into an administrative grid, the ability of a given set of local practices to be aligned with the categories of the state.[20] These groups have incorporated state slogans into their programming and have demonstrated their acumen in negotiating among various levels of government. The CSB fostered their links with Barreto's office and used their strength as an organized group to obtain funds for refurbishing their premises, to pay for buses to take them to events, and to sponsor conventions and forums. The mayor's office paid for a computer center on the premises of the organization's headquarters, providing seventy-four new computers. At this center, the CSB holds classes in computer literacy for residents of the parish and other parishes in Caracas. Catia T Ve also has a large building for its premises and receives most of its financing from

CONAC and PDVSA, which helps with the large expenses of maintaining a television station. State funding provides a steady source of income, and through their contacts these stations have more political clout. For example, Naomi Schiller recounts that when a reporter from the commercial channel RCTV confronted a young Catia TVe reporter and broke his camera in July 2005, the incident received wide coverage on state television broadcasts on VTV and Vive TV, and the then minister of information and communication, Andres Izarra, called an official press conference on the issue.[21] Although the reporter was never compensated for the attack, Catia TVe used their contacts and access to media time in order to publicize their encounter with the opposition reporter.

Communicators from Radio Negro Primero also strategically made themselves legible to various state institutions. After gaining authorization from the state, Radio Negro Primero moved to spacious new premises fitted out with a media cabin, Internet stations, and several new computers. The activists from the station submitted projects to various state institutions such as the Intergubernatorial Fund for Decentralization (FIDES) and the National Commission of Telecommunications (CONATEL). They were successful in receiving numerous grants which helped cover their bills and facilitated the purchase of further equipment and the financing of media courses. The core budget of the station is around 4.5 million bolívares ($US2,143) per month, which includes bills for rent, electricity, water, and a nominal salary for full-time staff. The station uses the grants and some small state advertising to cover this budget.

The workers at Negro Primero have tried to use forms of democratic assembly to manage their relationship with the government. At one point, the government decided to install Infocentres, or small Internet booths with Web links to government sites, on the premises of Negro Primero. There was disagreement among workers in the station, so an assembly was called to discuss it, and after arguments for both sides were presented, the workers finally agreed to allow it. Making the decision on their own gave them a sense of agency over the installation of Infocentres. Radio Negro Primero also earns money through cooperatives; workers have an audiovisual cooperative where volunteers edit videos and DVDs and an editorial cooperative which produces publications, and these services and products are sold to government agencies to raise money for the radio.

Other radio stations combine smaller amounts of government funding with their own funds and local community contributions. Radio Perola had an agreement with the Ministry of Popular Power for Communication and Information (MINCI) and CONATEL, whereby they received a computer, a mixer, and a new transmitter. But according to Carlos Carles, the majority of the equipment used in Radio Perola was bought or secured by members of the station and the neighborhood. Some community radio stations stretch the funds they receive from the government. Radio Comunitaria de Petare received 24 million bolívares ($US11,429) toward station functions for a period of six months from the cooperative created by Chávez, which they stretched to last thirteen months. Radio Activa la Vega received nine million bolívares ($US4,286) from the National Council for Culture (CONAC) to buy new equipment but they used the money to buy second-hand equipment and with the leftover funds bought four antennas, which they donated to other stations. These radio stations rely heavily on voluntary labor and donations of equipment and resources. As Francisco Pérez from Radio La Vega said, "Sometimes I do work here and there, and if I earn good money I put it towards the station funds. Likewise, the other day, Gilberto had some work painting a house and put in twenty thousand *bolos* [$US9.50]." Unlike the larger and better financed community radio stations like Negro Primero, Radio La Vega is a small operation squeezed into a tiny room with the console piled on top of the computer tower and stacks of boxes and books taking up most of the space. Radio La Vega is not able to put together the programming of the larger stations, but there is a strong sense of ownership by the members of the media collective, due to their personal financial contributions.

Likewise, Radio Macarao has received state support in setting up the station, but they prefer to maintain the everyday running of the station through the contributions of local businesses. Radio Macarao received authorization at the end of 2005 and in March 2006 the media collective began to build new and larger premises for the station. They were given twenty-seven million bolívares ($US12,857) by CONATEL for basic infrastructure and received another grant from MINCI for electricity, air conditioning, and equipment, such as a new higher potency transmitter, a larger antenna, a computer system, recording equipment, and a high-quality microphone. The technicians from MINCI installed the equipment and trained the members of the collective to use it. These grants from institutions helped the radio to begin functioning in its new premises, but

24 Radio Comunitaria de la Vega, Sector Los Mangos. PHOTO BY THE AUTHOR.

they do not cover everyday expenses such as rent, services such as electricity and water, and payment of the operators and technicians.

To pay the monthly bills, Radio Macarao raises money through advertisements from the government, fund-raising events in the neighborhood, and contributions and advertisements from local businesses. Radio stations are permitted to sell five minutes of airtime per hour to local commercial enterprises. As a community radio station, the law prevents them from selling airtime to large corporations. The amount the station charges for the publicity depends on the kind of business. In Radio Macarao, larger businesses pay a monthly fee of 600,000 bolívares ($US186); established middle-size businesses such as a bakery, a shoe shop, or an auto repair shop pay a monthly fee of 200,000 (US$95) or 300,000 bolívares ($US143); and small businesses pay around 100,000 bolívares ($US48). Radio Macarao has been successful in building a broad base of local financing. About 60 percent of their monthly income comes from fifty local businesses, and another 40 percent comes from state advertising from the Ministry of Finance, MINCI, and the national water company Hidrocapital. Through these transactions, radio stations tap into the vibrant informal economy that exists at the margins of the formal economy.

At times there can be conflicts between the desire to build a base of financing through local businesses and the potency of the transmitter. Un Nuevo Día has a transmitter of 10 watts, which reaches most of the homes in the surrounding hillside shanties of the Catia parish. But there are no businesses in this barrio, and the transmitter does not reach to the central area of Catia where the local businesses are situated. Luis Peña, a member of the station, said, "If we go around soliciting publicity, what am I going to say to the owner of the bakery if he asks me whether the radio will be heard in his sector? I have to say no." To reach the center of Catia the radio would need a transmitter of at least 100 watts. This would give the station broader reach and possibilities of publicity, but it would reduce its highly local nature, which has had a strong base in the barrio from the start.

Foreign funding is another source of income that is becoming increasingly important for financing community media. The newspaper *Sucre en Comunidad* has several digital cameras and a computer, and some of this equipment was donated by foreigners who sign up for Gustavo's barrio tours through their website www.el23.net. A Brazilian organization donated a transmitter to Radio Alí Primera, which they purchased in Rio Grande do Sul and sent to the southern state of Amazonas, and the volunteers of Alí Primera made the fourteen-hour journey south to the Amazonas to pick up the transmitter. Although these alternative means are not easy, activists pursue them as a means of expanding and diversifying their resource base.

While some community media are more closely connected to the Chávez government through funding structures, others seek alternative means to reduce their dependency on the state and become self-financing. "The idea is not that we should be community media sustained by the state, but rather we have the capacity to be self-sustaining," said Carlos. "Because if they give you money and they give you your daily bread, they begin to ask, why are you doing this, why are you doing that? We prefer autonomy in what we do." This insistence on autonomy is often at odds with the actual practices of stations such as Radio Perola that do accept state funding. But media producers are also aware of the compromises they may have to make to continue receiving state funding. Gustavo noted that there are major contradictions in receiving funding from officials such as the city mayor Juan Barreto, because that may prevent the media from criticizing the mayor when basic services are not functioning. Or if the community

25 Advertisements from *Sucre en Comunidad*, September 2002.

newspaper is criticizing the oil company PDVSA about not maintaining its gas installations in the barrio, PDVSA may retract its funds. For these reasons, Gustavo has worked hard to secure a diverse base of advertising from local businesses and service providers in 23 de Enero for *Sucre en Comunidad*, including plumbers, radiator cleaners, grocery stores, bakeries, printers, Internet cafes, and clothes stores from the parish.

Different units of community media often collaborate and cooperate; stations donate resources to each other and assist with financing when they are able, and producers may work at multiple stations. But this is generally within the context of defined media associations. As community media flourished after the 2002 coup, they began to group together in defined national media associations, such as the Bolivarian Bloc, the Asociación Nacional de Medios Comunitarios, Libres y Alternativos (National Association of Alternative and Community Media, ANMCLA)—led by stations such as Radio Negro Primero and Radio Perola—and the Red Venezolana de Medios Comunitarios (Venezuelan Network of Community Media)—led by Catia TVe. Between associations there can be conflict and competition for resources. Luis Peña, from the Venezuelan Network, related that he had encountered problems with one of the other community media associations, which had used their contacts in CONAC to exclude the other community media producers; now the Network does not receive any financing from CONAC. Fernando Pinto from ANMCLA also agreed that the associations had a tendency to be sectarian.

Community radio stations prefer to train their members in the technical aspects of managing the station rather than rely on officials from CONATEL. The Christian radio station Fe y Alegría has carried out workshops for community radio stations on technical aspects of radio. Fe y Alegría trained three teenagers from Radio Al Son del 23; they are responsible for sound levels, engineering, and production during broadcasts. These teenagers are also teaching other workers at the station how to manage the technical aspects. Beyond the radio, these youth are also working on the webpage for the radio and have been creating and editing short videos. At Radio Negro Primero, workers hold workshops in technical aspects of radio for other community radio stations, and those trained in technology often help out at other radio stations. Most stations recognize the importance of training their workers in technical aspects in order to defend the autonomy of the station. In a few cases, lack of technical knowledge has compromised the ability of community workers to manage the station. After receiving authorization from CONATEL, Radio Rebelde in Catia found that the regulatory agency began to restrict access to persons they deemed lacking the correct technical expertise. As Jesús Arteaga, an activist, noted, "It was highly undemocratic, a radio managed without community input . . . It didn't stimulate organization of any kind and the community was not represented in the board of directors." In June 2004, the station was without a signal for several weeks due to a technical problem, and because of the monopoly over technical expertise by a small group of people assigned by CONATEL, the activists were unable to resolve the problem. Technical knowledge can be used as a form of maintaining control by a small elite and excluding broader participation in the running of the station.

Community media collectives—and the social movement webs of assemblies, committees, and cultural groups in which they are located—

make up a highly variegated field. I have explored the differences among these media-based social movements along three key axes: the degree to which they are positioned in the local space of the barrio, their ability to facilitate democratic debate and collective decision making in the running of the station, and their access to state funding and technical knowledge. In the next sections, I show how these differences shaped the interactions of community media groups with state regulatory institutions.

COMMUNICATIONS LAWS AND ENCOUNTERS
WITH STATE REGULATORS

While the government has authorized and funded community media as an alternative to commercial media consolidation, the field of communications is one directly exposed to the requirements of global markets. The need to attract foreign investors and provide a stable environment for capital has led to market-based calculations and sanctions being applied by state regulatory agencies to community radio stations. As they interacted with state regulatory bodies, community media producers experienced the disjunctures between the state's inclusionary rhetoric, its liberal formalism of rules and regulations, and instrumental market rationalities. While some media collectives played down these contradictions, others strategically deployed the rhetoric of the state against its liberal and neoliberal exclusions.

Communications in Venezuela have been open to forces of deregulation and privatization since the late 1970s, as part of a global implementation of free trade policies in media industries.[22] In 1979, President Rafael Caldera assigned Channel 5, a state-owned channel, to the Caracas Dioceses. This arbitrary designation was in defiance of Article 1 of the Telecommunications Law of 1940, which requires decisions regarding communications to be made by the state, not the president.[23] During the neoliberal turn under Pérez, the state media apparatus in place since 1940 underwent substantial transformations. Telecommunications were seen as a cornerstone of neoliberal policy, crucial to attracting investors to all sectors of the economy. In March 1991, Congress ratified the privatization of the National Telephone Company of Venezuela (CANTV). In October 1991, a new Law of Telecommunications was passed, which sought to stimulate private investment in communications and deregulate media services.

The 1991 law created CONATEL as a new autonomous regulatory body which took over from the Ministry of Transport and Communications (MTC) the technical functions of assigning frequencies, granting concessions and permits, and applying administrative sanctions.[24] Given the neoliberal climate that favored free markets and a user-pays system, CONATEL was also assigned the task of promoting competition in the telecommunications sector. These technical responsibilities and competition-related tasks combined to make CONATEL a powerful instrument for policing the airwaves and enforcing the new regulatory regime in the interests of private media corporations and commercial stations.

Throughout the 1990s, successive governments continued the expansion of concessions to media corporations, leading to the centralization of the media in a small number of conglomerates. According to Elizabeth Fox and Silvia Waisbord, the Venezuelan media market is dominated by Venevisión and TVC, which receive the biggest share of advertising revenues and have the largest audiences.[25] Private television at a national level is monopolized by the Cisneros group (Venevisión) and the 1BC group of Phelps-Granier (Radio Caracas Televisión). Out of forty-four regional television networks, nearly all are linked by chain to private networks Venevisión, Radio Caracas Televisión,[26] Televen, and Globovisión. Of these groups, Cisneros, Phelps, and Televen receive 70 percent of all television advertising revenues.[27] This small group of corporations also controls radio-electric spaces and the national press. The political effects of this concentration of media ownership were dramatized during the coup against Chávez in 2002. Some popular communicators saw the events of the coup as evidence of the problem, potency, and force of media concentration, but also its crisis.[28] The events of the coup generated a powerful collective response that immobilized the opposition and revealed the limits to private control over communications technology.

The Chávez government has sponsored community media as a means to counter consolidation by pluralizing the field of media and allowing for greater citizen participation. But communications policy under Chávez continues to be oriented toward a global market as the sector seeks to attract foreign finance and investment. Most telecommunications service companies in Venezuela are related to foreign companies by ownership or contract, and of the three largest providers Bellsouth Telcel and Movilnet are U.S. owned, while CANTV was renationalized in April 2007. The field of telecommunications has experienced significant growth and foreign investment since 1999. This is partly due to the expansion of areas such as fixed-line telephone services, cell phones, wireless services, and Internet and satellite services.[29] Overall revenues for the telecommunications sector in 2007 were $US8.64 billion.[30] Income from the telecommunications sector is a major contributor to gross national product (GNP); in 1997 it represented 2.3 percent of GNP and by 2007 it had grown to 4.26 percent.[31] State agencies structure the field of telecommunications in contradictory ways, regulating the field to provide a stable environment for private investors, while at the same time enhancing equity and universal access.

One area where these competing interests are manifested is in the Law of Telecommunications passed in 2000 under Chávez. This law bore strong similarities to its predecessor passed in 1991, and to the 1996 Telecommunications Act passed in the United States, which sought to lift media regulations and ownership restrictions, promote free competition among media providers, and reduce the interventionist role of the government.[32] The language of the 2000 law passed under Chávez reiterates these concerns with free competition and it minimizes the idea of government as representative of the public interest. Private investors lauded the Chávez government for its work in deregulating the field of communications. The CEO of NetUno, a leader in the fixed-wire industry in Venezuela, stated, "We are very fortunate to have a telecom law as modern, thorough, and well-written as anywhere. This has really allowed for the process to open up."[33] At the same time, the law reflected the anti-neoliberal agenda of the Chávez administration. It sought to eliminate monopolies on telecommunications activities, and it guaranteed the right to communication as a basic human right. It promoted the ability of individuals to establish community television and radio networks, and it gave CONATEL the authority to grant administrative authorization to these stations. But the capacity of CONATEL to democratize the field of media was limited by its continuing need to appeal to and protect corporate media interests as a condition of growth and investment.

The tensions between promoting equity and market growth are also apparent in the administration of the radio spectrum. Under the Law of Telecommunications, the radio spectrum was designated as a range of radio frequencies divided into bands and sub-bands. These are considered the public domain of the state and use must be granted by means of a concession. The radio spectrum can be used by the public and private sectors to deliver radio, radar, and mobile telephone services. In a growing telecommunications market, there is increased demand for the limited resource of radio frequencies. In Europe, the assigning of frequencies has taken place through a system of free competition, where private companies bid at auctions for licenses. The Venezuelan government has so far resisted the option of auctioning off licenses, but it continues to guarantee a "free competition regime among the service operators by means of eliminating the monopoly of the State over telecommunication activities and the conception of public service."[34] Despite the nominal public ownership of the airwaves, producers must still compete for licensing, and those with fewest resources—such as community media—are most likely to be the losers within a structure of free competition.

Due to the key role of the telecommunications sector in contributing to national growth and the need for the state to position the industry in order to attract investors, all areas of the sector—including community-based media—are submitted to market-based rationalities. State agencies assign funding through a utilitarian accounting of the returns they provide. As community media producers clashed with bureaucrats on subsequent occasions, it seemed that a neoliberal rationality was not the only logic, and that disciplinary techniques were also in play. The abstract liberal concepts of procedure, rule of law, and impartiality were deployed by technocrats as a means of what Michel Foucault refers to as disciplinary power, or technologies of power that induce compliance by means of bureaucratic regulations and routines.[35] Technocrats sought to create a stable field for attracting investment and penalize those who violated the rules of the game. CONATEL, as the national regulatory agency charged with administration of the radio electrical spectrum, is expressly delegated by the law "the power to grant, revoke, or suspend administrative authorizations [habilitaciones administrativas] and concessions."[36] According to the CONATEL website, "together with the Superintendent for the Promotion and Protection of Free Competition (Pro-Competition), CONATEL will be responsible for promoting investment in the sector and safeguarding free competition, while also being an effective arbitrator of controversies that emerge between operators of communications."[37] Technocrats from CONATEL made recourse to the liberal language of procedure and impartiality as they adjudicated between the interests of private and community media stations, and as they policed the boundaries between authorized and unauthorized stations. But these abstract concepts assumed the participation of rational, autonomous individuals who shared equality under the law. Media activists contested this formal language of democracy, arguing that it functioned as a means of protecting hierarchies of existing power.

In the following subsections, I explore various interactions between community media producers and state regulators. While the more closely state-aligned media such as Catia TVe tended to elide the contradictions inherent in the post-neoliberal state, the less-structured, more autonomous groupings such as Radio Perola, Radio Macarao, and others collided with the neoliberal rationalities and liberal formalism of state agencies. The debates between popular communicators and technocrats from CONATEL revealed the antagonistic worldviews about culture, communication, and the social at the heart of communications policy.

Debates over the Authorization of Community Media, 2002

Following the 2000 Telecommunications Law, community media organizations continued to seek inclusion in the drafting of legislation pertaining to media, and in 2002 several groups participated in a process of debate over the Regulation of Open Community Public Service Radio and Television law. In order to gain authorization, CONATEL proposed that the stations meet requirements in four fields: social, legal, technical, and economic. The social aspect requires an analysis of the social conditions and necessities of the community; the legal component is related to the registration of the community radio or television station as a foundation; the technical part requires a study by CONATEL of the radio spectrum and assigning a frequency to the station; and the economic involves a study of the local market to assess the possibility of self-sustainability. Community media activists welcomed certain aspects of the Regulation, such as the promotion of self-financing, which would contribute to the autonomy of radio stations and the stimulation of local businesses. But at the same time, members of radio stations Radio Perola, Radio Negro Primero, Radio Macarao, and others who were involved in drafting the authorization procedures voiced criticisms of the neoliberal rationalities involved. Media collectives were to be structured along the lines of corporations: they had to present their projects in instrumental terms of resolving problems in the community, and they were asked to justify the benefits and returns of investment in their project. In contrast to the language of statistics and diagnosis, they put forth a strong, community-based vision of what validates an alternative radio station. They opposed the instrumental neoliberal rationality of utility, and they rejected a technocratic analysis of the social.

One of the major areas of contention in the drafting of the authorization procedures was over the legal components. Article 12 of the Regulation says that in order to present itself for authorization, a community radio or television station must form a "foundation," with a board of directors and a general director. The language borrows from broader neoliberal development discourses of international agencies and private funders, who have sought to refashion community organizations along the lines of corporations. Rafael Hernandez argued that the corporate model of a board of directors, who are responsible for running the organization and making decisions, goes against the collective and nonhierarchical forms of decision making that some of the community radio stations are trying to build. Carlos Carles said that they would prefer a general coordinating committee or an assembly as the highest decision-making authority, rather than a general director. In the legal component of the authorization procedures, there was also provision for a recall referendum to revoke the leadership of the station. The "community" is defined in vague and general language as those who reside in the neighborhood. Popular communicators also critiqued this vague definition, saying that the label of "community" could be appropriated by a group with specific economic or political interests who want to remove the leadership. For Rafael, the community must be clearly defined as those who work in the radio, support it, and attend events, and criticisms should be brought up in assemblies and meetings.

The social component of the authorization procedures most strongly reflected the neoliberal rationality of the Regulation. In order to obtain authorization, the members of the station are asked to justify the media project in instrumental terms: "Describe the principal necessities, wants, and existing problems in the community where the service of a community radio station will be installed and demonstrate the bridge, path, or mechanisms that will be implemented to facilitate the solution of these problems in a positive manner." Like the cultural activities described in the previous chapter, the community radio stations are supported by state institutions not for their intrinsic value as creations by the community but in terms of utilitarian calculations of the returns they will provide. There is no doubt that the government wants the media to be socially useful to the community, but this goal of social benefit intersects with other rationalities of cost and benefit calculation that are being driven by the broader market orientation of the communications sector. The residents of the neighborhood are imagined in passive terms: they are "beneficiaries" who will receive the "services" provided by the station, rather than active participants in the activities of the station.

As part of the social component, the members of the station are asked to carry out a "social diagnostic," which consists of the application of a predetermined methodological instrument, or a quantitative survey, that collects data on educational level, occupation, participation, problems and necessities of the community, and knowledge of the television or radio. The community radio members are required to collect data in the barrio using this quantitative instrument, then codify and tabulate the data, and finally to analyze and interpret their results. As Yúdice has shown, the requirements for this kind of quantitative data come from the market incentives that structure funding bodies. In order to assess the numerous projects that come to institutions for evaluation and funding, these agencies must be able to measure the benefits and returns that justify investment in a project.

Instruments for measuring culture and community media projects are modeled after market indicators that allow economists to measure the health of the economy and the types of structural interventions that will be required.[38] This diagnostic approach conflicts with the approach to knowledge production among barrio-based media groups. Carlos Carles described how heated debates arose during meetings over this issue. "They proposed techniques of demonstrating statistical data," said Carlos. "Against this, we proposed local knowledge, oral narrative, historical memory, and the everyday work of the community." The approach chosen by the community media groups highlighted the alternative epistemologies that were emerging from their community-based work. These criteria were not incorporated into the final authorization process, which required media collectives to put together a document of several hundred pages of data. Yet historical memory, everyday work, and local knowledge constituted an alternative set of values that Carlos and other community groups continued to appeal to in their negotiations with bureaucrats.

Radio Perola, Radio Macarao, and others involved in the authorization process questioned the paradoxes of communications legislation under Chávez. Meanwhile, some such as Catia TVe sought to minimize these contradictions and enforce the regulatory regime put in place by CON-ATEL by policing the boundaries between authorized and unauthorized stations. Through interactions involving the formation of a cooperative to disburse state funds, various media collectives positioned themselves differentially in relation to state agencies such as CONATEL. On November 14, 2004, CONATEL invited community media organizations to a meeting to discuss the formation of a cooperative to administrate a grant of five thousand million bolívares given by Chávez for community media groups. Radio Perola, Catia TVe, and other authorized stations were among the twenty-six represented at the meeting, but no unauthorized stations had been invited. CONATEL advised the gathering that Bs 74 million was to be allocated for the creation of the cooperative, Bs 3,000 million for the purchase of equipment, and the rest for operational costs of rent, services, personnel, and training programs. They then opened the floor for discussion of the proposal.

Ely Flores and Carlos Carles from Radio Perola agreed with this distribution and further proposed that part of the money be set aside to help unauthorized stations to complete the arduous process of authorization. Appealing to the rhetoric of the Chávez government, Ely argued that the work and social practice of the unauthorized stations fit perfectly within what the "Compañero President" and MINCI have called the "Bolivarian dream" and should be strengthened as part of the sector of community radio and television. She went on to say that the unauthorized stations had been unjustly excluded from the proceedings by CONATEL and that the proposal should be debated by all community media. Ely said that the division between authorized and nonauthorized stations served only to divide the movement. She suggested that the meeting be postponed so that the unauthorized groups could also be a part of the discussion.

Representatives from Catia TVe argued that the proposal should be discussed that same night, and the directors of the cooperative should be selected. Ely and Carlos were strongly opposed to this suggestion; they wanted to see a broad and majoritarian debate that involved not only the unauthorized stations but also stations outside Caracas in Mérida, Falcón, Sucre, Aragua, and other regional states that are typically excluded from such deliberations. In response, Ricardo Márquez from Catia TVe and others such as Radio Tamanangue Libre and Radio Tarma who were part of the Venezuelan Network of Community Media reiterated the urgency of making a decision and moving forward. Of the twenty-six stations invited that day, twenty-four voted in favor of discussing the proposal that night. There was one abstention and Radio Perola cast the only vote against discussing the proposal that night. Following this vote, Radio Perola left and refused to be a part of the discussion. The other groups present went on to select the directive of the cooperative and voted in favor of the proposal.

The following week, Radio Perola produced a document describing the events of November 14 and circulated it among local and regional stations affiliated with their own media network ANMCLA.[39] The document lauded the Chávez government's promotion of alternative media but argued that these media should not replicate the dominant model of media consumption, where "a station sends 'messages' to a receptive public who passively receives them." By contrast, "communication is a public and collective process," it is "the constitution of a public space." In keeping with its notion of communication as a sphere of public dialogue and debate, Radio Perola wanted to see the administration of the funds not decided by a small group of authorized stations, thus reinforcing the dominance of Caracas-based, legally recognized stations, but deliberated on by a broader movement of community media. On this point Radio Perola differed with collectives such as Catia TVe and other members of the Venezuelan Network, whose own association was divided into authorized stations that were regular members with voting rights and unauthorized stations that were associate members with no voting rights in assemblies of the association.

This role played by Catia TVe in the CONATEL meeting on November 14 was replicated on other occasions, where the station acted as mediator, channeling discontent and urging moderation. Schiller recounts that following the confrontation between the RCTV reporter and the young Catia TVe reporter described earlier, Catia TVe called a meeting of community media collectives. While members of Radio Negro Primero, Radio Libre, and Radio Perola, among others, spoke about the need to take to the streets to pressure the government to take action, Marquez from Catia TVe urged a moderate approach and encouraged the group to work through official channels. As Schiller argues, the approach of Catia TVe producers stemmed from their conviction that the Bolivarian state did provide means of redress to resolve the situation in their favor and advocate on behalf of their interests. The other stations did agree to follow Marquez's leadership, partly because they recognized his ability to access these official channels.[40] Through various events, Catia TVe emerged as broker between state institutions and community-based media groupings. Catia TVe producers drew on their considerable authority among alternative media producers to promote the legitimacy of the Bolivarian state, at the same time as they sidelined the more radical proposals of these groups.

The Occupation of CONATEL, May 10, 2005

The regulatory role of CONATEL came strongly to the fore on May 10, 2005, when CONATEL took actions against a community radio station. On that day, functionaries of CONATEL, together with five army officials, entered the studios of Radio Alternativa de Caracas and suspended live transmissions by confiscating their transmitter. The personnel did not identify themselves or explain their act, other than to say that they were carrying out a "sanctionary administrative procedure," because the transmissions were illegal.[41] They began to interrogate José Lyon, the technical coordinator of the station, and he was arrested and detained without explanation.

In response to this aggression, radio collectives across Caracas held a popular assembly and decided to occupy the offices of CONATEL to demand an explanation from CONATEL officials. The show of solidarity for Radio Alternativa was a testament to the unity that community radios were able to forge in times of crisis, despite their sectarianism and jostling for power at other times. Radio Alternativa was not a part of ANMCLA and it had its differences with the media association, but they came together with a common purpose in confronting the functionaries. At the offices of CONATEL, the activists broke through a barrier of the national guard and entered the offices, repeating slogans about free communication. Functionaries arrived two hours later to speak with the radio activists, and the activists outlined their demands, which included the authorization of Radio Alternativa de Caracas, the return of the transmitter, the organization of a forum to debate issues of the authorization of community radio stations, and a public apology for the violation of human rights by the functionaries in the acts of aggression against Radio Alternativa de Caracas.

The actions of CONATEL were linked to the usurpation of the Radio Alternativa frequency 94.9 FM in September 2004 by a radio station known as Llanera Capital, owned by Eduardo Manuitt, the Chavista governor of Guárico. When the Radio Alternativa activists complained to CONATEL about this act of usurpation, CONATEL's response was to shut down both stations. After the occupation on May 10, CONATEL suggested that Llanera Capital should remain with the frequency of 94.9 FM, and that Radio Alternativa could resubmit their request for authorization, but with no guarantees. Radio Alternativa should also be willing to confine its broadcasting to its own parish.[42] The media activists asked why the governor of Guárico should be permitted a radio station that covers all of Caracas. They questioned the interests of CONATEL in supporting the governor over the interests of the community radio stations. They also probed why the army should be brought in to take a small community radio station off the air.

The events of the occupation on May 10 were filmed by ANMCLA as a means of publicizing and documenting what took place. When I was visiting the offices of ANMCLA six months later, Fernando and Carlos put the recording on and we watched it together. The videotape began with a heated debate between the CONATEL functionaries and the activists over the meaning of "administrative procedure." One of the functionaries, Héctor Borges, was seated at the head of the table, and over a cacophony of voices and responses, he spoke in a loud and controlled voice. "I am part of this procedure, and I am going to respect it." Pointing his finger down at the table, Borges slowly repeated the phrase several times for emphasis, "I'm going to respect it, I'm going to respect it, I'm going to respect it."

Carlos Carles responded to him. "You can say that you committed an error, look, we're human, we make mistakes. The word brings us together, it humanizes us, it makes us better people, it allows us to share our feelings, our experiences. When we here are speaking of our transmitter, we are not talking about something technical, we are talking about the potency of our word, of our rights to communication. This is sacred." Carlos went on, talking about all the laws and articles of the constitution that exist to protect human rights, while ordinary citizens still find it difficult to defend themselves. As Carlos spoke, Borges scratched his furrowed brow and studied papers on the table.

After a few more interventions, Angelica from Radio Alternativa de Caracas spoke. "When there is no paperwork, there's nothing legal," she said. "When the army hid their identity, took away our compañeros, took the transmitter, where is the administrative procedure?"

Ali from Radio Ali Primera was standing behind the table, and he entered into the discussion, gesturing with his arms for emphasis as he spoke. "This is the 'procedure' of the Fourth Republic, when functionaries trampled on and assassinated citizens, and hid their names so they could not be identified. That's exactly what the functionaries did. What is the difference between what you call 'procedure' and that of a state that repressed and persecuted us? We are the defenders of this proceso, we went out into the streets, precisely to demonstrate this."

Carlos Lugo added, "Once again, it has been demonstrated that this process is unjust, you haven't given me a procedure for a discussion of the radio electric spectrum . . . Because we're going to see aggression on the part of those economic groups who today have 90 percent of the radio electric space hostage . . . We demand an open and direct discussion about the radio electric spectrum and if you're going to bring into question our compañero, you have to bring into question all the radio electric space in the hands of that 90 percent."

For functionaries, the language of regulations and procedures is a means of controlling the undisciplined media activists and producing obedience. As the Comaroffs have argued, compared to previous administrations that gave little autonomy to the law, neoliberal administrations often emphasized the rule of law and the primacy of rights—even when the spirit and letter of the law were violated by the authorities themselves.[43] The activists turn the language of procedure back onto the functionaries. Angelica notes that the functionaries do not comply with their own principles of due procedure when they enter a space without identification and remove a transmitter without just cause. Drawing on the language of procedure used by the bureaucrats, the participants ask for a debate to define new norms for regulating radio-electric space and creating access for the community radio stations. But at the same time, they reject this technocratic language of administration, which does not speak to the human and experiential side of the community work in which they engage.

Another functionary present at the meeting, Marcelo Quintana, was standing behind the table among some of the participants. Dressed in a white shirt and black tie, Quintana clearly stood out from the others present. Speaking slowly and with emphasis, Quintana said, "I think that the idea is to find solutions. We have advanced in some things, but you can't be putting so much pressure on us. We are involved in a process that is giving quality of participation." As he continued with his intervention, Quintana began to speak more rapidly, and he shrugged his shoulders and motioned with his hands as if brushing away something in the air, a gesture that communicated a disavowal of the things he felt he was being accused of by the media activists.

Flor, a young media activist from Apure, stood up from her seat to respond to Quintana. "We have a lot of work to do and we aren't in air conditioning," she said, gesturing around the room. "Most of us work in the heat of the sun . . . We don't know where CONATEL is coming from, what are the interests that CONATEL defends. In the face of this, we meet in assemblies, as we always do, as the people do in all our struggles. Because on April 11, when they brought down the government, we went into the streets, putting our lives at risk. In that moment we thought that it was the only way we could reclaim our rights. We can't wait at home for them to resolve some problem and then the government is overthrown. And now, we don't want them to overthrow the force that we have as we are constructing an alternative. We don't expect that CONATEL, do what it may with good or bad intention, should dictate the experiences of community radio. Because the way in which you work doesn't work for us." Flor connects the defense of Radio Alternativa by radio collectives with the popular defense of Chávez during the coup, thereby claiming moral authority for the occupation. She contests Quintana's claim that CONATEL is creating "quality of participation" with her own understanding of participation as the mobilization that emerged during the days of the coup.

Borges responded, "I'm a functionary, I won't say if something is good or bad, if they have the right or don't have the right. Because the administrative procedure is precisely a form of acting by public administration to avoid any kind of indiscretionality of functionaries. When procedures are followed, firstly, the assumption of innocence is respected." At this point the room erupted, with multiple people speaking at once. "Secondly," continued Borges, "we respect the rule of law." The interjections in the room grew louder, as people angrily refuted Borges's statements. "Third," said Borges, speaking forcefully amid the clamor of voices. "Third, third, third," he repeated slowly as he waited for the room to become quiet. "This is a farce," shouted someone from the back. "Let me speak," Borges requested. "If you're not going to let me speak, tell me." The room became quiet. "The laws are there," he went on, "so that whenever I act as an administrator, I don't act capriciously."

The technocrats' adherence to notions of procedure, rule of law, and impartiality correspond to what Iris Marion Young has described as the moral reasoning called for in impersonal public contexts of law and bureaucracy. Drawing on feminist and postmodern theory, Young argues that claims to impartiality feed cultural imperialism by parading the experiences of privileged groups as universal, and the conviction that bureaucrats can make impartial decisions serves to legitimate authoritarian hierarchy.[44] The detachment and dispassion required for impartiality can only be achieved by abstracting from the particularities of feeling and standpoint.[45] In contrast to the impartial view from nowhere, Angelica and Carlos made impassioned appeals to the bureaucrats to put aside their impartiality and to adopt a different approach that recognizes the particularity of the barrio groups and their situatedness within a power hierarchy of class and marginality.

Angelica, clearly exasperated, stood up and interjected, "There is commercial radio and alternative radio, that is something contestatory. You have to say it. They are two things completely distinct."

Carlos stood up next to her and, gesturing toward himself and others around the room for emphasis, entered into a long and engaging intervention, "You can't talk about them in the same terms, one of our stations is not equal to one under Cisneros. Because it is to know the heritage of this people, it is to know the struggle of this people, you understand? We do our work with principles of social justice . . . A compañero was made out to be a delinquent in this scenario. Is it just that a compañero who has five years struggling for authorization be treated in the same way as commercial media?"

"Things are clear. If you can't understand them, we're not in dialogue. Tell me, in what part of the world has a bourgeois rule of law served for the poor of the earth? . . . The state has one function, the community has another. We are required to say the truth in a democratic system. It is our duty and we are not the elected or anything. We are the ones who live here with all the contradictions. We are the ones in contact with daily reality. The ones who have problems [*tenemos peo*] with the malandros. The ones who have problems with the police. The ones who have problems with the Adecos at the base. We are our own people. What we care about is transport, housing, health, education. That is the concept of politics that we work with, that we discuss when we discuss regulations. It has to be intrinsically and genetically linked to the popular, the community, the social."

"For us, politics has nothing to do with parties, nor with politicians, nor with positions, nor with functions, nor with functionaries, nor with the institutions. Our politics is transport, housing, health, education, food, it's what we do in our lives every day. So, if these are the terms in which we have to discuss, don't ask me to act like a state, because I'm not one . . . We need ten thousand radios on the air, community or not, because we need the people to talk, and to talk in their own language. That's our proposal. But for you, every law has to regulate, has to structure . . . Don't ask me to act like you, to have your rationality. What do we have in common and what do we not—from that point we'll advance . . ."

"We don't have any other option, only to struggle, to struggle for dignity, for this country, and I ask that we talk in these terms. The terminology of the bureaucrat, that this is an administrative procedure, 'I'm not going to say if this is just or not because I'm a bureaucrat and this is a legal process,' that's fine, those are the laws, I understand you perfectly. But what happened to this compañero, this hurts me. This doesn't affect you in some law, it affects you in your heart. This is what we have to discuss. We are here talking about all of these laws, let's talk about the forum of regulation, we're not lawyers, but we can demonstrate to you, these are the radios of La Vega, Caricuao, and El Valle. We're not the kids [*chamos*] of las Mercedes, mummy's and daddy's kids. We're the people who sometimes don't even have food on the table. That's why we connect with Chávez, because he sees people with his eyes, he sees who ate or not, and if you didn't eat, here, take this little piece of food at least. The guy comments, he understands what the people are saying. But to you, we write, we comment, but you don't hear us, you don't hear us, you don't understand us. We have suffered quietly our indignities, we've spent four months coming here and we've hardly had any response."

While the functionaries appeal to a notion of liberal law that assumes the equality of all participants, Angelica and Carlos point out that the playing field is not level and community radio stations cannot be treated in the same way as corporate media stations, such as those owned by media mogul Gustavo Cisneros. As Suzana Sawyer has observed in the case of disputes between technocrats and indigenous leaders in Ecuador, for marginal sectors the liberal logic of universals cannot be easily reconciled with histories of discrimination in a racially stratified landscape.[46] Community media activists are not free-willed, autonomous individuals on the same footing as the technocrats and private media owners. Rather they are the poor and marginalized, "the people who sometimes don't even have food on the table." For Carlos, the appeal to universals like rule of law and procedure erases the difference and particularity of the urban poor.

What comes to the fore in this discussion are two distinct visions of politics: one based on administrative regulations, technocratic rationalities, and rule of law and the other based on the politics of everyday life, cultural heritage, the histories of community struggles, and feeling. Carlos asks, how can dialogue take place when the two parties are speaking different languages and come from distinct conceptual universes. In contrast to the language of procedures, laws, and impartiality, Carlos repeatedly brings up affect and emotion as a central aspect of community politics, and he links this to Chávez, as someone who can relate to this politics of feeling.

Ely Flores specifically describes the attitude of the functionaries as one of male arrogance: "We have explained to the functionaries of CONATEL, and to the Cuban company who has the equipment, and MINCI, and the arrogance of the men who tell us we have to change!" The attitude of state officials is contrasted with qualities of feeling, nurturance, and care that are being identified with community work.

As the meeting at CONATEL concluded, the participants sought to reach an agreement with the functionaries, emphasizing the illegality of what had taken place with the closing of the radio station. Carlos Lugo commented, "We have always said that the design [of regulations] should be decided by the community, not imposed by technocrats. And here are a series of technocrats assigned to this, and they've created the notion over and above us that they are the ones who have to design it." The functionaries did not agree to the authorization of Radio Alternativa or the return of its transmitter, but they did consent to organize a forum to debate the issue and they agreed to make a public apology. Some of the participants continued to debate issues of legality and illegality with the functionaries, while others such as Carlos Carles were less interested in engaging the bureaucrats on these terms. The takeover demonstrated the ways in which new forms of collective action conflict with the rationalities of a hybrid post-neoliberal state. It also showed the determination of the activists to put forth a community-centered perspective as the basis for dealings with state institutions, and a refusal to "act like a state," that is, to enter into discussion on the terms posed by the functionaries.

EMERGING BLOCS OF POLITICAL AGENCY

New forms of protagonism in contemporary Venezuela have produced a series of conflicts—over cultural representations, over media ownership and control, and over access to the state itself. Barrio-based organizations have sought to counter derogatory and negative imagery of barrio residents in the mass media by constructing alternative images through fiestas and murals, and they have contested the excessive concentration of private media by creating their own low-power radio and television stations. As barrio-based movements seek greater inclusion in the state, they find that the state apparatus itself is a site of competing interests, and they are vulnerable to incorporation and management by state agencies. Social movements have been able to bolster their autonomous presence by building a dense network of assemblies, media collectives, cultural groupings, and committees that are immersed in everyday life and historical memory. The Western-derived imaginary of civil society is an impoverished category for capturing the diversity of associational life in the barrio; rather, the mestizo Bolívar, the fierce chief Guaicaipuro, or the renegade Negro Primero are invoked in the murals, the radio stations, and the altars of popular fiestas as the basis for a radical social vision.

The field of community media is itself highly variegated, and over the course of the early millennium there has been the formation of distinct media alliances, each with its own ethos, visions, and agendas. These differences became more salient as community radio stations worked more closely with the state agency CONATEL. Certain stations—mostly affiliated with ANMCLA—emphasized collective structures over corporate models of leadership and oral narrative over statistical data. In a meeting to allocate state funds, differences emerged between representatives from

ANMCLA and others such as Catia TVe, affiliated with the Venezuelan Network—the latter playing a mediating and disciplinary role in relation to unauthorized stations. In an occupation to protest CONATEL's confiscation of a community radio's transmitter, media activists countered the liberal formalism and appeals to impartiality of the bureaucrats. These events revealed a clash of worldviews between a utilitarian, technocratic approach of state regulators and a perspective based in everyday work and situated, local knowledge coming from certain community radio stations.

Amid the plural and contestatory streams of thought that have emerged from the contemporary process of social change, community-based media collectives have sought to create an alternative pole based in human creativity, everyday life and work, and subterranean cults of popular history. This pole thrives as an undercurrent in the barrio assembly high in the hillside shanty, in the informal spaces of homes and discussions among comrades, the handmade broadsheet, and on the airwaves of a small radio station with a 10-watt transmitter. At times it gathers momentum and becomes a strong and forceful flow that contends and negotiates in the halls of power. At other times it is relegated to the margins, left on the outside with its nose pressed to the glass of the CONATEL offices in the spacious middle-class suburb of Las Mercedes.

6 | The Takeover of the Alameda Theater

"Good evening, residents of San Agustín. We are meeting today, trying to commemorate a little of those times, of the Grupo Madera. Because for those who remember, we lost the Teatro Alameda, but we realized a dream on April 13, 2004 when we took it over and created the Casa Cultural Alameda. And in a joint program with the Cinemateca Nacional we're going to have a cycle of Cinema under the Stars. Bring your chairs, your girlfriends, and your popcorn, and we'll provide the film."

Outside the Casa Cultural Alameda, along the main street of San Agustín del Sur, some coordinators of the Casa had set up a projector to show Jacobo Penzo's film *El Afinque de Marín* (1980). Penzo, a documentary maker, had come to Barrio Marín in the 1970s wanting to shoot a film about musicians in Caracas. His visit to Marín coincided with the vibrant historical moment of the Grupo Madera, and his documentary chronicled their attempts to create spaces of community resistance. The coordinators had organized the screening of Penzo's film in March 2005 as a way of linking their own occupation of the abandoned theater with the history of revolutionary cultural movements of San Agustín. Residents from sectors and barrios across the parish had turned out for the showing: older people and small children, couples and families, men and women. As the film began, there was silence and darkness, punctuated only by the occasional passing cars and the soft glow of light emanating from the screen. During the film, people whispered to each other and pointed at the screen. They laughed, nodded silently, smiled as they recalled some forgotten memory, and some had tears streaming down their faces.

The film begins with a tribute to the residents of San Agustín: "In 1971, it was announced that certain barrios of the parish San Agustín would be demolished to construct a park. Thanks to their active resistance, the residents of El Mamón, El Manguito, La Ceiba, La Charneca, Hornos de

Cal, Negro Primero, and Marín stopped the destruction of the old Caraqueño communities. This documentary is intended as an homage to those barrios and a recognition of the dignity and cultural vitality of its residents." The film is remarkable in its treatment of the barrio, especially given that the narrative of "history as progress" was a dominant paradigm in film and documentaries of the time. For instance, in her film *De cierta manera* (One Way or Another, 1974), the black Cuban filmmaker Sara Gómez explored the efforts of the Cuban revolution to eradicate the subcultures of marginal, mostly black populations who occupied slum areas such as Las Yaguas. Gómez employs the metaphor of a wrecking ball smashing into old buildings, signaling the destruction of an old way of life in order to pave the way for the new. The narrator in Gómez's film disparages the marginal sectors for promoting "a code of parallel social relations, a source of resistance, a point of endurance and a rejection of social integration." By contrast, rather than seeking the elimination of marginal cultures as the only solution to the so-called culture of poverty, Penzo celebrates the vibrancy of barrio groups who contested policies of urban remodeling.

The images on the screen are a testament to the vitality and strong sense of community in San Agustín of the 1970s. A young man sporting a black tracksuit and short Afro cruises through the streets of the barrio on a motorbike, two congas strapped on either side of his bike. He waves at people, stops for a chat, and taps lightly on the congas as he weaves his way through the lanes and narrow streets. A group of men stand talking animatedly on a street corner in their tight jeans, broad lapel shirts, and aviator sunglasses. Musical legend Mandingo appears in a pair of orange striped sweatpants, giving a demonstration of drums such as the culo 'e puya and the mina. A youthful Alejandrina Ramos, a silver star pinned to her Afro, talks about the importance of music in the life of the community.

Scenes from the film capture something of the extraordinary musical crucible that San Agustín has been historically. In a series of continuous shots, a young girl and boy sit talking, while in the background a man works out dance steps. A group of men sit on a front stoop and one of the men plays pianos chords on his legs. A woman stands in the street fixing the rollers in her hair. A small boy perches on a car hood, smiling and playing imaginary congas. A group of children come running down a set of concrete stairs, and some slide backward down the iron railings. The film conveys a sense of community presence in the streets and public spaces of the barrio, and the beat of the tambores that underlies the rhythm of life.

During the projection of the film for barrio residents, distinct modalities of memory were apparent. Some older and middle-aged residents who had lived through the period looked wistfully at the screen, perhaps remembering a particular concert, event, or feeling associated with the moment. The film evokes a sense of nostalgia for a simpler time. The musicians seem so youthful, their lives uncomplicated and happy. The response of the younger residents showed the ways that memory is transmitted in nonverbal ways. On screen, a group of young boys seven and eight years old play the drums in a small group. Watching the film, a young boy tapped out the same rhythms on his brother's back. The Grupo Madera lived on through their music, through annual commemorations and ritual activities. Every year at the anniversary of the accident, residents set up speakers and broadcast the music of Madera in the barrio. In schools of the barrio, young children sing and perform "La Negra Lorenza." According to one resident, "The children themselves identify with the song, they say, 'Let's do the dance of the Negra Lorenza.'" Residents find ways to remember and collectively transmit their stories, through oral narrative but also through music and images.

At the same time, the viewing of the film was a mourning or requiem for what had been lost. Daniel James describes the complex nature of such events that are not only mourning for loved ones but "mourning for a physical and social space that was lost and with it, perhaps, the possibility of recovering through memory the identities and experiences evoked by this mourning."[1] The showing of the film functions as a memorial for the dynamic young members of the Grupo Madera who tragically lost their lives in the Orinoco, a year after the film was released. It must be painful for the older residents to watch the energy, commitment, and passion of the musicians and to be reminded of their deaths. The residents are also expressing sadness at the loss of an entire way of life, for the days when they could be in the streets without the fear of crime, violence, and delinquency. Perhaps most poignant is the loss of many young boys of the barrio. The men of the barrio, including Yajaira's brother Jaime, watch themselves and their friends on the screen as young boys playing the drums or dancing, and they see so many of their playmates who have since been killed in the streets. Watching the Penzo film at home with some friends from San

Agustín, I noticed that throughout the film people named those young boys who had since died as a result of drugs or violence.

I observed the residents viewing this film through a short film by María Laura Vásquez, since I was not present in Venezuela at the time. My interpretations of the residents' responses are mediated not only by the filmmaker but also by my own partial knowledge of their memories and collective experience. As James says, "There may well be meanings beyond the hermeneutic reach of even the most empathetic viewer or listener."[2] From my work in the barrio over the previous years, as well as my knowledge of San Agustín, I had a sense of the depth of attachment of residents to this cultural history. There are some aspects that I could never access, and some feelings and memories so personal that for an outsider such as me it would be impossible to translate or describe. But I see these questions of collective memory as fundamental to understanding the takeover of the Alameda Theater by the San Agustín residents, and the symbolic role of the theater and of culture more broadly in the lives of the residents.

This book has explored the mobilization of historical memory, identity, and place by urban social movements, as they contest the utilitarian logics of the hybrid state. Memory and place also guided the political actions of residents as they occupied the Alameda Theater in April 2004 and declared it cultural patrimony of the parish. But over the course of the following year, both the Alameda Theater and the Grupo Madera became the subject of bitter disputes, as rival factions in the barrio—partly the result of state and party intervention—fought to align these symbols with their own projects. The institutionalization of the space by the state and the emergence of a small clique within the leadership eventually led to an abandonment of the space by the residents. How can we understand the failure of the theater to embody the hopes of the residents? Why did the theater succumb to the control of a small faction of local elite interests, excluding broader participation? Under what conditions might state agencies succeed in absorbing and deactivating vibrant social spaces?

FROM THE ALAMEDA THEATER TO THE CASA CULTURAL ALAMEDA

"I remember when the entry used to cost twenty-five centavos, and we'd go to see artists like Pedro Infante, María Félix, Andrés Soler, Sonia López and Sonora Matancera live. Apart from this, we went to the theater to see

movies like *Los peligros de Nioca* and *El tesoro de la isla misteriosa* . . .
When I was eleven years old, the entry cost fifty centavos . . . The theater was visited as much by musicians as by artists and journalists, there
was Vitas Brenner, who just died in Germany, Jerry Well, Cheo Feliciano,
Ismael Miranda, Larry Harlow, Ray Barreto."[3]

"I remember that I would take my children when they were small. They
showed children's movies, we paid one bolívar. They were silent movies,
they were very fast to watch. Many artists of high status came. They still
have photos of this."[4]

"After the presentations of Pedro Infante, we'd go to the Bar Cuba, very
close to the theater, to celebrate with a glass of clear *caña*."[5]

" 'El Morocho del Abasto,' 'La Novia de América,' Libertad LaMarque,
el Azúcar de Celia Cruz, the performance of 'La Tongolele,' the flavor
of 'Bárbaro del ritmo,' Benny Moré, the grace of Virginia Lopéz, Jorge
Negrete."[6]

"I remember that my father used to say that when the artists presented
there (I was very young at the time), you'd see great cars there in San
Agustín, there were, well, the Cadillacs of the time, Pontiacs, and all those
cars that were in style at the time."[7]

"After a presentation, we'd go to a party close by to the theater. It was in
the house of Jhony Pérez, also a musician by profession, who became a
good friend. So much so that I baptized one of his girls.[8]

"It was Sunday 19 April, 1963. It was 2.45 p.m. There was 15 minutes to
the start of the film, 'The Robot vs the Aztec Mummy.' From all sectors of
the cerro, young people and children came down, in their Sunday clothes
and best shoes on their way to stand in line at the ticket booth to buy the
ticket of 75 centavos, which was the price of a matinee from 3 to 5pm."[9]

The quotes from residents of San Agustín indicate the centrality of the
Alameda Theater in the cultural and social life of the barrio. The Alameda
Theater was founded in 1944, the third theater to be built in Caracas, after
the Teatro Nacional and Teatro Municipal in the City Center.[10] The Alameda Theater functioned as both concert hall and cinema hall during the

1940s and 1950s. It acted as a magnet for musicians, orchestras, and big-name performers from around Latin America and the Caribbean. Pedro Infante, Celia Cruz, Daniel Santos, Yolanda Montes "Tongolele," Benny Moré, Jerry Well, Mauricio Silva, Joel Ramírez, Cheo Feliciano, and Jorge Negrete all performed there. These artists interacted with barrio residents in the many bars and clubs that surrounded the theater during this time and contributed to the cultural vibrancy of the barrio. As local historian Antonio Marrero observed, "The kids who grew up in this era seeing Pedro Infante, seeing Jorge Negrete, seeing Daniel Santos in their community, they began to rub elbows with them, and this helped them to define their own artistic sensibility." At the same time, the theater played an important role in regional musical trends, giving a new shape to Latin American music, as artists formed relationships with one another and created enduring musical ensembles.

The theater also screened a variety of films, such as *Tarzan, Beauty and the Beast, Battle of the Titans, Snow White and the Seven Dwarfs, Captain America, Fu Manchu,* and the films of the Mexican comic actors Cantinflas, Tintan, Resortes, and Viruta y Capulina.[11] As with other cinemas in the barrios, such as the Cine Dupuicito in La Vega and the movie house of the Cristo Rey complex in 23 de Enero, residents would go to the movies on Sundays as a form of recreation. Mexican cinema was especially popular in that time, as Edgar "El Gordo" recalls: "Mexican cinema has more to do with our culture even if it's very machista, but at least we had Cantinflas who is an expression of the political situation in Latin America, we could see Pedro Infante in *La escuela de vagabundos,* all of that expressed a way of life that exists in Latin America." At between 25 centavos and 1 bolívar, the cinema was relatively affordable for most barrio residents.

During the movement against the dictatorship in the 1950s, the theater played a political role in supporting the insurgency. Carmen Veitia recalled, "We carried out assemblies in the salons of the Alameda Theater, we had sessions of collective lectures, discussions, and seminars."[12] However, once the dictatorship was overthrown and the AD came to power, the theater, which was owned by the corporation Cines Unidos, ceased functioning in 1965 and was turned into a depository of films. Since then, several groups declared their intentions to rescue the theater. As part of their plan for urban remodeling in the 1970s, the government sponsored Centro Simón Bolívar (CSB) proposed to buy the theater and convert it into a great cultural center for the community.[13] This was not realized, and when the CSB was expelled from the parish and the Grupo Madera began their cultural work, they also proposed to recuperate the theater. In 1977 there was one attempt to occupy the theater, but the residents were removed forcibly by the national guard.[14]

The theater remained closed for thirty-seven years. During the 1970s and 1980s, the three other cinemas in San Agustín were also shut down, along with cinemas in many barrios that were all centrally owned by Cines Unidos. This elimination of entertainment venues coincided with a period of deindustrialization that left the urban landscape bereft of public and community spaces. People became afraid to leave their houses after dark or even to be in the streets for fear of being attacked by gang members or security forces. Cinema complexes were built in malls in middle-class neighborhoods, such as the Centro Sambil in Chacao, and cinema became accessible only to the middle and upper classes, who could afford the high prices of films.

From being a symbol of the cultural life and internationalism of the people of San Agustín in the 1950s, the disrepair and shabbiness of the theater was a testament to years of social dislocation, neglect, and the loss of public spaces suffered by barrio residents. The narrow lanes behind the theater leading to el Afinque de Marín were littered with syringes and reeked of urine. In the humid climate, the films rusted and produced noxious chemical fumes. The outside façade of the building gave an indication as to its interiors. Windows were smashed in and bricked up. The outside ledges were overgrown with moss and the original green tiles were painted over with patches of white paint and gray cement. The sign centered over the front doorway that used to read "Alameda" was missing the "A" and the "l," and the "d" dangled upside-down from the base of the sign.

On April 13, 2004, an assembly of 278 residents from San Agustín del Sur met in the Afinque de Marín to decide on whether to occupy the theater. For eight months prior to the takeover, various groups in the parish had been proposing it, and they formed a coalition known as the Comisión General de Grupos Organizados de la Parroquia San Agustín (General Commission of Organized Groups of the San Agustín Parish). The date was symbolically linked with the coup against Chávez two years earlier, although, as one of the leaders Nelson relates, "This night was by coincidence Tuesday April 13; the rescue of the president happened on April 13, so the rescue of the Alameda Theater was this same day, but of this year." The

26 Alameda Theater. PHOTO BY THE AUTHOR.

date of April 13 provides a symbolic reference point for the actions of the residents. During the assembly, community leaders explained to a nervous but jubilant crowd their proposal to take over the theater. There was a vote and the residents decided unanimously to occupy the theater.

When the residents arrived at the theater, the Metropolitan Police (PM) were blocking the entrance, but the leaders began to speak with the police, and eventually the police stepped back. "They spoke to us politely," said Nelson, "because they realized that this was a cultural occupation supported by the people, by the community." The residents went into the theater and others stayed outside, placing banners over the entrance that read "San Agustín occupies its spaces," "The Alameda is ours," "Culture for the People," and "The community supports the occupation." As some of the residents entered the back rooms where the reels had been locked up for many years, they were assaulted by the overpowering fumes of the rusting films, and several of them suffered respiratory problems for over a month from breathing these fumes.

The next morning, April 14, musicians played the tambores in front of the theater to indicate that the theater now belonged to the residents. Several of the leaders signed an act, which declared:

We, the undersigned, on the aforementioned date and at 9.00 a.m, after an extraordinary assembly of 278 people in the Afinque de Marín, behind the Alameda Theater, decided unanimously to take over the installations of the old Alameda Theater. The conditions in which we found the theater are recorded on video film, on the same date. The aim of the takeover is the total recuperation of the structure for the creation of a cultural complex for the parish of San Agustín.

A month later, there was a visit from one of the owners of Cines Unidos. As another leader of the occupation recalls, "They were never against us, but they wanted to know why and for what reasons we did what we did."[15] This leader told the owners that they wanted to write new statutes so that the theater would be administered, cared for, and organized by the residents. Barrio residents sought to negotiate with the owners and the state, because as Nelson told me, "If you make a mistake here, you're a dead man."

Residents involved in the takeover made constant references to the constitution, as giving them the right to take over spaces that are not being used and convert them into centers for the community. José Luis said, "When we did this occupation it was peaceful, by the norms of the constitution." I searched the constitution for such a clause, but one does not exist, and I realized that they were broadly interpreting Article 70, which states: "There are medium for the participation and protagonism of the people in the exercise of their sovereignty, in the political . . . and in the social and economic: the instances of citizen attention, self-action, cooperatives in all forms including financially, savings banks, community enterprises and other associative forms guided by values of mutual co-operation and solidarity." The mention of participation and protagonism in the constitution has provided the impetus for these kinds of occupations, which have also taken place in other parishes such as La Vega and 23 de Enero. On April 13, 2002, when Chávez was restored to power after the coup attempt, the residents of La Vega briefly occupied a police module. In the sector La Cañada of 23 de Enero, the Coordinadora Simón Bolívar (CSB) organized residents to take over the local unit of the PM and they turned it into a cultural center. The residents feel that there is more latitude under the Chávez government to carry out these kinds of acts, but some leaders

27 Discussions with barrio residents involved in the takeover. PHOTO BY AUTHOR.

worry about the impact of too much state presence. Totoño, a long-term leader in San Agustín and member of the cofradía, warned from the start of the occupation: "We need to be responsible for the space, for what will happen to it."[16]

The residents also made reference to the language of cultural patrimony, mentioned in the Organic Law of Culture. The law describes culture as a nonalienable good: "The goods of patrimony as goods that are outside the commercial realm, that cannot be sold or alienated by title or by the competent authority for its administration." The law—passed under Chávez in December 2000—prohibits the transference of public patrimony into private hands and it rejects a notion of patrimony as private property. In discussions with the owners of the theater, the residents appealed to the law, claiming that the theater was not the property of any one individual but it was the "cultural patrimony" of the people of San Agustín. According to Cástor, "It is the community who is working to restore and reclaim the building, therefore it cannot be taken away from us." Residents draw on the notion of public patrimony that is mentioned in the law; however, they frame it as "collective cultural patrimony" that is part of the historical memory of San Agustín. This is akin to what Nina Laurie, Robert Andolina, and Sarah Radcliffe note in the case of the Cochabamba water uprisings in Bolivia, where indigenous groups sought to defend their collective water rights as their cultural heritage, which was being threatened by market forces.[17] Private interests have increasingly dominated the administration of culture in Venezuela, and barrio residents have generally been excluded from participation in decisions related to this administration. But in the act of the occupation, the residents took on the task of defining cultural patrimony themselves and resisting its administration by private interests. Their appeal to the law was similar to the "insurgent citizenship" that Holston describes in the case of the urban poor in Brazil, in that it drew on the accepted aura of social legitimacy and power of the law, showing the competency of the poor and their dignity as bearers of rights.[18]

The theater began operating as the Casa Cultural Alameda almost immediately after the takeover. The leaders formed an organizing council which consisted of general coordinators and personnel in charge of security, finances, and general services. One reason for the creation of these posts was to give the leaders greater legitimacy before state institutions. For instance, when I went with Cástor to the state institution Fundarte, I noticed that he pulled out an official-looking badge with his name, personal identification number, and "Casa Cultural Alameda" written underneath. He introduced himself as a member of the board of directors of the Casa Cultural Alameda and asked to see someone in the office. The badge seemed to be a way of signaling the authority and presence of the residents in their dealings with institutions.

As they began to recuperate and rehabilitate the space, the leadership of the occupation relied heavily on the volunteer labor of residents and fundraising activities. The council members organized courses for local residents in dance, percussion, and painting to generate money. They opened a concession stand on the premises to sell snacks and drinks. At the same time, the leaders tried to access state funds. "They haven't helped us like they should," the finances director Wendy complained initially. "We've submitted applications, we've gone to all the institutions, we've done a

28 Concession stand in the Casa Cultural. PHOTO BY AUTHOR.

million things and we've not had any response."[19] Given the long time it took for institutions to respond, the mayor of the Libertador Municipality Freddy Bernal gave four million bolívares ($US1,905) worth of construction materials. The city council also guaranteed certain basic services such as water and electricity for the Casa Cultural.[20] During the recall referendum, the Casa Cultural became an organizing nucleus for the Comando Maisanta, or the electoral units working in the barrios toward Chávez's victory. This strategic alliance with the state has been noted in other initiatives such as the fiestas, popular assemblies, and the radio stations. One of the participants in the takeover used the metaphor of a trampoline to describe state support: "The project of the Alameda depends on the persistence of the community and our links with the state, which is the trampoline for organized groups."[21] The leadership distinguished this kind of support from traditional clientilism, where local groups are dependent on the state for resources and are not organized autonomously.

There was a renewed vibrancy around the Casa Cultural for many months in the wake of the occupation, as it became a central meeting place for residents of the parish. The Casa Cultural was integrated into the community work of groups in the sector, with meetings of the Land

29 Evenings in the Casa Cultural. PHOTO BY AUTHOR.

30 Evenings in the Casa Cultural. PHOTO BY AUTHOR.

Committees, Health Committees, the Missions Robinson I and II (literacy), as well as classes, music workshops, and an eye clinic, which gave free eye examinations and prescription glasses to residents who needed them. Every day around 6.30 p.m. after work and school, residents would come to the Casa Cultural to participate in meetings or just to socialize with the other residents. In the evenings, the rooms would be filled with people having their meetings. The general congregation of people in the open meeting spaces would spill out onto the streets. The Casa Cultural hosted two exhibitions, one on the architecture of the Central University of Venezuela, and a second on historic and contemporary photos of San Agustín. They organized bolero concerts, comedy nights, theater and dance performances, among other events.

THE TAKEOVER WITHIN THE TAKEOVER

However, within six months of the functioning of the Casa Cultural, organizational weaknesses were becoming apparent as the leadership fragmented into different factions and state institutions stepped in to fill the gap. The connections with the state became less of a strategic alliance and more of a dependency. From the broad coalition of community leaders and groups that had carried out the occupation, a small elite was emerging— people who had been central to the occupation but who had little experience in community organizing. This elite began to siphon off resources for their own personal benefit and use their base in the Casa Cultural to launch a campaign for local government. Long-term leaders such as Totoño and Pelon were gradually edged out, provoking bitterness and resentment among the residents.

The factions opening up in the leadership were based on a growing division between conceptions of political work and community work. On one occasion, a woman from the Health Committee came into one of the rooms of the Casa Cultural and asked two male leaders if they could carry out their business in another room so that the Health Committee could hold their meeting. One of the men responded, "We're all in this revolution together, we can share this room." When she left the room, the other remarked, "She's not a real revolutionary like us." The divisions opening up in the theater seemed to be gender based, with the emerging clique consisting of all men and the committees consisting of nearly all women. By disparaging the woman leader as "not a real revolutionary," the male leader was creating a hierarchy between community work being carried out by mainly women residents, and political militancy, as supposedly represented by this leadership. One of the male leaders expressed their claims to the theater in gendered terms: "The theater is like a beautiful woman. You've got her and others want to dress her, claim her as their own, but she is your wife." This statement revealed the notions of male dominance guiding the small elite; like women's bodies, the theater is conceived as an object of exchange and ownership.

During the July 2005 local municipal elections, the small clique running the theater used it as a base to run an electoral campaign, promoting themselves as candidates for local parish council. They had joined the Tupamaros party, and the walls of the Afinque de Marín and other prominent walls were covered in murals advertising their candidacy. The political party Tupamaros is loosely connected to the militant underground movement of Tupamaros that originated in the parish of 23 de Enero in the 1980s. After Chávez came to power, the party was formed in order to contest elections. Although the Tupamaros party saw itself to the left of Chávez's party, the MVR, it retained a hierarchical and vanguardist orientation like the MVR. The decision of the clique to affiliate with the Tupamaros was surprising to many residents of the barrio, since the Tupamaros had never had a base in San Agustín. Totoño described what was happening as an example of "politiquera," or politicking, as the small elite was mainly interested in extending its power and utilizing the theater for electoral goals. Totoño countered the hierarchical logic of politiquera with an appeal to feeling and emotion, stating, "Real politics comes from the heart, not from the pursuit of power."

The small elite that took control of the theater was emboldened by its connections with state institutions and its growing ability to access state funds. By the middle of 2005, the Casa Cultural had ceased to be a central hub of activity for barrio residents. Besides a few classes and meetings that took place there, it was fairly quiet. The concession stand had fallen into disuse. At the same time, the government had created an infocenter in the Casa Cultural, was using the rooms of the Casa to house various international guests, and was giving money for further renovations of the restrooms and facilities. The notion of self-financing seemed to have been relinquished.

There was a widespread sense of disappointment and betrayal among residents of San Agustín, although none felt empowered to confront the small elite openly. In the spaces of everyday life and community gatherings, people expressed their criticisms. At a funeral for an older woman from Marín, the women were more interested to talk about the politics of the theater than the passing of their friend. "The Teatro Alameda is being taken over by a small group and they are very corrupt," said one woman. "Just last week, the government sent televisions and VCRs to the theater, to be used in educational instruction for the older people who can't make it to the missions. One of the leaders took the equipment for himself and distributed it among his family." "Now he's running for alderman, and it will be terrible if he wins, because he'll have access to even more resources," responded another. One woman suggested that they make an official complaint, but they were too scared. "Anyway, the current aldermen and council people are also corrupt and alcoholic, so what difference will it make?" said someone. Later that week, a number of women were gathered in the kitchen of a friend in San Agustín and began talking about collecting testimonies and signatures from all the women to put to the head of the literacy mission in San Agustín. But as one said, "What good would that do? She herself is corrupt and has eliminated the scholarships for a number of students in order to keep the money herself." The degree of corruption that emerged in the state-sponsored programs in San Agustín, with the theater itself at the center of the scandal, was an indication of the weakness of community networks.

A few weeks later, the residents organized an homage to the Grupo Madera in the Afinque de Marín on the anniversary of their tragic accident. On the same night, the new Grupo Madera, a group created by Noel Márquez, one of the original members of Madera, was performing in the Poliedro for the closing of the International Youth Festival. There was a sense of bitterness among the residents that the current Grupo Madera was capitalizing on the name of the original group and that they had become government spokespersons; indeed their hit song "Uh Ah Chávez no se va" (Uh Ah Chávez won't go) was the anthem of the Chavista movement. People used the event as a platform to make their denunciations of Márquez and the current Grupo Madera. Felipe Rengifo Mandingo, a member of the original Madera living in Germany, sent a recorded message reclaiming the Grupo Madera as cultural patrimony of the country. "Why should Noel Márquez, who is not a native of Marín, nor of

San Agustín del Sur, direct an institution as sacred as the group and the Foundation Madera, which is patrimony of the country?" Mandingo accused Márquez of using the name of Madera to enrich himself personally through state subsidies. He went on to say that Márquez was corrupt and a drug addict.

After the recording finished, others climbed onto the stage to voice their agreement. At times, the situation bordered on farce. One woman from the audience got up and said that all the people making accusations were themselves drug addicts. People whispered in the audience that this woman would know, as she herself was a drug dealer and supplied drugs to most of them. Even as the concert began, the women of the barrio were grouped together in small circles recounting and discussing the issues, reminiscent of the day in the funeral home. Some argued that this was just clashes of ego between male leaders of the parish and others disagreed, saying that it did relate to the formation of political factions within the community. One of the surviving members of the original Grupo Madera, Nelly Ramos, stood quietly watching the events. She leaned over to me and commented, "This is all a form of catharsis. It is the way we have of relieving tensions and speaking to the grief and the divisions that exist within our community."

The historic symbols of the parish of San Agustín—the Grupo Madera and the Alameda Theater—had become contested sites among various factions in the community. As David Harvey has argued, places are sites of collective memory that hold the possibilities for different futures. But such heterotopic spaces are also susceptible to being absorbed by the dominant praxis; "the production of space and place is shot through at every moment with the dynamics of indeterminate social struggles whose outcomes depend upon the shifting currents between social groups."[22] State and party intervention fed the internal divisions existing in the community to convert the theater and the memory of the Grupo Madera into instruments for political incorporation.

The occupation and the homage to Grupo Madera brought to the fore a series of oppositions through which people located themselves: male–female, politickers–community, and politics in pursuit of power–politics from the heart. While it seems that over time a particular community-based vision was defeated and relegated to the informal channels and microspaces of the barrio, at the end of that day of the concert, it seemed to be revived for a moment. After the various musical groups left the stage, the organizers of the event played the song "Canción con todos" by the original Grupo Madera. *"From this barrio has emerged my feeling and my expression that I show you now . . . Share your pain, and also your happiness, to the strong beat of the drum."* There was silence in the Afinque, and then slowly the older men and women came up to the front to dance. Young children placed a wreath of flowers at the foot of the Grupo Madera mural. An old man with a soft white Afro and a cane smiled as he stepped into the spotlight and moved his hips in time to the music, winking at two elderly women dancing near him. On the corner, a group of young boys tapped out the drum rhythms of the song—da-da, da-da-da. The cofradía brought out live drums and began playing along to the song, and after it was finished they continued playing until late in the night.

The occupation of the Alameda Theater represented a taking back of community spaces that had been lost through decades of social decline, government neglect, and privatization. It is one example of a broader trend of popular protagonism that aims to revitalize public space and take back the streets for the community. At the base of this action was the historical memory of the Alameda Theater, the musical life of the parish, the vibrant years of the Grupo Madera and the dignity and pride that they represented for ordinary residents, as well as the multiple losses suffered by the community. While they could never reverse the painful defeats and losses of the past few decades, the residents could try to take control of their present. As they renamed the theater as their culture house and reclaimed it as collective cultural patrimony, the residents linked their collective memories to the hope for a different kind of future.

The subsequent takeover by a small internal leadership, and state occupation of a space left dormant by the community, points to the fragility of this community-based vision. A self-appointed leadership marshaled the resources of the theater for their own personal benefit as they sought to win political office. Early on in the occupation, leaders such as Totoño were warning that the residents needed to take responsibility for what would happen to the space. But it was precisely the absence of strong organizational structures, linked to popular assemblies and other forums for accountability and deliberation, that facilitated the rise of an undemocratic current within the leadership. The story of the Alameda Theater produces questions about the potential for local and sometimes fragmented place-based movements to launch a challenge to broader structures of power. While mobilizing the "power of place" can be an important political strategy, argues Harvey, the politics of localism is not an answer to the ever-present threat of reactionary and exclusionary dangers.[23] How is it possible to both preserve accountability at the base and transcend local concerns? How can social movements create an enduring interface with the state, without losing their grounding in the local? The next chapter explores these questions by looking at the forms of citizen accountability and alliances that are being created by social movements.

III STATE-SOCIETY MEDIATION

We come from another cosmology, another episteme, another form of constructing knowledge.

—MADERA, RADIO NEGRO PRIMERO

Tell me, in what part of the world has a bourgeois rule of law served for the poor of the earth?

—CARLOS CARLES, RADIO PEROLA

Throughout this book, we have seen struggles between, on the one hand, social movements drawing on place-based consciousness, historical memory, and oral narrative to justify claims over public space and access to resources, and, on the other hand, administrators who deploy instrumental and quantitative approaches in their management of community-based programs and organizations. Fiesta organizers and residents who occupied the Alameda Theater affirmed the spiritual, everyday dimensions of culture against utilitarian notions of culture as a tool for political integration or an input for building social capital. Community media producers confronted state regulatory agencies, proposing local knowledge and historical memory over the state requirements for quantitative data, and they contested the liberal formalism of rules and regulations with appeals to feeling and emotion. But in the case of the Casa Cultural Alameda, we also saw the ways that localism can privilege parochialism and entrenched interests, leading to the failure of a transformative agenda. Social movements mobilize identity and place against the abstractions of civil society, the homogenization of media and social life, and the liberal logic of universals, yet meaningful change may also depend on the reincorporation of a broader politics of rights and social justice.

This chapter explores the extent to which social movements have been able to create sustainable structures of representation and accountability. The lack of institutional mediation, which has provided the grounds for urban social movements to grow and flourish, also proved to be problematic as these movements found themselves without the kind of union representation or party structures that could defend their interests against the state. The problems of accountability have been most apparent as the postneoliberal state continues to search for foreign investment, introducing market-based logics in certain demarcated zones. This crisis came to a fore with the government's plan to increase coal mining in Zulia with the aid of multinational companies, undermining the livelihoods of indigenous people in the area and subjecting them to a toxic environment. As before, the contradiction between the anti-neoliberal rhetoric of the state and the reality of its continued accommodation of foreign investors produced criticisms from social movements. In the case of the coal mining, it led to the emergence of new urban-rural coalitions which organized resistance in the form of marches and protests. In this chapter, I explore the coalitions that are being built from the ground up, and I evaluate their potential to function as new forms of institutional linkages.

Some scholars have argued that functioning institutional channels between state and society depend on a strong procedural democracy. Procedural democracy, derived from Western experiences of representative government, is based on the rule of law, free and fair elections, and a separation of powers between the executive, legislative, and judicial branches of government. The changes carried out by Chávez during his administration have provoked concern among some political scientists and Western-based human rights organizations that this procedural democracy is being eroded.[1] Javier Corrales argues that the new constitution, which was approved by popular referendum in December 1999, expanded the executive branch at the expense of the other branches by concentrating power in the presidency.[2] According to Jennifer McCoy, since Chávez has been in power he has systematically attacked institutional structures by intervening in the court system through the constituent assembly and disbarring several judges, appointing Supreme Court members by decree, and increasing the power of the military by removing congressional oversight over military promotions.[3] And in 2004, critics such as Human Rights Watch add, Chávez carried out actions to control Venezuela's judicial branch by increasing the size of the Supreme Court from twenty to thirty-two members, thereby further undercutting the separation of powers and undermining the rule of law.[4] Although some observers have refuted these claims,[5] most assessments of the Chávez government from outside continue to be based in the language of procedural democracy.

Yet in some criticisms coming from urban social movements, this explicit focus on procedural democracy is a limited means of ensuring government accountability and institutional mediation, as it reduces citizen participation to elections once every six years. Fernando Pinto, a young media activist, explained to me that, moreover, it removes decision-making power from the people: "What liberal democracy has done is separate who decides from who votes: you vote, but you lose the real capacity to decide about the things that affect you." In contrast to the focus among some with procedural democracy, urban social movements in Venezuela are concerned with *substantive* democracy, defined by John and Jean Comaroff as "a civic culture in which participatory politics would be the stuff of everyday life."[6] While procedural democracy relies on multiparty elections as a means of ensuring accountability and trusts in branches of government to monitor each other as the principle of separation of powers, others have spoken about the need for social accountability that counts on social movements and organizations to monitor the government.[7] Without this kind of accountability from below, as one observer noted, the participatory democracy being touted by the Chávez government can be "just as illusional and formal as liberal democracy."[8] Rather, it is at the level of everyday life and culture; the local publics created through popular assemblies, radio programs, and fiestas; and through community-based organizations that the urban poor develop their own meanings of democracy, as substantive and participatory democracy. In the accounts given in this book, we can see the multiple ways in which a substantive democracy is being practiced, often through vernacular cultures of participation and critique. First, even if the state is the central site of political power,[9] the exercise of power is actually negotiated, through a culture of questioning authority and a dislike of autocracy. This was apparent in the relation of Carmen Teresa and Yajaira to Chávez—they looked up to him as an authority figure at the same time that they chided him when he appeared on television and they expressed their concerns when they disagreed with him. Likewise, Blanca Eekhout from Catia TVe and Guadalupe from CSB physically approached Chávez at various events to complain about lack of funds for their radio stations. Even the relation of the people to the patron saint San Juan reflects a culture of negotiating authority: his religious status depends on his ability to provide for his followers.

Second, rumors and private gossip serve as a check on leaders, who may seek to amass wealth or hoard goods under a system of redistribution. After Chavista mayors Freddy Bernal and Juan Barreto came to office as mayor of the Libertador municipality and city mayor respectively, people grumbled and complained about their inefficiency and lack of attention to everyday problems. Similarly, when a small clique in the Casa Cultural Alameda began to siphon off television sets and other items sent to the Casa by the local mayor's office, the women of the barrio noticed, and they began discussing this whenever they gathered at funeral homes and in kitchens. At times the critiques became more public, and during the homage to the Grupo Madera in the Afinque de Marín, the musician Mandingo made open accusations that Noel Márquez was using the name of the original musical group in order to enrich himself personally. As Roger Lancaster noted in revolutionary Nicaragua, the microdiscourses of rumor are where the populace organizes its own covert and informal powers. Rumor, murmurings, and gossip act as a vigorous leveling mechanism that holds in check the emergence of new class and status stratification.[10] The people hold leaders and each other accountable to their own rhetoric of egalitarianism, honesty, and revolutionary self-discipline.

Third, doing reports on radio stations and other forms of community media is a way of making politicians and corporations responsive to local needs. Community radio and newspapers reported on instances where the mayor had not provided basic services such as garbage collection, or PDVSA did not maintain its gas installations in the barrio, or the government did not respond to a flooding tragedy. In addition, barrio residents have sought to interface with the state and demand measures of accountability through the mechanism of "Contraloría Social" (Social Control). In November 2004, Chávez encouraged citizens to form units of Contraloría Social in their neighborhoods in order to exercise some degree of vigilance and control over state-sponsored social programs. An example of how this means of citizen oversight functioned can be seen in the parish of La Vega. Some unemployed workers from the Carretera Negra sector of La Vega formed a construction cooperative and approached Fundabarrios, who had a large endowment of funding to repair houses in the barrios. The residents carried out a census in the sector and determined that thirty families were in need of repairs to their homes, and they proposed to Fundabarrios that the work on the thirty houses be assigned to the cooperative. Only twelve families were approved for repairs, and of these, only four houses were given to the local cooperative. The remaining eight houses given to outside contractors were left half finished, and the contractors absconded with the money. The members of the cooperative and the affected families formed a unit of Contraloría Social, and they occupied Fundabarrios, demanding that the situation be addressed. A supervisor from Fundabarrios was sent to the Carretera Negra, but the outside contractor lied, and the matter was not pursued further. The Controlaría Social unit then worked with the cooperative to repair the houses that had been assigned to the contractors.

A culture of negotiation, critique, and social control from below is an important feature of a substantive democracy, but as we have seen, it is not sufficient to ensure that voices from below are heard in the halls of official politics. Individual chastisement, rumor, and gossip may in fact act as a safety valve to channel discontent rather than bring about change. Controlaría Social may only be a stopgap measure for what is a larger systemic problem. Social movements themselves are highly localized and fragmented. There are multiple groups in the barrios with an organic leadership and alternative visions, but they do not often communicate with each other. They united around specific tasks such as the election of Chávez, defeating the coup against Chávez, and the recall referendum, but they have faced greater difficulty in sustaining a common agenda to represent their own interests before the state. Rather, a functioning substantive democracy may depend on the ability of social movements to build broad-based coalitions, especially across the urban-rural divide.

STATE-SOCIETY LINKS UNDER CHÁVEZ: THE FORMATION OF ANMCLA

Since his first public appearances during the coups of 1992, Chávez had established a strong personal connection with the masses, but he was less successful in creating enduring institutions that could mediate the relationship between state and society. The Chávez government attempted to build the links between state and society through a series of methods. Initially, the government strengthened the MVR, thinking that Chávez's party would be the main vehicle for state-society interactions. For his first year in government, Chávez operated solely through the party, and most nonparty activity was not considered important. However, the MVR proved to be bureaucratic, hierarchical, and removed from the lives of ordinary people. Margarita López Maya describes how the MVR was originally conceived as an electoral front controlled by Chávez's clandestine cell, the Movimiento Bolivariano Revolucionario 200 (MBR-200).[11] Since the founders of the MVR did not consider it to be a party, they did not create democratic structures and procedures for internal debate or training of members. The hierarchical structure of the party consisted of Bolivarian coordinators at the municipal and regional level, and a national directorate with decision-making power, consisting of civilian and former military leaders.[12] Yet the electoral successes of the organization thrust it into the spotlight and gradually reduced the significance of the MBR-200.[13] The MVR frequently attempted to intervene into local initiatives, mobilize the base in support of various electoral initiatives, and absorb independent expressions into its fold.

Given the failures of the MVR, Chávez then tried to promote local units of participation such as the Círculos Bolivarianos (CBS) and between 2001 and 2003 there were around 200,000 CBS formed across the country. But according to their own members, the CBS collapsed due to "incapacity, neglect, exhaustion, and evolution."[14] In their place, new structures were created such as the Unidades de Batalla Electoral (Units of Electoral Battle, UBES), which successfully organized people to defend Chávez in the referendum of 2004. After the referendum, these were converted into the Unidades de Batalla Social (Units of Social Battle, UBSS). But as Carlos Lugo described it, while the CBS, UBES, and UBSS originally facilitated popular participation, they were eventually taken over by political parties and institutions, and the transference of power to the local level that some groups hoped for did not happen.

Chávez also attempted to bypass the traditional institutions, with their high levels of nepotism and corruption, by creating the missions, which sought to channel resources directly to the community. The missions did have some degree of success in avoiding the bureaucracy of the institutions. For example, in the Barrio Adentro program of local health clinics, people in the barrios arranged to find housing for Cuban doctors, and they themselves built and supervised the health modules. Likewise, with the soup kitchens, resources arrived directly from the government, without the delay and red tape of the health and social welfare institutions. But at times, the missions reproduced the paternalism, corruption, and hierarchy of the institutions. The Universidad Bolivariana de Venezuela (Bolivarian University of Venezuela, UBV) is a case in point. At one point a small faction took over control of the UBV in Caracas and began to use undemocratic methods in its running, excluding the teachers and students from decision making. They would call for "asambleas informativas" (informative assemblies) to advise the teachers about the direction of the institution, and in their frustration of being left out of decision making, several teachers resigned. The continuing hegemony of a vanguardist logic in attempts to organize popular movements from above resulted in growing disillusionment with these methods.

In this context, media associations have provided an important vehicle for uniting diverse social movements and allowing them to interface with the state. Given the growth of communications technology and the changing sites of working-class politics from the factory to the barrio, it is not surprising that media associations should play a role in building a coalitional politics. Radio, especially, has functioned as an organizing nucleus for diverse committees and movements in the barrio. Media collectives are fluid and dynamic and can respond quickly to specific situations. The media association that has been most concerned with building strategic alliances among urban social movements is the Asociación Nacional de Medios Comunitarios, Libres y Alternativos (ANMCLA). ANMCLA has its roots in a loose network of radio producers known as Banda Ciudadana that was formed in 1992. According to Fernando, the idea of the network emerged during the social explosions of the early 1990s, as a means of communicating what was happening on the ground during the coups of 1992 and beyond. The group gave workshops on radio to people in Catia, Caricuao, and La Vega, helping to start the radios in those areas. After Chávez was elected in 1998, the activists from Banda Ciudadana entered into a series of discussions around the Law of Telecommunications and the Regulation of Community Media, and they realized that they needed to unify their forces and build a more coherent organization.

The popular communicators began meeting in 2001 to discuss the idea of creating an organization, and in 2002 they formed ANMCLA. Prior to the coup of 2002, the group had been mostly an idea; as most of the members were involved in their own individual collectives and community organizations, the broader grouping had little resonance. It was only after the coup of 2002 that ANMCLA began to function as an organization. In December 2003, it held a conference in the northwestern Andean town of Mérida, uniting media collectives from across the country. Certain aspects of the organization were agreed on from the start: that ANMCLA was not a party or a union but a social movement; that it had to function as a way of integrating all its struggles, not only in the area of communication; it had to work to multiply the media in the hands of popular sectors; and last, it had to connect with all of the long-term social movements that predated Chávez and help them to create community media. It was by connecting with these long-term groups, especially in rural areas such as Yaracuy and Zulia, that ANMCLA grew so rapidly, says Fernando, advancing through its connections with consolidated social forces. The organization integrated movements of urban barrio communities with indigenous movements, the miners' struggle, and the peasant movements. ANMCLA was defined as an integral community project with four main areas of struggle: communication, defense, production, and social life.

The founders of ANMCLA were concerned that social movements needed a national organization that would allow them to counter the centralization of power in the private media, in the state, and in corporations. But how to create a national group without losing local specificity and the force of history and place at the base of their movements? How can they maintain plurality and autonomy of local groups in a broader organization? These are the issues that ANMCLA activists have raised and continue to grapple with in their everyday work.

ANMCLA as an organization has engaged in several kinds of protest and deliberative activities as a way of realizing its vision of a substantive democracy. One form of action, connected with the resignification of public space, is marches and mobilizations on the streets. Fernando says, "The street is the space to rediscover ourselves as a power, as a force." During the tense days of the petrol strike in 2001 and beyond, both Chávez supporters and the opposition took regularly to the streets. This was important, as Fernando notes, as "all the heavy political events, at least in Venezuela, have been lived in the street." But in 2005, ANMCLA began calling marches in defense of the interests of its members, such as mobilizations against the Chávez government's plan to increase coal mining in the state of

Zulia. The organization engaged in "tomas," or occupations of state institutions, to protest the mistreatment of its members and the capriciousness of state officials. ANMCLA also organized regional and national meetings as a forum for deliberation over the direction and goals of the organization. Regional activists in one meeting criticized the ANMCLA leadership for itself being highly centralized. In these debates we see how the problems of centralism, hierarchy, and autonomy play out even within an association of community-based groups.

IN DEFENSE OF WATER AND LIFE: STRATEGIES OF MOBILIZATION

The appeals among some urban groups for a model of politics and knowledge production based in everyday life and cultural heritage are being echoed among rural and indigenous peoples who are calling for an alternative model of development that is sustainable and protects the way of life of indigenous peoples and the biodiversity of the environment. Indigenous people in the northwestern state of Zulia, including the Añú, Barí, Wayuu, Yukpa, and Japreira communities, formed an organization called Front for the Defense of Water and Life (Frente por la defensa del agua y la vida, FRENDAV), which sought to defend their natural resources against the exploitative coal mining in their region that continued after Chávez was elected. These indigenous communities, residing along the Andes range Sierra de Perijá on the border with Colombia, are independent from the Yanomami, Guajibo, Warao, and Piaroa indigenous groups located in the southern Amazon region of the country. FRENDAV held a meeting in December 2003 at Isla de San Carlos to criticize the Free Trade Area of the Americas (FTAA) or Area de Libre Comercio de las Americas (ALCA) that was being proposed by the United States. They urged the Chávez government not to sign the ALCA treaty, whose principles were already apparent in the concessions being made to mining companies for expanded coal mining in their region that depleted natural water supplies and eliminated biodiversity. Unlike the indigenous movements of Bolivia, Ecuador, and Colombia which were resisting the development projects being carried out by transnational corporations and their governments, FRENDAV was concerned that indigenous movements in Venezuela were demobilizing in the face of promises by the Chávez government that it would protect their interests, when this was far from clear.

The name of the movement, "For the Defense of Water and Life," signals its affinities with other indigenous movements, such as the Mobilization for Life (Movilización por la Vida) in 1994 in Ecuador against a proposed neoliberal agrarian law, and the Bolivian Coalition in Defense of Water and Life (Coordinadora de Defensa del Agua y de la Vida), which emerged to contest a new law introduced in October 1999 to allow the privatization of water in Bolivia. One of the leaders of the Coordinadora, Oscar Olivera, recounts that when the Coordinadora was formed among irrigation farmers and union leaders in the central Bolivian city of Cochabamba, it took its name from the comment by one irrigation farmer, who said, "Let's not have just 'water' in our name, but 'life' as well, because they are taking everything away from us. All that's left to us is the water and the air."[15] Like the Coordinadora, FRENDAV built alliances between indigenous and urban barrio communities, organized in ANMCLA. As they worked together, these groups discovered their commonalities and they developed a critique of the prevalent model of economic and social development that requires some of the most vulnerable sectors to be sacrificed in the name of a broader plan.

When Chávez was elected to government, he adopted many of the contracts and concessions to mining companies that had been granted under previous governments. But following the restructuring of the oil industry in 2003 to promote joint ventures where the state has majority ownership, the Chávez government has made efforts to develop state control over key sectors such as bauxite, iron, and coal. In the southeast state of Guyana, where the majority of the country's mines, hydroelectricity capacity, and steel works are located, the state is revising mining contracts and concessions to also move toward joint ventures. Gregory Albo argues that in a hostile global context, the ability of Venezuela to diversify depends on planning capacities at the center and the development of independent capacities in new agencies, but old state structures have been a significant obstacle to this.[16] And although the state is attempting to control the significant natural resources of the country and restrict the license of multinational companies to exploit these resources, its broader strategy remains based upon an export-oriented model of development where those who profit from and consume resources are still mostly foreign corporations and citizens. These contradictions came to the fore with the proposal of the Chávez government to increase coal mining in the state of Zulia.

In October 2004, just months before signing a trade agreement with Cuba under the auspices of an anti-neoliberal, pro-sustainable development model known as ALBA (Alternativa Bolivariana para las Américas), the Chávez government announced plans to increase coal mining in Zulia. Venezuela extracts 8.5 million metric tons of coal per year, which is predominantly for export to the United States and Europe.[17] Eighty percent of this coal comes from two mines located north of the Manuelote water reservoir in Zulia, the Mina Norte and the Mina Paso Diablo. These mines are controlled by joint ventures with private consortiums where the government is a minority partner. Extensive coal mining in these locations has already displaced local indigenous people. In 2004, Corpozulia, the regional development corporation of the national government, planned to open coal mines along the Cachirí and Socuy rivers to increase extraction of coal from 8,000 tons to 30,000 tons. Maracaibo, the capital of Zulia, home to over two and a half million people, is dependent on the sources of water that come from these two rivers. The government plan to increase production involved the investment of hundreds of millions of dollars for the construction of a megaport for the extraction and transport of coal by multinationals. Corpozulia also planned to build a thermoelectric plant of 500 megawatts, fueled by coal to supply electricity to the state.[18] The indigenous Wayuu, Barí, and Yukpa people from the area were concerned that the plans would increase water contamination and health risks for the mostly indigenous population of the region which depends on scarce water supplies. They argued that the proposal violated the Kyoto Agreement and several articles of the Bolivarian constitution that guarantee a clean and safe environment and protection of indigenous resources.

In March 2005 and January 2006, ANMCLA brought together urban media activists with indigenous groups in mobilizations in Caracas to protest the plans. On March 31, 2005, a group including over six hundred indigenous people marched from the Plaza Morelos to the Miraflores Presidential Palace. They presented a letter of protest to Chávez, noting the pulmonary illnesses suffered by mining workers, the threat to the water supply, and the accidents occurring during the transport of coal.[19] As in the Water Wars in Bolivia, the protesters focused on protecting customary usage.[20] In a statement to the press, the activists claimed that the extraction of coal constitutes a violation of the rights of the indigenous people "whose culture and mode of life are absolutely connected with nature."[21]

Posters at the march read "Coal Miners of Maché, Socuy, and Yachirá Out: In Defense of Water!" and "No to Coal, Yes to Life and Nature." The indigenous protesters wore traditional outfits, including grass skirts, beads, painted faces, and woven baskets on their heads, and many of the women were bare chested. They emphasized their identity as indigenous people, as a way of staking claim to water as a resource that belongs to them as a collective right. In contrast to a development model based on large-scale industrial projects and modernist ideals of progress, the protesters emphasized Andean cosmologies and the defense of their cultural heritage as indigenous people.

The urban protesters who joined the indigenous people on the march similarly drew on the language of Andean spirituality and cultural heritage. The march was a dramatic expression of the ways that the urban poor deploy indigenous identity as a means of framing their resistance. In chapter 4 we saw how barrio residents like El Indio create murals and narratives about the mythic indigenous chiefs as a way of articulating issues of urban poverty. We went on to look at how icons of the chiefs are used in the names and narratives of urban community radio stations. On the day of the march, the concerns of the protesters, both rural indigenous and urban nonindigenous, were framed as a question of indigenous rights. As Nancy Postero has argued in the context of Bolivia, this is not simply a strategic use of indigenous identity but rather "a new form of coalitional politics that is emerging as the most important form of social movement protagonism."[22] Although most of the protesters in the march were indigenous or, in the case of the urban poor, with some mixture of indigenous background, they did not mobilize as indigenous people but rather they united around a common sense of exclusion and marginality. The number of indigenous groups directly affected by the mining plan was very small, some fifty households or so, which makes this kind of coalitional politics even more important to make their voices heard in national politics.

The protesters took on the language and symbols of the Chávez government itself, to challenge its plans for coal mining. In the press statement, they cited articles from the Bolivarian constitution of environmental protection (Article 129), individual and collective rights to quality of life (Article 127), the role of the state to guarantee a contamination-free environment (Article 127), and maintaining the cultural, social, and economic integrity of indigenous groups (Article 120) that are being violated by the plan to increase coal mining. According to the statement, the plans for coal mining conflict with the spirit of the government-proposed endogenous development projects that seek to promote the principle of self-determination for all peoples.[23] In both the March 31 and the January 27 marches, the "No to Coal" signs used the "No" symbol of the pro-Chávez campaigners during the recall referendum as a way of signaling the ways they have supported Chávez, who must now live up to his promises. Protesters carried signs with slogans such as "Venezuela: Now It Is for Everyone," and "There Is No Fatherland without Us," appealing to the official mottos of inclusiveness being touted by the government. The signs referred to Chávez as *compañero*, and many of the protesters said that they had come because they wanted Chávez to know what was going on in Zulia.

But at the same time, the protesters were highly critical of the model of development that is represented by the coal mining and, by extension, that undergirds the Bolivarian project. In their press statement, they said, "The plans for coal mining in Zulia are part of an exogenous strategy that weaken self-determination, and moreover, are in keeping with a hegemonic economic and productive model in the world, that identifies development with economic expansion and a growth in the consumption of energy."[24] One of the posters at the march had an image of the Grim Reaper, draped in the American flag, which read, "Exploiting Coal Is Death!!! And Money for Transnationals." In contrast to the government slogan, "Another World Is Possible," the protesters claim, "Another Integration Is Possible." Social movements in the barrios have long been engaged in struggles against contamination and pollution, and some see the Chávez government as no different from its predecessors regarding environmental policy. One barrio resident related, "When I hear Chávez on TV saying that the production of automobiles has risen 30 percent in the last year, I don't feel happy, because it only means more traffic and more pollution. Why should I feel happy that Chevron is making more money, when I've had a sore throat for the last month?" But it has been extremely difficult to make these kinds of arguments publicly. Government propaganda declares that PDVSA has been reclaimed from multinational corporations and now belongs to the people, in slogans such as "PDVSA: Now It Is for Everyone." To some degree, government rhetoric has associated an improvement in standards of living of the urban poor with greater exploitation of natural resources.

The march raised the question of what democracy looks like and who makes decisions in a democracy. In the press release, the protesters state that Article 120 of the constitution gives indigenous people the right to participate in decision making in issues regarding their social, economic, and cultural integrity, but in the case of the mining the decisions are being made by the authorities in collaboration with transnational companies.[25] Rusbel Palmar, a leader of a Zulia indigenous organization, said, "The coal infrastructure plans have not been presented to indigenous people. These plans cannot be done without consultation with indigenous people."[26] The government decision highlighted the lack of accountability of officials to their constituents. The press release states, "The majority of sectors of the Yukpa, Barí and Wayuu people, among the others affected, reject the projects for the exploitation of coal, and that their voice is not being adequately heard by the authorities, which constitutes a violation of the right to participation and the democratic principle of popular protagonism."[27] By mobilizing in the street, the people are not just protesting the government's plans; they are also shaping a new vision of what substantive democracy should look like. As the people organized, they created alternative structures of decision making that challenged the monopoly of the state and transnational corporations.

Through mobilizations, protesters also reclaim the streets as the site of politics and a space for renewing local power. In contrast to the large marches of 300,000 and 500,000 people supporting Chávez during the oil strikes of 2002, after the referendum people began to mobilize autonomously. "At a certain point we noted that all the marchers were coming out in support of the proceso, or rather, Chávez as the central element," Fernando commented to me. "But we began to lose the capacity of our autonomy to fight our fight, as there are many contradictions within the development model of the Bolivarian government . . . And the struggle against coal mining has been emblematic because it highlights the model of export development, condemning of the environment." ANMCLA continued supporting other marches, such as a peasant march later in 2005. "The idea is to unify the movements who are fighting for autonomy, to give them voice and force," said Fernando. "Because if not, you have a discourse monopolized by government spokespersons." The marches have had some degree of success in raising popular awareness about environmental concerns, and also in halting the plans. After the March 31 protest, the government ordered two commissions, which found that the protesters were correct about the contaminating impact of the mining. The Ministry of the Environment and another special commission in Miraflores issued statements and reports supporting these findings. But the government has not acted strongly on these findings. As of May 2006, it had postponed plans to increase coal mining to 30,000 tons, leaving it at 8,000 tons, but it had not met protester's demands to reduce it to zero. The protesters think that the government will continue pushing for the increase of production, which requires them to be vigilant and ready to take to the streets. ANMCLA has played a crucial mediating role in organizing the marches, building coalitions between rural and urban sectors and providing a common platform for groups seeking more autonomy. Further important coalition building is still needed to reach out to and involve mining workers, who have been pitted against indigenous groups by mining corporations.

REGIONAL ASSEMBLIES AND ALLIANCE BUILDING

While rural and urban groups came together for marches and protests, their attempts at building more long-term alliances can be seen through the regional and national assemblies held by ANMCLA. These assemblies have been a means for coming up with alternative platforms and agendas, debating future actions, and also for interrogating questions of internal democracy within the organization itself. Between December 2003 and April 2006, ANMCLA held five national assemblies which brought together media groups from around the country. It also held several smaller regional assemblies. I have chosen to focus on a smaller regional assembly held in Aragua in February 2006, as it reveals much about the vision of participatory politics that the media activists are proposing, as well as some of the limitations they face.

The three-day assembly in the Campamento Rancho Grande in Aragua was attended by sixty or seventy activists from Miranda, Aragua, Carabobo, Caracas, and Vargas, in preparation for an upcoming national meeting projected for April. There were older activists, students, housewives, people from all walks of life. The meeting was a forum to debate the goals and aims of the activists and to discuss the three points that had been put forth by the leadership. These were Carlos Carles's suggestion that ANMCLA should be a revolutionary organization, committed to building an Indo-Afro-American socialism; Fernando Pinto's proposal for the creation of local units of self-defense, as an alternative to the School of the

Americas model inherent in the government notion of army reserves; and Alfredo Flores's plan for local production and the building of self-sufficient communities. Those present at the meeting discussed these points, but some also raised concerns about the functioning of ANMCLA and the focus of decision making in a small, Caracas-based, and mostly male leadership.

To get to the Campamento, I had to take a bus from Caracas to Maracay, and then I took a taxi, which dropped me off on a small country road. I had to walk through a small stream and then I came to some small streets leading to the Campamento. When I arrived at the camp grounds, the assembly was taking place inside a large hall, where participants were seated in concentric circles, similar to other assemblies I had witnessed.

Madera was speaking, addressing the question of strategy before the state. "We need analysis, what are the solutions that we have as a movement before the state?" He went on, "This is a state that is creating more and more direct dependency. We have to revise this. What position are we going to take as a popular movement, as an organic movement, as a movement of action, marking out lines of defense against imperialism not only from the point of view of organization, but also production. There is a vicious action in this moment on the part of the state towards the communities. It is demobilizing us, everything that has to do with the Mission Vuelvan Caras, everything that has to do with the Núcleos Endógenos.[28] In reality, these are not proposals that support a self-productive, substituting work, in an organic way. It is a form of destroying us, and we, as a popular movement, could be carrying these vices to our own communities, where we can already see the influence of the Junta Parroquial, the MVR. In this conference, let's put on the table a synthesis and put forward proposals or our positions as a popular movement and we'll do a final assembly at the end."

After Madera made his intervention, an older woman, Marta, spoke up. "I see disorganization, disunity, incoherence. My suggestion is the construction of popular power. At this moment, we have the Consejos Comunales [Communal Councils] above us and it turns out that the law supporting them and the organizational structure of the Consejos Comunales includes almost all areas of production. So, it seems that we could be struggling, always functioning as parallel organizations. I am concerned about the proposal of a national platform. I think that we can achieve much from the Consejos Comunales, and we have to take advantage of this process that's in the works, while fighting with everyone so that they don't absorb the popular power of the popular communities at the base. My proposal is that we define well what is unity and national organization, and the confluence and congruence between our organizations and our plans, because if not, ANMCLA will be left on one side and other organizations on the other. This worries me. I see that here today, nobody talks about Consejos Comunales, and I'm afraid that we'll become an island. And imperialism sees us all as the same thing and will crush all of us."

The participants debated issues of strategy and their relationship with government supported units of popular participation, such as the Consejos Comunales. In 2003, Chávez had made a call for people to form Consejos Comunales. But at that time, the city of Caracas was under the control of opposition-identified mayor Alfredo Peña, who was hostile to the idea. The idea of the Consejos Comunales was to create avenues for local governance outside the control of the corrupt and party-dominated Juntas Parroquiales, linked with the mayor. Under Chávez's plan, the Consejos Comunales would be linked to a parallel structure known as the Consejo Local de Planificación Público (Local Council of Public Planning), independent of the mayor and Juntas Parroquiales. In February 2006, Chávez announced that he would be giving money for the creation of Consejos Comunales, which is why Marta was suggesting that they take advantage of this. The question of whether to create an entirely distinct structure of mediation or participate in government-sponsored units was a strongly debated issue. For Marta, the Consejos Comunales must themselves be seen as terrains of popular struggle. But for others such as Madera, the threat of cooptation and demobilization was very present.

Ely Flores made a lengthy intervention in favor of autonomous organization. She specifically addressed the February 4 march and their decision not to attend. February 4 was the historic date of Chávez's first coup attempt, and a large march was being held in Caracas. The decision of the activists to attend the assembly in Aragua rather than the march in Caracas was criticized by some within Chavismo, and during the forum the participants also addressed the reasons why they chose to attend this meeting rather than the march.

"Why are we gathered here, why are we gathered here as an organization?" Ely asked the assembly participants. "There they are saying that it's February 4, that we are a force, that we have to march, that we have to participate. But we are still looking for spaces of popular participation of the people. That's fine, communal production is one of our proposals, it is our proposal, it's something that comes from way back like many other things. But then, we have to ask, who are we? Where are we going? Who directs and designs politics? And how are we going to participate? Because really, popular participation doesn't exist, why? The Núcleos Endógenos are a failure, because they're dependent on a government who decides how the people are going to organize. 'If you want to do culture, do dance, organize,' but they're not even from our communities. 'It doesn't matter, we'll form a cooperative with whomever.' So, with the government alone this will never work. It depends on us. We are not just media, we are organized communities who use media as a way of being heard, to frame our proposals, to make public the experiences we are constructing. Radio is nothing if there's no social organization at its base. That's why I say I'm concerned."

"I think that the march is important, but I think that this is more important, because here we are organizing, we are constructing our spaces of popular power, not marching only when they call us. And they'll keep utilizing us, and they'll keep manipulating us. And the same will happen with us that happened to the UBES, that happened to the Circulos Bolivarianos, nobody talks about the UBES. That's why we are calling these working groups, we can sit together and come up with a plan of action so that we can construct the popular power that we are talking about. The same state talks about popular power, but when you ask people what this is, they can't tell you. These things have to be in our discussion so that we can advance as a movement, not only as radio and television, but as a social movement, as a people. We, who have a little more formation than others in our community, have to construct the real popular power. It's not the missions, not Robinson, not Sucre. That's fine, you have to participate, but we have to construct our own references. We can't be dependent on anyone who will give you the money when they feel like it, but when it's not in their interest they take away everything."

Ely's intervention, which was followed by loud applause from the audience, reveals the contested meanings of participation coming from social movements. How can the radio activists encourage self-generating, autonomous participation when the discourse of participation has been monopolized by the government and identified with the government-organized marches and organizations? As Julia Paley describes in the context of postdictatorship Chile, social movement actors see "participation" as a tool used by the government "to appropriate popular organizations for its own ends."[29] In contrast to the attempt by the state to absorb and demobilize social movements, Ely sees the need for popular movements to "construct our own references." While state-sponsored bodies like the missions are named for official Republican heroes such as Robinson, Sucre, and Ribas, community activists draw on popular historical memory and the locale of the barrio in order to frame their activities.

After Ely's speech, Marcelo, a young man, urged them to move toward the "mesas de trabajo" (working groups), in order to open up the discussion. "I think that the mesas, as smaller forums, are spaces where more people can talk," said Marcelo. "It shouldn't be that Carlos Carles spends two hours talking. I want to propose that the working groups be spaces for discussion." The methodology of mesas was one employed by ANMCLA at their assemblies to encourage a "culture of debate," as "the free flow of ideas which involves confrontation of diverging opinions and a plural communication free of coercion."[30] The participants also sought to democratize decision making through the mesas, encouraging collective participation in the "elaboration, planning, and execution of programs, plans and projects."[31] The format of the working groups did allow for greater input from others, particularly the women and younger people. Specifically, participants in the mesas brought up the issue of the de facto leadership that had emerged in the organization and the need to extend decision-making responsibility to others.

In the mesa de trabajo where I sat in, there was a brief discussion about procedure and the group voted to follow a list method, where people would indicate to the moderator if they wished to speak, and those who had not spoken already would be placed before those who had. People began the discussion by pointing out what they saw as problems that had emerged in ANMCLA. Nancy Quiroz, an older woman from Aragua, began the discussion by saying that ANMCLA needs to decentralize.

Another woman, Arlenia from Miranda, agreed with Nancy. "The proposals and financing are always coming from Caracas, but regional communities need to come up with their own proposals. We need to think about consolidating local networks so that we are autonomous."

Marcelo interjected, "What is the relationship between social movements and state power? The state is a chair where we sit, but we need to destroy the chair and all sit on the floor. In ANMCLA there is a tendency to centralize big responsibility, decision making, the political line, and resources in a few people. This reproduces problems of centralization. How can responsibility be divided more evenly?"

An older woman, Mariela, sitting to the left of Marcelo, responded to his question. "We need to decentralize work by devolving more responsibility to working groups. Many people think that Chávez is the ultimate leader, but we need to work towards building local power bases."

Another young man, Erikson, added, "The problems of centralization in the organization could be addressed by communicating more, by making better use of email to pass along information."

"But," responded another woman, Lydia, "the problem is that information and organization is usually concentrated in a few leaders—Fernando, Ely, and Carlos—and it's often hard to find out information about the marches and other activities." She was sitting next to Ely and glanced over at her a few times during her intervention.

Summing up the point, an older woman, Graciela, said, "We need to be conscious of where we came from, and how we can be community and organic communicators. This needs to be linked to questions of citizenship, of permanent formation."

One old man present voiced his agreement: "I'd like to support the notion of decentralization. ANMCLA as an organization is too focused in a small leadership."

Most of those present in the working group seemed to agree that ANMCLA had problems of centralization, and that a de facto leadership made many of the decisions regarding the organization. They drew on the notion of building local power that was introduced in the plenary, and Carlos Carles's suggestion that ANMCLA should be a revolutionary organization, as a way of bringing up issues of decentralization within the organization. Ely, in turn, responded by saying that this was not only the fault of Caracas-based leaders but that it was also necessary for regional and other leaders to honor their commitments and assume responsibilities. When they do not comply with their work, Ely commented, the burden then falls on the Caracas-based leaders.

With the exception of Ely, the relationship between leaders and base in ANMCLA was strongly gendered. It was women who constituted the majority of everyday workers, while men were concentrated in the leadership. As a community-based organization, ANMCLA differed from Chavista organizations, which tended to operate with a much more vertical notion of politics. But even in the community spaces, it is still men who tend to occupy leadership roles. Although women have always played an important role in everyday work in their communities, the gendered division of labor which underlies women's participation in community work also restricts them from having time for the kinds of education and reflection that the men of the community have had available to them. Where men can gather to discuss, read, or attend lectures, women are often at home with the children, or taking care of other domestic responsibilities such as cooking and cleaning.[32] Women face ongoing challenges in becoming leaders in their communities, but community-based organizations like ANMCLA provide spaces where these issues are raised and debated.

During the discussion, Marcelo added that the issue of internal centralization and hierarchy was compounded by working closely with the government. The administration and allocation of resources generates new hierarchies and concentrates power in fewer people. Marcelo argued, "When you begin to work within state power, you start creating hierarchies. ANMCLA still depends on the state. This is a double-edged sword, as we get resources, but self-government is the challenge. How can we maintain autonomy before the state, but make use of the resources available? It is a question of needing to maintain a strategy of direct action."

The participants were concerned with the degree of agency and autonomy they could retain within a state-led process of transformation. They agreed that they needed a strategy of direct action, such as the marches and takeovers; and they needed to pursue diverse paths both within and outside of state institutions as a way to build their movement without being isolated. The meeting demonstrated some of the pitfalls of trying to build cross-regional coalitions to represent the interests of community organizations, especially the dangers of isolation and problems of centralization.

Urban social movements engage in everyday wars of position with cultural institutions, the private media, media regulatory agencies, and mining corporations over issues of culture, access to media, the meanings of development, and visions of what democracy itself should look like. They question the abstract and formal principles of impartiality, rule of law, and procedural democracy invoked by Western observers and technocrats as a means of masking forms of privilege and domination. Instead of relying on the separation of powers and regular elections expected to produce limited accountability under a system of procedural democracy, urban social movements are calling for accountability from below that brings social pressures to bear on the Chávez government to ensure that it carries out its mandate. This logic of accountability differs from that of a middle-class civil society, with its postulation of a sharp boundary between state and society. Rather, the metaphors used by urban movements to describe their relation to state power—as one of strategic ambiguity, as a trampoline, and as a chair—recognize the porous nature of society's interface with the state.

Media activists from Caracas, indigenous groups, and others are concerned with substantive democracy that gives poor and disenfranchised sectors the ability not just to vote for the candidates of their choice in elections but to have decision-making powers over the issues that affect them. In battles with state development agencies over coal mining in Zulia, indigenous groups appealed to the constitution, which gives them the rights to make decisions over questions of cultural and economic integrity. By increasing coal mining from 8,000 to 30,000 tons, the government was violating this right. Democracy, for urban social movements, was to be realized through mobilizations in the streets, occupations of state institutions, and regular assemblies and meetings. The activists from ANMCLA sought to redefine the nature and meaning of participation, as not only government-sponsored rallies that mobilized people in support of the state but also the building of self-generating and autonomous movements.

Central to this new kind of participation was the need to construct an alternative set of references, as Ely said at the meeting in Aragua. From the murals to the fiestas and the mobilizations, this is what urban social movements were engaged in doing. Over the course of their battles with the private media and technocrats in the administration, social movements came to develop and voice a distinct vision of politics based on everyday work, cultural heritage, feeling, and historical memory. During the marches in defense of water and life, the protesters drew on Andean cosmologies and indigenous cultural heritage as a means for unifying their diverse struggles.

At the same time, the experiences of the regional ANMCLA assembly cautions us against romanticizing community-based movements, which are themselves shaped by gender and regional inequalities. Several women at the meeting criticized the predominantly male and Caracas-based leadership of the organization for centralizing power and not allowing the regional centers the same level of decision-making power in the organization. The political culture of paternalism and hierarchy was being reflected in ANMCLA, even as it instituted structures such as the mesas de trabajo to decentralize and encourage decision making at the base. If anything, the stories told here should convey that democracy is always a work-in-progress, and the struggles for participation and calls for inclusion reverberate even at the very margins of the margins.

Conclusion

Moments of social change are hard to capture in all of their dynamism and fluidity. Often all we can hope to glimpse are the broad shapes of actors in motion and the traces of possibility that are left in the air. Shifts in paradigm are not discernible simply through the rhetoric and slogans of a few charismatic leaders, or through the clashes on the streets between opposing groups. Rather, they are registered in small seismic shifts of consciousness, in the everyday wars of position that are fought out in areas that earlier were not contested and now are. The balance of forces is constantly shifting. New centers of power emerge for a time and they multiply into diverse streams of activity or they are suffused with the habits of the old order and collapse into themselves. And as this process unfolds, it partakes of life, the throb and hum of the city streets dense with vendors and slowly moving crowds, and the pulse of a reggaeton beat, a life which never ceases but weaves itself into the evolving and vital spaces of revolution.

Throughout this book we have looked at the spheres of everyday life—the fiestas, life histories, music, rhythms, murals, barrio assemblies, and popular radio—in order to understand the dimensions of urban popular politics during the historic presidency of the radical leftist leader Hugo Chávez. In these final reflections, I consider some broader questions about the contemporary political landscape and changing sites of social struggle. Is Latin America entering a phase of recomposition and regrouping of forces? Are cities set to be the site of new social movements, or are we seeing the development of an urban vanguardism? What might a world after neoliberalism look like? I offer some brief speculations here, but I hope that these questions will be further answered by future work that is deeply informed by ethnography and a political sociology of movements on the ground.

Between the mid-1970s and the mid-1980s, numerous governments across Latin America and the Caribbean adopted macroeconomic stabilization policies in an attempt to control inflation and regain investor confidence following the debt crisis. During this period, Latin America was at the forefront of a cycle of international protest against austerity measures that was unprecedented in scope.[1] At the end of the 1980s, structural adjustment measures were formulated into a coherent and extensive set of neoliberal principles known as the Washington Consensus, and reforms were urged on Latin American countries. The decade of the 1990s was marked by attempts to consolidate the neoliberal model throughout the region.

The neoliberal model was widely proclaimed to be a panacea that could resolve the foreign debt crisis and spark economic growth through reviving the private sector. During the 1990s, money brought in through privatizations temporarily increased the public sector cash flow and incoming foreign investment led to economic growth.[2] Laws promoting decentralization gave increased scope for participation at the local level of government in countries such as Bolivia. Neoliberal reforms were carried out in different ways in the various countries of Latin America, with earlier and more sustained reforms taking place in Chile, while countries such as Uruguay and Costa Rica maintained a greater role for the public sector in providing welfare.

By the late 1990s, however, the consequences of neoliberal reform were being felt in several places. In Argentina, capital flight took place due to external shocks, prompting a sharp recession that began in 1998. Unemployment and poverty rose to critical levels, and economic growth stagnated, leading to further capital flight. As people tried to retrieve their savings from banks, the government of President Fernando de la Rúa put a freeze on all banking. In December 2001, large demonstrations in the streets led to de la Rúa's resignation from office. In Bolivia, following large popular protests against the decision in 1999 to privatize the water supply in Cochabamba, a round of strikes spread across the country in 2000 as workers, teachers, and *cocaleros* (coca growers) protested trade liberalization policies and the neoliberal agenda of the government.[3] In September 2003, protesters occupied the capital city of La Paz, demanding the recovery of natural gas reserves from transnationals and the nationalization of natural gas. As a result of the protests and the repressive response of the army, which left hundreds wounded and over thirty dead, President Sánchez de Lozada resigned in October 2003. There were large protests against privatization in Costa Rica, Peru, and Guatemala. From 2004 to 2007, there were nationwide mobilizations across Central America against free trade agreements.[4] Several leaders challenging the neoliberal orthodoxy to greater and lesser degrees came to power: Hugo Chávez in Venezuela in 1998, Lula Inacio da Silva in Brazil in 2003, Néstor Kirchner in Argentina in 2003, Tabaré Vázquez in Uruguay in 2004, Evo Morales in Bolivia in 2005, Daniel Ortega in Nicaragua in 2006, and Rafael Correa in Ecuador in 2006. The national mobilizations, the ousting of neoliberal politicians, and the election of left-wing leaders marked a deeper rejection of the neoliberal model than the earlier cycle of protests.

During the first years of the twenty-first century, there was a shift from protests and mobilizations as a reaction against neoliberal reforms to a new phase of recomposition and regrouping of social forces.[5] The popular fiestas, radio stations, local assemblies, street protests, and occupations that are part of the fabric of associational life in this period are testimony to the creativity and inventiveness of the urban poor, in the face of harsh deindustrialization, the loss of public spaces, economic depression, and the atomization of everyday life. The potentially devastating crisis of marginality, where the urban poor are segregated, vilified, and excluded, has given rise to alternative forms of social cooperation. The locale of the barrio has become a primary marker of identity and belonging. The condition of informality itself has promoted alternative forms of economic cooperation, as informal workers become the cells of a new supportive economy.[6] This period of recomposition marks a shift to a stage where neoliberalism seems to have lost its "taken-for-granted" position and alternative social and political models seem possible once again. This is a highly uneven and shifting process across the region, but in countries such as Venezuela, Ecuador, and Bolivia it may be possible to point to the emergence of post-neoliberal orders, where leaders are seeking to implement policies radically in opposition to prevailing neoliberal orthodoxies.

Like the earlier wave of protest cycles, the locus of post-neoliberalism seems to be in Latin America, while in many other regions of the world neoliberalism still reigns as the dominant social and economic paradigm. This unique position of Latin America may owe to its status as what Greg

Grandin has called "empire's workshop," the place where the United States acquired its conception of itself as an empire, a school where it learned how to execute violence through proxies, and a staging ground for experiments with free-market nation building.[7] Among the first to be hit by the effects of structural adjustment policies, Latin American countries were also the first to react with protest, and several are now at the forefront of attempts to construct alternative social and political orders. Whether the construction of a new model is realized or instead a permutation of the neoliberal order takes place, and whether this will generate a new round of global recomposition and regrouping, is still unclear.

CITIES AS SITES OF A NEW POLITICS

The specifically urban location of the barrio, favela, periferia, or villa miseria has become a central site of working-class politics. From a temporary residence that housed rural workers who came to the city in search of work, to a step on the ladder to greater social mobility as opportunities expanded during the period of ISI, to becoming a sign of the city's chaos, poverty, and decline following the debt crisis: the barrio has increasingly come to be seen as the space of belonging and the source of identity for new social actors. Others have described how during earlier eras of national-populist politics across Latin America, the factory was central to the production of working-class politics and consciousness. In his study of the militant workers of Chile's El Teniente copper mines, Thomas Klubock writes, "The union hall served as the central social space in which workers and their families gathered for cultural events, as well as for political meetings."[8] Today, union halls and party offices have receded in importance, as the percentage of the population engaged in formal wage labor declines. As Holston notes, it is in the realm of the *oikos*, the zone of domestic life of remote urban peripheries, where the struggle for daily rights begins: "demands for a new formulation of citizenship get conceived in terms of housing, property, plumbing, daycare, security, and other aspects of residential life."[9] The popular slogan "La nueva fábrica es el barrio" (The new factory is the barrio) points to these changing sites of working-class politics across Latin America in a neoliberal era.[10]

The shift from the factory to the barrio has also led to changing subjects of popular struggle. In this book, I have traced the subjects of social protest in the barrios from worker to guerrilla and party militant, then as informal worker and *vecino*, or neighbor. While the terms *compañero* (friend) and *camarada* (comrade) are frequently used among barrio residents, the most commonly used is *vecino*, both as a way of addressing another person ("Hola vecino") and in discussing someone in the third person ("La vecina de San Agustin"). These moves away from the proletariat as a key subject of working-class identity reflect the new sites of labor, deliberation, and political action in which popular sectors are engaged.

As the map of class power has been redrawn over decades of neoliberal reform, the losses sustained by marginal classes are evident in the urban landscape. The privatization of public areas, the militarization of the barrios, and social dislocation have led to shrinking spaces for collective life in the city. The construction of new models of sociability in a post-neoliberal era is strongly connected with the redimensionalization of public space. Fiesta organizers and muralists sought to establish a presence in the streets, even in the face of threatened violence from the police. Community radio hosts organized karaoke contests near the subways and promoted fiestas in the plazas. Through involving young people in sports, vacation programs, and the radio, community media activists sought to demilitarize the barrios. Guided by the memory of the vitality of San Agustín in earlier periods, residents occupied the Teatro Alameda and turned it into a cultural center. In the mobilizations against coal mining, urban and indigenous groups took to the streets to protest the government plans. Movements of cultural identity are linked to claims over public space, redirecting the uses of plazas, streets, and abandoned lots toward the interests and needs of the people who reside in the territory.

Cities are increasingly functioning as the sites of a new politics across the world. Especially in large global cities such as New York City, there is a massive demographic transition toward a concentration of African Americans and third world immigrants who are devalorized and marginalized.[11] New forms of social movement organizing such as the immigrant rights movement, the independent workers center movement, and movements for housing democracy have strong bases in the city. As traditional trade union politics has become less able to relate to the diversity and complexity of the urban workforce, union organizations covering domestic workers, street vendors, taxi workers, and restaurant workers have formed to give voice to largely undocumented, informal, and immigrant urban sectors.

The incorporation of the urban poor into social movements with a progressive political voice and presence is not a foregone conclusion. In many urban centers, street gangs and mafias dominate the streets. In Brazil, the massive popular movements of liberation theology from the 1970s and 1980s have been largely replaced with short-term, project-oriented NGOS and evangelical churches.[12] We may not be able to identify any single logic of radical politics in urban areas, yet as Mike Davis argues, there are nonetheless "myriad acts of resistance."[13] Black musical forms such as rap and Afro Reggae formulate a critical analysis of marginality and structural poverty through an oppositional culture of the streets. Evangelical culture can provide the idiom for expressing collective identities and developing a critical consciousness about one's place in the world. In some cases, movements such as Afro Reggae in Brazil have collaborated with NGOS to criticize class privilege, racism, and corruption through a consumer-media politics.[14] But if and how these cultures could articulate together in a broader movement in pursuit of social justice remains to be seen.

Building a new form of coalitional politics has become the most urgent task facing fragmented and at times isolated urban movements. As we have seen in this book, cultural identity has provided a means for uniting diverse urban sectors and linking them to their rural counterparts. Urban murals elaborated images of the mythic chiefs as symbols of marginality and exclusion. While creole discourses celebrated the vanquished indigenous chiefs as the foundations of the modern state, in contemporary counternarratives the chiefs are reconfigured as emblematic of indigenous resistance. Indigeneity and Andean cosmology have provided tropes capable of bringing together urban and rural sectors and creating a sense of collectivity. These coalitions have been particularly important in the case of the campaigns against coal mining, where the affected indigenous groups are small in numbers. Urban and rural groups succeeded in constructing a broader front to protest the issue of coal mining, linking it to an analysis and critique of modernizing development.

Within this new coalitional politics, the question of internal power relations is also important. As was seen in some of the regional ANMCLA meetings, there was a tendency for vanguardism and centralization among urban groups, which was resented by some of their rural and regional counterparts. The concentration of resources in urban areas, the privileged access by urban sectors to political connections, and the greater facility of communications in urban areas led to the emergence of a de facto leadership in ANMCLA who often took decisions on behalf of other sectors. Might these informal urban vanguards be replacing the party vanguards of earlier revolutionary movements? ANMCLA had the structures and spaces for discussion where these issues could be raised, but it is something that the organization is constantly grappling with.

POST-NEOLIBERAL VISIONS

At the heart of a transition away from a neoliberal order are the post-neoliberal visions that have crystallized in the experiences of social movement organizing over the last few decades. The instrumental rationalities of technocrats in state institutions, with their emphasis on expediency and universal, quantifiable knowledge, have generated countervisions that emphasize local knowledge, oral narrative, and historical memory. This pattern of oppositions was played out in the numerous sites that I have explored throughout the book. It was apparent in the interactions between fiesta organizers, who saw culture as a spiritual and religious matter, and arts administrators, who sought to utilize the fiestas for instrumental purposes such as resolving the necessities of the community. In the dealings of San Agustín residents in the Casa Cultural with an arts administrator, the residents emphasized culture as the everyday, which is linked to their family, their sector, and daily lives, as compared to a concept of culture as a resource and as a commodity, which was proposed by the administrator. When community radio activists encountered state officials of CONATEL, during the drawing up of legislation for community media and later in the occupation, they brought out cultural heritage, local knowledge, feeling, and everyday work in response to the technocratic analysis of the social, quantitative data, and the impartiality of the officials.

The tensions between these competing visions reflect the contradictions of a revolution fought from within the structures of a neoliberal state apparatus, as well as Venezuela's continued subjection to a global market economy. Urban social movements are making demands—over public space, for inclusion in the state, for social rights, and for a redistribution of resources—that cannot be accommodated within the framework of the present order. This conflict came to the fore during the occupation of CONATEL, when community media activists accused technocrats of representing the interests of media corporations and continuing to police the airwaves to keep out community media. Pointing to Chávez as their representative within the state, community activists struggle to identify who the state represents, whose interests are being protected by the impartiality of bureaucrats, and on whose side the army and state officials will be willing to intervene. They find that it is not always in the interests of ordinary people, and this realization is generating a greater impetus toward self-organization and autonomy.

But on a deeper level, these struggles reveal the continuing predominance within the Chavista project of an Enlightenment notion of progress and knowledge construction historically associated with colonialism and European capitalism. As Han Yuhai has argued, Enlightenment thought emphasizes the need to form a "rational community" through "an intelligentsia in charge of a certain system of knowledge, a bourgeoisie in charge of a market, and a bureaucracy in charge of various administrative and juridical mechanisms." This framework undervalues "cultural life," which includes "religion, ritual, drama, storytelling, popular history, local speech practices, and so forth."[15] It is precisely through the politics of everyday life, the fiestas, storytelling, music, drums, historical memory, murals, barrio assemblies, and popular radio examined in this book that the urban poor make their presence felt. In the marches against coal mining, indigenous groups put forth Andean cosmologies as an alternative to a modernist notion of development that views progress in terms of economic expansion and greater exploitation of natural resources.[16]

Social justice and political transformation do not depend only on coming up with new policies and legislation as the Chávez government has done. Rather, they require generating alternative rationalities to counter the market-based rationalities that have come to structure political and social life. By emphasizing local knowledge, oral narrative, and historical memory against the rationalities of administrators, social movement actors were formulating these post-neoliberal visions. Ultimately, this points to the role played by local actors in mediating and contesting global configurations of power. While state-society alliances can alter the trajectory of neoliberalism, state-centric solutions remain subject to the internal and external constraints of global capital.

The post-neoliberal social imaginary that animates urban movements spells the possibility for an alternative order. Boosted by his success in the recall referendum in 2005, Chávez began talking about a socialism of the twenty-first century, including nationalizations of private industries and services, state-led development, and regulation of the banking and financial sector. Socialism of the twenty-first century, quipped Carlos Carles, sounds like the slogan of a transnational corporation. Indeed, one could see in the Plaza Venezuela a large banner reading, "Private Business Supports Socialism of the 21st Century." By contrast, Carlos Carles, Edgar "El Gordo," and others have talked about an Indo-Afro-American socialism, based on not just nationalization but community control; not just worker management of existing industries but an alternative system of production; and not led by party militants or bureaucrats but by organic leaders of the community. Rather than a blueprint for a future society mapped out from above and carried out by bureaucrats, this vision of socialism is one where the direction toward a new order will come from the creative force of everyday life. We cannot say with any certainty what a post-neoliberal future will look like. The narrative continues to unfold through the energies and interactions of multiple actors, the everyday decisions they make in a constantly shifting field of structures and relations, and the fortuitous circumstances and unintended consequences they encounter along the way.

In the end, it is people who make history, but not under circumstances of their own making, as Marx said famously. This book has explored the obstacles, conditions, and material circumstances that shape and limit the protagonism of the urban poor. But it has also sought to explore their agency to remake their daily worlds. The people I write about here will go on making history for many years after this book is published: their stories do not finish here. As I was finishing this book, Palmiro, the community activist and Maria Lionza devotee from Petare, had joined the mayor's office and was working for the government. He had moved his office headquarters from the fried chicken shack Mirapollo to Superbueno, a popular vegetarian restaurant close to Capitolio. Juan Contreras also had a full-time position in the mayor's office, and he spent most of his additional time in the new headquarters of the CSB, directing programs and training youth. Gustavo had started up a cooperative with his son in the southeastern state of Miranda, and they traveled regularly to work there. Freddy had also recently returned to his native place to work with cooperatives there. He continued his work with El Gordo in La Vega, particularly among young people of the parish, trying to develop a future generation of leaders.

Carlos and Ely added twins to their growing family and organized several vacation camps for children of the parish. Johnny and Yajaira were active in creating communal councils in the parish of El Valle and had joined the United Socialist Party of Venezuela (PSUV) as aspiring militants. Yajaira has many chapters yet to add to her "bestseller."

Notes

INTRODUCTION

1. Historians have described the ambivalence that slaves and mixed-race sectors felt toward the independence movement as led by creole elites such as Bolívar, who was one of the most wealthy slave-owning cacao producers. This was why some popular sectors participated in countermovements such as that led by Boves. See, for instance, Bergquist, *Labor in Latin America*, 199; Carrera Damas, *Historiografía marxista Venezolana y otros temas.*

2. Roberts, "Social Correlates of Party System Demise and Populist Resurgence in Venezuela."

3. Ellner, "The Contrasting Variants of the Populism of Hugo Chávez and Alberto Fujimori."

4. Levine, "The Decline and Fall of Democracy in Venezuela"; Molina and Pérez, "Radical Change at the Ballot Box"; Molina, "The Presidential and Parliamentary Elections of the Bolivarian Revolution in Venezuela"; Ramírez Roa, "La política extraviada en la Venezuela de los años '90."

5. Molina and Pérez, "Radical Change at the Ballot Box," 105.

6. Levine, "The Decline and Fall of Democracy in Venezuela," 254.

7. Weyland, "Economic Voting Reconsidered," 844; Naím, "The Real Story behind Venezuela's Woes."

8. "Susceptible": McCoy, "From Representative to Participatory Democracy?," 293; "ripe": Canache, "Urban Poor and Political Order," 47; "charisma-hungry": Weyland, "Economic Voting Reconsidered," 843; "unorganized": Roberts, "Social Correlates of Party System Demise and Populist Resurgence in Venezuela," 36.

9. McCoy, "From Representative to Participatory Democracy?" 270.

10. For a few examples of this broad and diverse literature, see Boudin, González, and Rumbos, *Venezuelan Revolution* ("Participatory Democracy" chapter); Alex Holland, "Venezuela's Urban Land Committees and Participatory Democracy," February 11, 2006, http://www.venezuelanalysis.com (visited March 10, 2008); Michael Fox, "Venezuela's Secret Grassroots Democracy," November 30, 2006, http://www.zmag.org (visited March 10, 2008).

11. Duque, "Un gobierno, un proceso."

12. James, *Resistance and Integration*, 2–3.

13. República Bolivariana de Venezuela, Gobierno del Distrito Federal, *Anuario estadístico de la gobernación del distrito federal*, 2000.

14. Comisión Económica para América Latina y el Caribe, *Anuario estadístico de América Latina y el Caribe*, 2005, http://websie.eclac.cl/anuario_estadistico/anuario_2005 (visited April 14, 2007).

15. República Bolivariana de Venezuela, *Anuario estadístico*.

16. Ibid.

17. Ibid.

18. World Bank, "Project Appraisal Document on a Proposed Loan in the Amount of U.S.$60.7 Million to Venezuela for a Caracas Slum-Upgrading Project," September 28, 1998.

19. World Bank, "Gender in Urban Infrastructure Projects: The Case of the Caracas Slum-Upgrading Project: Executive Summary," http://www.worldbank.org.

20. José Roberto Duque, "En Caracas," *La Otra Caracas*, October 10, 2004.

21. Bolívar, "Rehabilitación y Reconocimiento de los Barrios Urbanos," 73.

22. Perlman, *The Myth of Marginality*.

23. Ray, *The Politics of the Barrios of Venezuela*; Susan Greenbaum, "Backgrounds of Political Participation in Venezuelan Barrios" (B.A. thesis, Department of Anthropology, University of Kansas, 1968); Lomnitz, *Networks and Marginality*.

24. Lewis, *La Vida*.

25. González de la Rocha et al., "From the Marginality of the 1960s to the 'New Poverty' of Today."

26. Ward, "Introduction and Overview."

27. Goldstein, *The Spectacular City*, 12.

28. Ibid., 13–14.

29. Sassen, "Whose City Is It?"

30. Davis, *Planet of Slums*, 178.

31. See Goldstein, *Laughter Out of Place*; Burdick, *Blessed Anastácia*; Ferrándiz, "The Body as Wound"; Smilde, *Reason to Believe*; Gutmann, *The Romance of Democracy*.

32. Auyero, *Poor People's Politics*.

33. Goldstein, *The Spectacular City*.

34. Holston, *Insurgent Citizenship*.

35. Alvarez, Dagnino, and Escobar, Introduction, 15.

36. Ibid., 15–16.

37. Smith and Low, Introduction, 1–16.

38. New social movement theorists go beyond a reductionist concept of politics and political culture as found in mainstream sociology and some resource mobilization theory to assess the multiple realms in which dominance is con-

tested (Alvarez, Dagnino, and Escobar, Introduction, 11). Although some scholarship on resource mobilization theory, such as Sidney Tarrow's "collective action frames" and Debra Friedman's and Doug McAdam's "identity incentives," is concerned with theorizing cultural processes, other work has been mostly concerned with institutional and structural processes and how movement demands are processed in institutional spheres (Alvarez, Dagnino, and Escobar, Introduction). Also, while resource mobilization theorists often assume the existence of collective identities, proponents of new social movements theory are interested in the construction and negotiation of identities (Stephen, *Women and Social Movements in Latin America*).

39. I do acknowledge that I am using different scales of analysis in my study. I am looking at the local scale of the city, specifically Caracas, and comparing this with the state, a national entity. My rationale for this follows from the explanation offered by others such as Bob Jessop that as a key site for both international financial operations and grassroots civic initiatives, the city becomes an interface between conflicting local and global flows. Therefore it is in cities that the key tensions and contradictions of neoliberal governance are felt in everyday life. See Jessop, "Liberalism, Neoliberalism, and Urban Governance."

40. Coronil, *The Magical State*, 4.

41. Ibid., 224.

42. Ibid., 89.

43. Ibid., 139.

44. Ibid., 146.

45. Ibid., 370.

46. Ibid., 375.

47. Parker, "Chávez and the Search for an Alternative to Neoliberalism."

48. Coronil, *The Magical State*, 385.

49. Parker, "Chávez and the Search for an Alternative to Neoliberalism."

50. Robinson, *Transnational Conflicts*, 12–13.

51. Coronil, "Magical Illusions or Revolutionary Magic?"

52. Parker, "Chávez and the Search for an Alternative to Neoliberalism"; Ellner, *Rethinking Venezuelan Politics*.

53. Leonardo Vera, "¡El balance es neoliberal!," July 23, 2001, http://www.analitica .com (visited April 20, 2008).

54. Petras and Veltmeyer, *Social Movements and State Power*, ix.

55. Foucault, "Governmentality."

56. Brown, "Neoliberalism and the End of Liberal Democracy."

57. Ong, *Neoliberalism as Exception.*

58. Contreras, "Cultura política y política cultural en Venezuela."

59. Ibid., 52.

60. Albo, "The Unexpected Revolution."

61. Weisbrot, "The United States and the World."

62. Wilpert, *Changing Venezuela by Taking Power*, 221–23.

63. Craig and Porter, *Development beyond Neoliberalism?* 21; Ong, *Neoliberalism as Exception*, 95.

64. Grimson and Kessler, *On Argentina and the Southern Cone*, 191.

65. Postero, *Now We Are Citizens*. For examples of theories of neoliberal governmentality, see Rose, *Governing the Soul*; Ferguson and Gupta, "Spatializing States"; Yan, "Neoliberal Governmentality and Neohumanism."

66. Coronil, "Magical Illusions or Revolutionary Magic?"

67. Gramsci, *Selections from the Prison Notebooks*, 234.

68. Lander, *Neoliberalismo, sociedad civil y democracia*.

69. In *Seeing like a State*, Scott observes the utilitarian rationalities in high modernist architecture, revolutionary vanguard parties, collectivization in the Soviet Union, and compulsory villagization in Tanzania.

70. Li, *The Will to Improve*, 278.

71. Hylton and Thomson, *Revolutionary Horizons*, 8.

72. Gould, *To Lead as Equals*, 3.

73. Stephen, *¡Zapata Lives!*

74. Universidad Central de Venezuela (Central University of Venezuela).

75. Scheper-Hughes, *Saints, Scholars, and Schizophrenics*, 12–13.

1. URBAN POLITICAL HISTORIES

1. Almandoz, "The Shaping of Venezuelan Urbanism."

2. Yarrington, *A Coffee Frontier*.

3. Almandoz, "The Shaping of Venezuelan Urbanism," 2074.

4. Ibid., 2085.

5. Marrero, *San Agustín*, 13–14.

6. Interview with Antonio Marrero, local historian, San Agustín, July 2005.

7. Marrero, *San Agustín*, 15.

8. Almandoz, "The Shaping of Venezuelan Urbanism," 2085–87.

9. Interview with Marrero, July 2005.

10. Ibid.

11. Herrera de Weishaar, *La Vega*, 195.

12. Bergquist, *Labor in Latin America*, 210–11.

13. Karl, "Petroleum and Political Pacts."

14. Rafael Quintero, "Un poco de provincia en la ciudad." In Vivir en Marín, http://www.nodo50.org (visited April 13, 2007).

15. Ibid.

16. Ibid.

17. Karst, Schwartz, and Schwartz, *The Evolution of Law in the Barrios of Caracas*, 17.

18. Marrero, *San Agustín*, 16.

19. Carrero, "La parroquia en la evolución político-administrativa de Caracas."

20. Ibid., 91.

21. Gosen, *El 23 de enero*, 7.

22. Coronil, *The Magical State*, 173.

23. Herrera de Weishaar, *La Vega*, 214.

24. Gosen, *El 23 de enero*, 7–10.

25. López Villa, "La arquitectura del 2 de diciembre," 172.

26. Gosen, *El 23 de enero*, 10.

27. Ellner, *Venezuela's movimiento al socialismo*, 34.

28. Felix Baptista and Oswaldo Marchionda, "¿Para Qué Afinques?" (B.A. thesis, Escuela de Antropología, Universidad Central de Venezuela, 1992).

29. Petzoldt and Bevilacqua, *Nosotras también nos jugamos la vida*, 275.

30. Coronil, *The Magical State*, 205–7.

31. Gosen, *El 23 de enero*, 10.

32. Karl, "Petroleum and Political Pacts," 80.

33. Karst, Schwartz, and Schwartz, *The Evolution of Law in the Barrios of Caracas*, 7–8.

34. Hurtado Salazar, *Dinámicas comunales y procesos de articulación social*, 34.

35. Ibid., 52.

36. Karl, "Petroleum and Political Pacts."

37. Hurtado Salazar, *Dinámicas comunales y procesos de articulación social*, 53.

38. Ibid., 34.

39. Ray, *The Politics of the Barrios of Venezuela*, 118.

40. Ibid., 114.

41. Susan Greenbaum, "Backgrounds of Political Participation in Venezuelan Barrios," B.A. thesis, Department of Anthropology, University of Kansas, 1968, 73.

42. Hurtado Salazar, *Dinámicas comunales y procesos de articulación social*, 63.

43. Karl, "Petroleum and Political Pacts," 85.

44. Hurtado Salazar, "La definición sociopolítica del barrio urbano," 120.

45. Lander, *Neoliberalismo, sociedad civil y democracia*, 17.

46. Ramos Rollón, *De las protestas a las propuestas*, 128.

47. Lander, *Neoliberalismo, sociedad civil y democracia*, 17.

48. "Encouraging": Brusco, Nazareno, and Stokes, "Vote Buying in Argentina"; "discouraging": Escobar and Alvarez, *The Making of Social Movements in Latin America*; "promoting": Coppedge, *Strong Parties and Lame Ducks*.

49. Roberts, "Social Correlates of Party System Demise and Populist Resurgence in Venezuela."

50. Hobsbawm, *Primitive Rebels*, 118.

51. On Argentina, see James, *Resistance and Integration*; Auyero, *Poor People's Politics*. On Nicaragua, see Lancaster, *Thanks to God and the Revolution*.

52. Coronil, *The Magical State*, 141.

53. Ibid., 218.

54. Interview with Luisa Alvarez, popular historian, San Agustín, May 2004.

55. Interview with Héctor Ramírez, political activist, La Vega, January 2004.

56. Guss, *The Festive State*, 98.

57. Ibid., 98–100.

58. Angulo Ruiz, *Francisco Wuytack*, 68.

59. Herrera de Weishaar, *La Vega*, 165.

60. Cited in *La Vega Resiste*, documentary directed by Marc Villá (Caracas: Consejo Nacional de la Cultura, 2004).

61. Herrera de Weishaar, *La Vega*, 168.

62. DISIP is the investigation unit of Intelligence and Prevention Services (Dirección de Investigación de los Servicios de Inteligencia y Prevención), akin to the Secret Service.

63. Juan Contreras, "La Coordinadora Cultural Simón Bolívar: Una experiencia de construcción del poder local en la parroquia '23 de Enero'" (B.A. thesis, Escuela del Trabajo Social, Universidad Central de Venezuela, 2000), 54–56.

64. Velasco, "We Are Still Rebels."

65. Marrero, *San Agustín*, 20.

66. Alejandra Ramos and Jesús Quintero, *Relato de una experiencia: Grupo Madera*, I Seminario Nacional de Investigación Participativa, 1980.

67. Interview with Totoño, San Agustín, January 2005.

68. Marrero, *San Agustín*, 20.

69. Quintero, "La lucha contra el desalojo del Centro Cultural Simón Bolívar." In Vivir en Marín, http://www.nodo50.org (visited April 14, 2007).

70. Ibid.

71. Ibid.

72. Marrero, *San Agustín*, 20–24.

73. Baptista and Marchionda, "¿Para qué afinques?"

74. Interview with Marrero.

75. Rengifo, "Embajador de San Agustín en Alemania," 162.

76. Ramos, "Trabajadora cultural a tiempo completo," 176.

77. Quintero, "El Grupo Madera." In Vivir en Marín, http://www.nodo50.org (visited April 14, 2007).

78. Rosas, *Objectivo Chávez*, 123–25.

79. López Maya, Smilde, and Stephany, *Protesta y cultura en Venezuela*; Ellner, "Obstacles to the Consolidation of the Venezuelan Neighborhood Movement."

80. Ellner, "Obstacles to the Consolidation of the Venezuelan Neighborhood Movement," 78.

81. Grohmann, *Macarao y su gente*, 41; Ellner, "Obstacles to the Consolidation of the Venezuelan Neighborhood Movement," 78.

82. Ellner, "Obstacles to the Consolidation of the Venezuelan Neighborhood Movement," 78.

83. López Maya, Smilde, and Stephany, *Protesta y cultura en Venezuela*, 63.

84. Ellner, "Obstacles to the Consolidation of the Venezuelan Neighborhood Movement," 78–82.

85. Ramos Rollón, *De las protestas a las propuestas*, 97.

86. Lander, *Neoliberalismo, sociedad civil y democracia*, 139–40.

87. Farías, "El papel de las organizaciones vecinales en el control y prevención de la delincuencia."

88. Friedman, *Unfinished Transitions*, 176.

89. Ibid., 186.

90. Ibid., 194.

91. García Guadilla, "Crisis, estado y sociedad civil," 41.

92. Penfold-Becerra, "Electoral Dynamics and Decentralization in Venezuela," 159–60.

93. Ciccariello-Maher, "Towards a Racial Geography of Caracas."

94. Coronil, *The Magical State*, 379.

95. Ellner, "Organized Labor and the Challenge of Chavismo."

96. Contreras, "La Coordinadora Cultural Simón Bolívar," 36.

97. Ibid., 37.

98. Buxton, "Economic Policy and the Rise of Hugo Chávez," 116.

99. Holston, *Insurgent Citizenship*; see chap. 7.

100. Velasco, "We Are Still Rebels."

2. POVERTY, VIOLENCE, THE NEOLIBERAL TURN

1. Comaroff and Comaroff, "Law and Disorder in the Postcolony," 5.

2. Silva Michelena, "La política social en Venezuela durante los años ochenta y noventa," 91.

3. Buxton, "Economic Policy and the Rise of Hugo Chávez," 115.

4. Levine, "Beyond the Exhaustion of the Model."

5. Coronil, *The Magical State*, 370–71.

6. Silva Michelena, "La política social en Venezuela durante los años ochenta y noventa," 92; Contreras, "Cultura política y política cultural en Venezuela," 41.

7. Contreras, "Cultura política y política cultural en Venezuela," 41–42.

8. Ibid., 43.

9. Coronil and Skurski, "Dismembering and Remembering the Nation," 314–16.

10. Ibid., 314–15.

11. López Maya, "The Venezuelan Caracazo of 1989."

12. Kornblith, *Venezuela en los noventa*, 122.

13. Buxton, "Economic Policy and the Rise of Hugo Chávez," 118.

14. See Strange, *The Retreat of the State*; Evans, "The Eclipse of the State?"; Hardt and Negri, *Empire*.

15. Robinson, *Transnational Conflicts*, 46.

16. See Meiskin Woods, "Unhappy Families"; Cox, *Production, Power, and World*

Order; Panitch, "Globalization and the State"; Jessop, "Globalization and the National State."

17. El Gran Viraje: Lineamientos Generales del VIII Plan de la Nación, Enero de 1990 (hereafter VIII Plan de la Nación), Presentación al Congreso Nacional, Presidencia de la República de Venezuela, Oficina Central de Coordinación y Planificación CORDIPLAN, 6.

18. Coronil, *The Magical State*, 382.

19. VIII Plan de la Nación, 1990, 6.

20. Mujica Chirinos, "Estado y políticas sociales en Venezuela," 241.

21. Gutiérrez Briceño, "La política social en situaciones de crisis generalizada," 226.

22. Ibid., 227.

23. VIII Plan de la Nación, 1990, 6.

24. Carvallo, "Los nuevos programas sociales," 150–51.

25. Buxton, "Economic Policy and the Rise of Hugo Chávez," 120–21.

26. Ellner, *Rethinking Venezuelan Politics*, 101–2.

27. Mujica Chirinos, "Estado y políticas sociales en Venezuela," 245–46; Gutiérrez Briceño, "La política social en situaciones de crisis generalizada," 228.

28. Silva Michelena, "La política social en Venezuela durante los años ochenta y noventa," 95–101.

29. Martínez, "Comentaristas," 221.

30. Portes and Hoffman, "Latin American Class Structures."

31. Coronil, *The Magical State*, 382–83.

32. Portes and Hoffman, "Latin American Class Structures."

33. Roberts, "Social Polarization and the Populist Resurgence in Venezuela," 60.

34. Ibid.

35. J. P. Leary, "Untying the Knot of Venezuela's Informal Economy," NACLA, December 6, 2006, http://nacla.org.

36. Buxton, "Economic Policy and the Rise of Hugo Chávez," 115.

37. Roberts, "Social Polarization and the Populist Resurgence in Venezuela," 59.

38. Wilpert, *Changing Venezuela by Taking Power*, 107.

39. Roberts, "Social Polarization and the Populist Resurgence in Venezuela," 59–60.

40. Hurtado Salazar, *Dinámicas comunales y procesos de articulación social.*

41. Leeds, "Cocaine and Parallel Polities in the Brazilian Urban Periphery."

42. Auyero, *Poor People's Politics*, 66.

43. Quinn, *Nuthin' but a "G" Thang*, 57.

44. Auyero, "The Hyper-Shantytown," 85.

45. Ferrándiz, "Jose Gregorio Hernández," 43.

46. Interview with Pancho, Centro Madre Erika, Petare, August 2005. Not more than a decade later, when a local popular clinic was opened by the Chávez government just a few blocks down, Madre Erika's intake had declined to 1,000 patients per week.

47. Duque and Muñoz, *La ley de la calle*, 161.

48. Interview with Freddy Mendoza, June 2004.

49. Salas, "Morir para vivir," 245.

50. Sanjuán, "Democracy, Citizenship, and Violence in Venezuela," 87.

51. Salas, "Morir para vivir," 244.

52. In his article "Towards a Racial Geography of Caracas," George Ciccariello-Maher notes that since Chacao attained municipality status in 1990, it is estimated to spend 25 percent of its budget on policing; it has an autonomous police force and a philosophy of law enforcement based upon constant surveillance.

53. Mujica Chirinos, "Caracterización de la política social y la política económica," 34.

54. Ibid.

55. Ibid., 35–37.

56. Ibid., 38.

57. Craig and Porter, *Beyond Neoliberalism?*

58. Ellner, *Rethinking Venezuelan Politics*, 112–13.

59. Dunning, *Crude Democracy*, 232.

60. Wilpert, *Changing Venezuela by Taking Power*, 105.

61. Ibid., 134.

62. Alejandro Botía, "Círculos bolivarianos parecen burbujas en el limbo," *Últimas Noticias*, March 20, 2005.

63. Ellner, "The Revolutionary and Non-Revolutionary Paths of Radical Populism," 24.

64. Botía, "Círculos bolivarianos parecen burbujas en el limbo."

65. http://www.infocentro.gov.ve (visited March 2006).

66. Buxton, "Social Policy in Venezuela."

67. Rodríguez and Ortega, "Freed from Illiteracy?"

68. Rosnick and Weisbrot, "Illiteracy Revisited."

69. Rodríguez, "How Not to Defend the Revolution."

70. Weisbrot, "How Not to Attack an Economist (and an Economy)."

71. López Maya, "Caracas."

72. Salas, "La dramatización social y política del imaginario popular."

73. Carrera Damas, *El culto a Bolívar*.

74. Salas, *Bolívar y la historia en la conciencia popular*.

75. Salas, "La dramatización social y política del imaginario popular," 205.

76. Ibid., 216.

77. García Guadilla, "Ciudadanía y autonomía en las organizaciones sociales bolivarianas"; García Guadilla, "La praxis de los consejos comunales en Venezuela."

78. Ong, *Neoliberalism as Exception*, 77.

79. http://www.pdvsa.com (visited March 18, 2008).

3. PERSONAL LIVES

1. Auyero, *Contentious Lives*, 7.
2. Behar, *Translated Woman*.
3. James, *Doña María's Story*, 124.
4. James notes this same narrative focus in his interpretation of the oral testimony of Doña María, a union activist in Peronist Argentina.
5. Bourgois, *In Search of Respect*, 141.
6. James, *Doña María's Story*, 185.
7. Auyero, *Contentious Lives*, 81.
8. Valdivieso, "Confrontación, machismo y democracia."
9. Bayard de Volo, *Mothers of Heroes and Martyrs*, 121.
10. Lind, *Gendered Paradoxes*; Morgen, "'It is the Whole Power of the City against Us'"; Bayard de Volo, *Mothers of Heroes and Martyrs*.
11. Stephen, *Women and Social Movements in Latin America*.
12. Gott, *In the Shadow of the Liberator*, 146.
13. Goldstein, *Laughter Out of Place*, 5.
14. Mercer, "Black Hair / Style Politics," 248.
15. Goldstein, *Laughter Out of Place*, 64.

4. CULTURE, IDENTITY, AND URBAN MOVEMENTS

1. Hobsbawm and Ranger, Introduction, 1.
2. Laitin, *Identity in Formation*, 20.
3. Hall, "Cultural Identity and Diaspora."
4. Li, "Articulating Indigenous Identity in Indonesia," 151.
5. Comaroff and Comaroff, "Millennial Capitalism."
6. Comaroff and Comaroff, "Law and Disorder in the Postcolony," 3.
7. Lander, *Neoliberalismo, sociedad civil y democracia*, 48.
8. Salamanca, "Civil Society," 99.
9. Medeiros, "Civilizing the Popular?" 147.
10. García Guadilla, "El poder popular y la democracia participativa en Venezuela."
11. Ibid., 100–8.
12. Yúdice, *The Expediency of Culture*, 97.
13. "Minuto a minuto," *El Nacional*, December 10, 2001.
14. "Minuto a minuto," *El Nacional*, January 29, 2002; "Agencia de aguas negras," *El Nacional*, March 15, 2002.
15. "Sociedad civil y sociedad política," *El Universal*, November 15, 2000.
16. "¿Son los círculos sociedad civil (III)," *Ultimas Noticias*, December 7, 2001.
17. "Sociedad civil y sociedad política," *El Universal*, November 15, 2000; Gerardo Fernández, "Sociedad civil," *El Universal*, April 2, 2003.
18. Elías Pino Iturrieta, "¿Sociedad civil?," *El Universal*, June 5, 2000.
19. See Duno Gottberg, "Mob Outrages"; Hernández, "Against the Comedy of Civil

Society"; Salas, "'La revolución bolivariana' y 'la sociedad civil'"; Cañizales, "Sociedad civil, medios y política en Venezuela"; Delgado Bello, "Urbanización es a barrio lo que sociedad civil a organización comunitaria," *El Universal*, September, 2002.

20. Duno Gottberg, "Mob Outrages," 118.

21. Hernández, "Against the Comedy of Civil Society."

22. I am grateful to Jesus "Chucho" Garcia and the Fundación AfroAmerica for providing me with copies of these images from their archives.

23. Jaimes Quero, *Mentalidades, discurso y espacio en la Caracas de finales del siglo XX*, 180.

24. Deloria, *Playing Indian*, 45.

25. Wright, *Café con Leche*, 44.

26. Rojas, *Civilization and Violence*, xxvi.

27. Herrera Salas, "Racismo y discurso político en Venezuela."

28. Contreras, "Cultura política y política cultural en Venezuela," 62.

29. See the pioneering work of Norbert Elias, *The Civilizing Process*, on the connections between processes of state formation and civilization.

30. Hale, "Cultural Politics of Identity in Latin America," 568.

31. Hale, "Neoliberal Multiculturalism," 12; Postero, *Now We Are Citizens.*

32. Postero, *Now We Are Citizens*, 6.

33. García, *Afrovenezolanidad e inclusión en el proceso bolivariano venezolano*, 34.

34. García and Duysens, *AfroVenezuelan Reflections*, 62.

35. Ana Barrios, Matilde Camasho, Albertina Rangel, and Sonia Tona, "Religiosidad popular urbana: Velorio de cruz de mayo en Marín" (B.A. thesis, Escuela de Trabajo Social, Universidad Central de Venezuela, 1988).

36. Guss, "The Selling of San Juan," 453.

37. Pollak-Eltz, *La negritud en Venezuela.*

38. Guss, *The Festive State*, 30.

39. Garcia and Duysens, *AfroVenezuelan Reflections*, 15.

40. Guss, *The Festive State*, 56.

41. García and Duysens, *AfroVenezuelan Reflections*, 15.

42. "Creolization": Mintz and Price, *The Birth of African-American Culture*; "syncretism": Comaroff, *Body of Power, Spirit of Resistance*; "innovation": Brown, *Santería Enthroned.*

43. Guss, *The Festive State*, 52.

44. Ibid., 56.

45. Lancaster, *Thanks to God and the Revolution*, 36.

46. Wright, *Café con Leche*, 3.

47. Alemán, *Corpus Christi y San Juan Bautista*, 40.

48. Ibid., 29.

49. García Canclini, *Transforming Modernity*, 10.

50. Alemán, *Corpus Christi y San Juan Bautista*, 298.

51. Goldstein, *The Spectacular City*, 177.

52. Guss, *The Festive State*, 100.

53. Ibid., 37.

54. Yúdice, *The Expediency of Culture*, 70–71.

55. Guss, "The Selling of San Juan," 456.

56. Guss, *The Festive State*, 100.

57. Ibid., 42.

58. Ibid., 94–96.

59. Ibid., 96.

60. Ibid., 111.

61. Ibid., 116.

62. Ibid., 102–3.

63. Salas, "En nombre del pueblo," 162.

64. These latter two companies had established cultural programs in Venezuela that predated Bigott by many years.

65. Guss, *The Festive State*, 123.

66. Yúdice, *The Expediency of Culture*, 11.

67. El Gran Viraje: Lineamientos Generales del VIII Plan de la Nación, Enero de 1990. Presentación al Congreso Nacional, Presidencia de la República de Venezuela, Oficina Central de Coordinación y Planicifación CORDIPLAN, 113.

68. Felix Baptista and Oswaldo Marchionda, "¿Para qué afinques?" (B.A. thesis, Escuela de Antropología, Universidad Central de Venezuela, 1992).

69. Proyecto Ley Orgánica de la Cultura, December 4, 2000.

70. Although in 2007 the name of the institution Fundef was changed to Encuentros de Diversidad Cultural (Meetings of Cultural Diversity).

71. Guss, *The Festive State*, 114–15.

72. Salas, "En nombre del pueblo," 167–68.

73. Cited in Isabel Cristina Calcaño, "El arte y la ley de mecenazgo: ¿Una muy necesaria . . . fantasía?" http://www.veneconomia.com (visited April 14, 2008).

74. Salas, "En nombre del pueblo," 164–67.

75. Yúdice, *The Expediency of Culture*, 12–13.

76. Wisotski, *El Pueblo es la Cultura*, 21.

77. Li, *The Will to Improve*, 235.

78. Laurie, Andolina, and Radcliffe, "The Excluded 'Indigenous'?" 253.

79. "Estas paredes hablan," *Patriadentro*, May 28–June 3, 2004.

80. Martínez and Rotker, "Oviedo y Baños," xxviii.

81. Deloria, *Playing Indian*, 36.

82. Barreto, "Perspectiva histórica del mito y culto a María Lionza," 24.

83. Taussig, *The Magic of the State*, 187.

84. Barreto, "María Lionza," 99.

85. Oviedo y Baños, *Historia de la conquista y población de la provincia de Venezuela*, 186.

86. Ibid., 234.

87. Ibid., 235.

88. Reyes, *Caciques aborígenes venezolanos*, 34.

89. Ibid., 35.

90. Ibid., 22.

91. Barreto, "María Lionza," 99.

92. Clifford, *The Predicament of Culture*, 338.

93. Herrera Salas, *El Negro Miguel y la primera revolución venezolana*, 19.

94. Salas, " 'La revolución bolivariana' y 'la sociedad civil,' " 263.

95. Ibid., 267.

96. Salas, *Manuel Piar*, 12.

97. Barreto, "Identidad, etnicidad, antropología," 11.

98. Barreto, "El mito y culto de María Lienza," 66.

99. Comaroff and Comaroff, Introduction, 20.

100. Sanjinés, "Outside In and Inside Out," 292.

5. BARRIO-BASED MEDIA AND COMMUNICATIONS

1. Urla, "Outlaw Language," 280.

2. Bennett and Entman, "Mediated Politics," 16.

3. Barbero, *Communication, Culture and Hegemony*, 208.

4. García Canclini, *Consumers and Citizens*, 23.

5. Duno Gottberg, "Las turbas sobre ruedas."

6. Martín-Barbero, *Communication, Culture and Hegemony*, 181.

7. Remedi, "The Production of Local Public Spheres."

8. Tanner-Hawkins, "Community Media in Venezuela."

9. http://www.onapre.gov.ve (visited May 5, 2008). The Bs F refers to the bolívar fuerte. On January 1, 2008, the Chávez government replaced the bolívar with the bolívar fuerte, at the rate of Bs F 1 = Bs 1000. The exchange rate with the U.S. dollar was fixed at Bs F 2.15 = $US1.

10. Dirlik, "Place-Based Imagination."

11. Huntemann, "A Promise Diminished," 78.

12. Newman, "The Forgotten Fifteen Million," 122.

13. Hayden, *Street Wars*, 270.

14. Escobar, "Place, Economy, and Culture in a Post-Development Era," 205.

15. Dirlik, "Place-Based Imagination," 29.

16. Olivera, *¡Cochabamba!*, 130.

17. Notably, this is a mostly Caracas phenomenon, as outside Caracas there are radio stations which are led by women.

18. Squalid ones, Chávez's term for opposition supporters.

19. Tanner-Hawkins, "Community Media in Venezuela."

20. Scott, *Seeing like a State*.

21. Schiller, "Catia Sees You."

22. Fox and Waisbord, "Latin Politics, Global Media," 6.

23. Mayobre, "Venezuela and the Media," 183.

24. http://www.vii.org/papers/vene.htm (visited June 28, 2007).

25. Fox and Waisbord, "Latin Politics, Global Media," 12.

26. On May 27, 2007, the Chávez government decided not to renew the broadcast license for Radio Caracas Televisión (RCTV). RCTV continued to offer a paid subscription service via cable and satellite.

27. Mayobre, "Venezuela and the Media," 182.

28. Interview with Roland Denis, national leader of Movimiento 23 de Abril, Proyecto Nuestra América (M-13), http://www.medioscomunitarios.org (visited June 6, 2007).

29. "Investment and Demand Fuel Venezuela's Telecommunications Race: Competition in Full Swing after Ending of Telecom Monopoly," *Washington Times*, 2002, http://www.internationalreports.net (visited April 7, 2008).

30. "Telecoms Roundup," *Business News America*, March 24, 2008, http://www.bnamericas.com (visited April 9, 2008).

31. Banco Central de Venezuela, http://www.bcv.org.ve (English version) (visited April 8, 2008).

32. McChesney, *The Problem of the Media*, 51.

33. Cited in "Investment and Demand Fuel Venezuela's Telecommunications Race."

34. Bruno Ciuffetelli Gentile and Juan Carlos Pondal Kleber, "Venezuela's Telecommunication Legal Framework under the New Telecommunications Law," http://www.bomchilgroup.org (visited April 14, 2008).

35. Foucault, *Discipline and Punish.*

36. Ciuffetelli and Pondal Kleber, "Venezuela's Telecommunication Legal Framework."

37. Marco Legal: Comisión Nacional de Telecomunicaciones, CONATEL, Fundamento Jurídico, http://www.conatel.gov.ve/marco_legal.htm (visited March 28, 2008).

38. Yúdice, *The Expediency of Culture*, 15–16.

39. "Escrito para reflexionar y debatir: Cuando lo urgente mata lo importante," November 21, 2004.

40. Schiller, "Catia Sees You."

41. "Ataque de radio comunitaria en Venezuela," http://www.indymedia.org.

42. Ibid.

43. Comaroff and Comaroff, "Law and Disorder in the Postcolony," 23.

44. Young, *Justice and the Politics of Difference*, 10.

45. Ibid., 97.

46. Sawyer, *Crude Chronicles*, 183.

6. THE TAKEOVER OF THE ALAMEDA THEATER

1. James, *Doña María's Story*, 149.
2. Ibid., 151.
3. Interview with Angel Ramirez, Barrio Marín, San Agustín, June 2004.
4. Interview with Graciela Suárez de Robles, Barrio Marín, San Agustín, July 2004.
5. Juanita Linares, cited in Molina, "El Alameda cuenta la historia de San Agustín," 3.
6. Merlina La Rosa, cited in Molina, "El Alameda cuenta la historia de San Agustín," 3.
7. Interview with Antonio Marrero, San Agustín, July 2005.
8. Cruz Mijares, cited in Molina, "El Alameda cuenta la historia de San Agustín," 3.
9. Quintero, Rafael. "Teatro Alameda." In *Vivir en Marín*, http://www.nodo50.org (visited May 10, 2007).
10. Interview with Carlos Villegas, Alameda Theater, San Agustín, May 2004.
11. Molina, "El Alameda cuenta la historia de San Agustín"; Quintero, "Teatro Alameda."
12. Cited in Petzoldt and Bevilacqua, *Nosotras también nos jugamos la vida*, 275.
13. Marrero, *San Agustín*, 21.
14. Interview with Irma Hypolite, San Agustín, July 2004.
15. Cited in "La Alameda: Abre sus puertas una casa cultural en San Agustín," *Agencia Bolivariana de Noticias*, April 15, 2005, http://www.nodo50.org (visited May 10, 2007).
16. Cited in *La Alameda de los sueños*, documentary produced by Consejo Nacional de la Cultura, 2005.
17. Laurie, Andolina, and Radcliffe, "The Excluded 'Indigenous'?"
18. Holston, *Insurgent Citizenship*, 241.
19. Cited in Montalbán, Olafo. "Autogestión comunitaria en la Venezuela bolivariana," http://www.nodo50.org (visited May 10, 2007).
20. Interview with Villegas.
21. Cited in "La Alameda: Abre sus puertas una casa cultural en San Agustín."
22. Harvey, *Cosmopolitanism and the Geographies of Freedom*, 56.
23. Ibid., 59.

7. THE NEW COALITIONAL POLITICS

1. See, for instance, the edited volume by McCoy and Myers, *The Unraveling of Representative Democracy in Venezuela*.
2. Corrales, "In Search of a Theory of Polarization," 107.
3. McCoy, "From Representative to Participatory Democracy?" 279–81.

4. Testimony of José Miguel Vivanco, executive director, Americas Division, Human Rights Watch, Washington, D.C., June 24, 2004, *http://hrw.org* (visited June 15, 2007).

5. See Grandin, "Countervailing Powers," 15. Grandin argues that the legislation had provided numerous mechanisms for debate over these actions, and furthermore they were justified because the court had failed to absolve military officers involved in the 2002 coup and the measures were essential to fulfilling the social mandate of the government.

6. Comaroff and Comaroff, "Postcolonial Politics and Discourses of Democracy in Southern Africa," 141.

7. Smulovitz and Peruzzotti, "Societal Accountability in Latin America," 147–58; Smulovitz and Peruzzotti, *Enforcing the Rule of Law*.

8. Albo, "The Unexpected Revolution."

9. Coronil, *The Magical State*.

10. Lancaster, *Thanks to God and the Revolution*, 144–51.

11. López Maya, "Hugo Chávez Frías," 83.

12. Ibid., 80.

13. Ibid., 83.

14. Alejandro Botía, "Círculos bolivarianos parecen burbujas en el limbo," *Últimas Noticias*, March 20, 2005.

15. Cited in Olivera, *¡Cochabamba!*, 27.

16. Albo, "The Unexpected Revolution," 7–8.

17. http://stocks.us.reuters.com (visited April 23, 2008).

18. Robin Nieto, "El costo ambiental de la explotación del carbón en Venezuela," http://www.voltairenet.org (visited June 23, 2007).

19. Sarah Wagner, "Venezuela's Indigenous Protest against Coal Mining in their Lands," http://www.venezuelanalysis.com (visited June 23, 2007).

20. Laurie, Andolina, and Radcliffe, "The Excluded 'Indigenous'?"

21. "Venezuela: No a la explotación del carbon en el estado Zulia," http://www.de rechos.org.ve (visited June 23, 2007).

22. Postero, *Now We Are Citizens*, 195.

23. "Venezuela: No a la explotación del carbon en el estado Zulia," http://www.de rechos.org.ve.

24. Ibid.

25. Ibid.

26. Cited in Nieto, "El costo ambiental de la explotación del carbón en Venezuela."

27. "Venezuela: No a la explotación del carbon en el estado Zulia," http://www.de rechos.org.ve.

28. The Núcleos Endógenos de Desarrollo (Nuclei for Endogenous Development) are specific communities where the government gives financial start-up support for projects involving agricultural or industrial production. Endogenous development implies that resources come from within the community who are

involved in planning and organization. A few years later, in 2004, the government added Misión Vuelvan Caras (Mission About Face), which aims to provide skills and training for those involved in the Núcleos Endógenos. Wilpert, *Changing Venezuela by Taking Power*, 79–81.

29. Paley, *Marketing Democracy*, 170.

30. Preparatory notes for III Foro Internacional y II Festival de Medios Comunitarios, Libres y Alternativos, 2005, courtesy of Carlos Carles.

31. Ibid.

32. Fernandes, "Barrio Women and Popular Politics in Chávez's Venezuela."

CONCLUSION

1. Walton, "Debt, Protest, and the State in Latin America," 309.

2. Grimson and Kessler, *On Argentina and the Southern Cone*, 71.

3. Postero, *Now We Are Citizens*, 196–97.

4. Almeida, "Defensive Mobilization," 124.

5. Grimson and Kessler, *On Argentina and the Southern Cone*, 191.

6. Altvater, "Globalization and the Informalization of the Urban Space."

7. Grandin, *Empire's Workshop*.

8. Klubock, *Contested Communities*, 287.

9. Holston, *Insurgent Citizenship*, 313.

10. The slogan was noted by Susana Wappenstein during a panel discussion at the Latin American Studies Association in San Juan, Puerto Rico, March 2006.

11. Sassen, "Whose City Is It?"

12. McCann, "The Political Evolution of Rio de Janeiro's Favelas."

13. Davis, *Planet of Slums*, 202.

14. Yúdice, *The Expediency of Culture*, 156.

15. Han, "Speech without Words," 374.

16. For more on the discourse of development, see Escobar, *Encountering Development*, and Saldaña-Portillo, *The Revolutionary Imagination in the Americas*.

Bibliography

Albo, Gregory. "The Unexpected Revolution: Venezuela Confronts Neoliberalism." Paper presented at the International Development Week, University of Alberta, Canada, January 2006.

Alemán, Carmen Elena. *Corpus Christi y San Juan Bautista: Dos manifestaciones rituales en la comunidad afrovenezolana de Chuao.* Caracas: Fundación Bigott, 1997.

Almandoz, Arturo. "The Shaping of Venezuelan Urbanism in the Hygiene Debate of Caracas, 1880–1910." *Urban Studies* 37, no. 11 (2000): 2073–89.

Almeida, Paul. "Defensive Mobilization: Popular Movements against Economic Adjustment Policies in Latin America." *Latin American Perspectives* 34, no. 3 (2007): 123–39.

Altvater, Elmar. "Globalization and the Informalization of the Urban Space." *Informal City: Caracas Case,* edited by Alredo Brillembourg, Kristin Feireiss, and Hubert Klumpner, 51–55. Munich: Prestel, 2005.

Alvarez, Sonia, Evelina Dagnino, and Arturo Escobar. "Introduction: The Cultural and the Political in Latin American Social Movements." *Cultures of Politics/ Politics of Cultures: Re-Visioning Latin American Social Movements,* edited by Sonia Alvarez, Evelina Dagnino, and Arturo Escobar, 1–32. Boulder, Colo.: Westview Press, 1998.

Angulo Ruiz, Luis. *Francisco Wuytack: La revolución de la conciencia.* Caracas: Fundación Editorial el Perro y la Rana, 2006.

Auyero, Javier. *Contentious Lives: Two Argentine Women, Two Protests, and the Quest for Recognition.* Durham, N.C.: Duke University Press, 2003.

——. "The Hyper-Shantytown: Neo-liberal Violence(s) in the Argentine Slum." *Ethnography* 1, no. 1 (2000): 93–116.

——. *Poor People's Politics: Peronist Survival Networks and the Legacy of Evita.* Durham, N.C.: Duke University Press, 2001.

Barreto, Daisy. "Identidad, etnicidad, antropología." *Boletín Americanista* 35 (1995): 7–21.

——. "María Lionza: Genealogía de un mito." Ph.D. diss., Universidad Central de Caracas, 1998.

———. "El mito y culto de María Lionza: Identidad y resistencia popular." *Historias de identidad urbana: Composicion de identidades en los territorios populares urbanos*, edited by Emanuele Amodio and Teresa Ontiveros, 61–72. Caracas: Fondo Editorial Tropykos, 1995.

———. "Perspectiva histórica del mito y culto a María Lionza." *Boletín Americanista* 39–40, no. 31 (1990): 9–26.

Bayard de Volo, Lorraine. *Mothers of Heroes and Martyrs: Gender Identity Politics in Nicaragua 1979–1999*. Baltimore: Johns Hopkins University Press, 2001.

Behar, Ruth. *Translated Woman: Crossing the Border with Esperanza's Story*. Boston: Beacon Press, 1993.

Bennett, W. Lance, and Robert M. Entman. "Mediated Politics: An Introduction." *Mediated Politics: Communications in the Future of Democracy*, edited by W. Lance Bennet and Robert M. Entman, 1–32. Cambridge: Cambridge University Press, 2001.

Bergquist, Charles. *Labor in Latin America: Comparative Essays on Chile, Argentina, Venezuela, and Colombia*. Stanford, Calif.: Stanford University Press, 1986.

Bolívar, Teolinda. "Rehabilitación y reconocimiento de los barrios urbanos: Su necesidad y riesgos." In *La cuestión de los barrios*, edited by Teolinda Bolívar y Josefina Baldó, 73–81. Caracas: Monte Avila Editores Latinoamericana, 1995.

Boudin, Chesa, Gabriel González, and Wilmer Rumbos. *The Venezuelan Revolution: 100 Questions, 100 Answers*. New York: Thunder's Mouth Press, 2006.

Bourgois, Philippe. *In Search of Respect: Selling Crack in El Barrio*. Cambridge: Cambridge University Press, 2003.

Brown, David. *Santería Enthroned: Art, Ritual, and Innovation in an Afro-Cuban Religion*. Chicago: University of Chicago Press, 2003.

Brown, Wendy. "Neoliberalism and the End of Liberal Democracy." *Theory and Event* 7, no. 1 (2003): 1–21.

Brusco, Valeria, Marcelo Nazareno, and Susan Stokes. "Vote Buying in Argentina." *Latin American Research Review* 39, no. 2 (2004): 66–88.

Burdick, John. *Blessed Anastácia: Women, Race, and Popular Christianity in Brazil*. New York: Routledge, 1998.

Buxton, Julia. "Economic Policy and the Rise of Hugo Chávez." *Venezuelan Politics in the Chávez Era: Class, Polarization, and Conflict*, edited by Steve Ellner and Daniel Hellinger, 113–30. Boulder: Lynne Rienner Publishers, 2003.

———. "Social Policy in Venezuela." Paper presented at Changes in the Andes conference, Center for Latin American Studies and Watson Institute for International Studies, Brown University, February 2008.

Canache, Damarys. "Urban Poor and Political Order." *The Unraveling of Representative Democracy in Venezuela*, edited by Jennifer McCoy and David Myers, 33–49. Baltimore and London: Johns Hopkins University Press, 2004.

Cañizales, Andrés. "Sociedad civil, medios y política en Venezuela: Una mirada a su interacción." *Políticas de ciudadanía y sociedad civil en tiempos de globaliza-ción*, edited by Daniel Mato, 151–66. Caracas: Facultad de Ciencias Económicas y Sociales, Universidad Central de Venezuela, 2004.

Carrera Damas, Germán. *El culto a Bolívar: Esbozo para un estudio de la historia de las ideas en Venezuela.* Caracas: Universidad Central de Venezuela, 1970.

———. *Historiografía marxista venezolana y otros temas.* Caracas: Dirección de Cultura, Universidad Central de Venezuela, Colección humanismo y ciencia 3, 1967.

Carrero, Manuel. "La parroquia en la evolución político-administrativa de Caracas (siglos XIX–XX)." *Tiempo y Espacio* 25–26, no. 13 (1991): 77–99.

Carvallo, Moisés. "Los nuevos programas sociales: Notas para un balance." *Política social: Exclusión y equidad en Venezuela durante los años noventa*, edited by Lourdes Alvares, Helia Isabel del Rosario, and Jesús Robles, 141–63. Caracas: Nueva Sociedad, 1999.

Ciccariello-Maher, George. "Towards a Racial Geography of Caracas: Neoliberal Urbanism and the Fear of Penetration." *Qui Parle* 16, no. 2 (2007): 1–33.

Clifford, James. *The Predicament of Culture: Twentieth Century Ethnography, Literature, and Art.* Cambridge, Mass.: Harvard University Press, 2002.

Comaroff, Jean. *Body of Power, Spirit of Resistance: The Culture and History of a South African People.* Chicago: University of Chicago Press, 1985.

Comaroff, John L., and Jean Comaroff. Introduction. *Civil Society and the Political Imagination in Africa: Critical Perspectives*, edited by John L. Comaroff and Jean Comaroff, 1–43. Chicago: University of Chicago Press, 1999.

———. "Law and Disorder in the Postcolony: An Introduction." *Law and Disorder in the Postcolony*, edited by Jean Comaroff and John Comaroff, 1–56. Chicago: University of Chicago Press, 2006.

———. "Millennial Capitalism: First Thoughts on a Second Coming." *Public Culture* 12, no. 2 (2000): 291–343.

———. "Postcolonial Politics and Discourses of Democracy in Southern Africa: An Anthropological Reflection on African Political Modernities." *Journal of Anthropological Research* 53, no. 2 (1997): 123–46.

Contreras, Miguel Angel. "Cultura política y política cultural en Venezuela: Un debate sobre las reconfiguraciones de la ciudadanía y la democracia en un espacio tiempo transformativo." *Debate sobre la democracia en América*, edited by José María Cadenas, 35–70. Caracas: Universidad Central de Venezuela, 2006.

Coppedge, Michael. *Strong Parties and Lame Ducks: Presidential Partyarchy and Factionalism in Venezuela.* Stanford, Calif.: Stanford University Press, 1994.

Coronil, Fernando. "Magical Illusions or Revolutionary Magic? Chávez in Historical Context." *NACLA* 33, no. 6 (2000): 34–41.

———. *The Magical State: Nature, Money, and Modernity in Venezuela.* Chicago: University of Chicago Press, 1997.

Coronil, Fernando, and Julie Skurski. "Dismembering and Remembering the Nation: The Semantics of Political Violence in Venezuela." *Comparative Politics in Society and History* 33, no. 2 (1991): 288–337.

Corrales, Javier. "In Search of a Theory of Polarization: Lessons from Venezuela, 1999–2005." *Revista Europea de Estudios Latinoamericanos y del Caribe* 79 (October 2005): 105–18.

Cox, Robert. *Production, Power, and World Order: Social Forces in the Making of History.* New York: Columbia University Press, 1987.

Craig, David, and Doug Porter. *Development beyond Neoliberalism? Governance, Poverty Reduction and Political Economy.* London: Routledge, 2006.

Davis, Mike. *Planet of Slums.* London: Verso, 2006.

Deloria, Philip. *Playing Indian.* New Haven, Conn.: Yale Historical Publications, 1998.

Dirlik, Arif. "Place-Based Imagination: Globalism and the Politics of Place." *Places and Politics in an Age of Globalization,* edited by Roxann Prazniak and Arif Dirlik, 15–51. Lanham, Md.: Rowman and Littlefield, 2001.

Dunning, Thad. *Crude Democracy: Natural Resource Wealth and Political Regimes,* New York: Cambridge University Press, 2008.

Duno Gottberg, Luis. "Mob Outrages: Reflections on the Media Construction of the Masses in Venezuela (April 2000–January 2003)." *Journal of Latin American Cultural Studies* 13, no. 1 (2004): 115–35.

——. "Las turbas sobre ruedas: Representaciones de la movilización política y imaginarios del motorizados en Venezuela (de 1950 al Caracazo y los círculos bolivarianos)." Paper presented at the 2006 Meeting of the Latin American Studies Association (LASA), San Juan, Puerto Rico, 2006.

Duque, José Roberto. "Un gobierno, un proceso." *Patriadentro* 1, no. 5 (May 21–27, 2004): 2.

Duque, José Roberto, and Boris Muñoz. *La ley de la calle: Testimonios de jóvenes protagonistas de la violencia en Caracas.* Caracas: Fundarte, 1995.

Elias, Norbert. *The Civilizing Process: Sociogenetic and Psychogenetic Investigations.* Oxford: Blackwell, [1939] 1994.

Ellner, Steve. "The Contrasting Variants of the Populism of Hugo Chávez and Alberto Fujimori." *Journal of Latin American Studies* 35, no. 1 (2003): 139–62.

——. "Obstacles to the Consolidation of the Venezuelan Neighborhood Movement: National and Local Cleavages." *Journal of Latin American Studies* 31 (1999): 75–97.

——. "Organized Labor and the Challenge of Chavismo." *Venezuelan Politics in the Chávez Era: Class, Polarization, and Conflict,* edited by Steve Ellner and Daniel Hellinger, 161–78. Boulder, Colo.: Lynne Rienner Publishers, 2003.

——. *Rethinking Venezuelan Politics: Class, Conflict, and the Chávez Phenomenon.* Boulder, Colo.: Lynne Rienner Publishers, 2008.

——. "The Revolutionary and Non-Revolutionary Paths of Radical Populism: Directions of the Chavista Movement in Venezuela." *Science and Society* 69, no. 2 (2005): 160–90.

——. *Venezuela's Movimiento al Socialismo: From Guerrilla Defeat to Innovative Politics.* Durham, N.C.: Duke University Press, 1988.

Escobar, Arturo. *Encountering Development: The Making and Unmaking of the Third World.* Princeton, N.J.: Princeton University Press, 1995.

——. "Place, Economy, and Culture in a Post-Development Era." *Places and Politics in an Age of Globalization,* edited by Roxann Prazniak and Arif Dirlik, 193–217. Lanham, Md.: Rowman and Littlefield, 2001.

Escobar, Arturo, and Sonia Alvarez. *The Making of Social Movements in Latin America: Identity, Strategy, and Democracy.* San Francisco: Westview Press, 1992.

Evans, Peter. "The Eclipse of the State? Reflections on Stateness in an Era of Globalization." *World Politics* 50, no. 1 (1997): 62–87.

Farías, Levy. "El papel de las organizaciones vecinales en el control y prevención de la delincuencia: Un testimonio desde Los 'Erasos.'" *Politeia* 17 (1995): 283–324.

Ferguson, James, and Akhil Gupta. "Spatializing States: Toward an Ethnography of Neoliberal Governmentality." *American Ethnologist* 29, no. 4 (2002): 981–1002.

Fernandes, Sujatha. "Barrio Women and Popular Politics in Chávez's Venezuela." *Latin American Politics and Society* 49, no. 3 (2007): 97–127.

Ferrándiz, Francisco. "The Body as Wound: Possession, Malandros, and Everyday Violence in Venezuela." *Critique of Anthropology* 24, no. 2 (2004): 107–33.

——. "José Gregorio Hernández: A Chameleonic Presence in the Eye of the Medical Hurricane." *Kroeber Anthropological Society Papers* 83 (1998): 33–52.

Foucault, Michel. *Discipline and Punish: The Birth of the Prison.* New York: Vintage Books, 1977.

——. "Governmentality." *The Foucault Effect: Studies in Governmentality,* edited by Graham Burchell, Colin Gordon, and Peter Miller, 87–104. Chicago: University of Chicago Press, 1991.

Fox, Elizabeth, and Silvio Waisbord. "Latin Politics, Global Media." *Latin Politics, Global Media,* edited by Elizabeth Fox and Silvio Waisbord, 1–21. Austin: University of Texas Press, 2002.

Friedman, Elizabeth. *Unfinished Transitions: Women and the Gendered Development of Democracy in Venezuela, 1936–1996.* University Park: Penn State University Press, 2000.

García, Jesús. *Afrovenezolanidad e inclusión en el proceso bolivariano venezolano.* Caracas: Ministerio de Comunicación y Información, 2005.

García, Jesús, and Bartolomé Duysens. *AfroVenezuelan Reflections: The Drums of Liberation.* Caracas: Fundación Afroamérica and CONAC, 1999.

García Canclini, Néstor. *Consumers and Citizens: Globalization and Multicultural Conflicts.* Translated by George Yúdice. Minneapolis: University of Minnesota Press, 2001.

———. *Transforming Modernity: Popular Culture in Mexico*. Austin: University of Texas Press, 1993.

García Guadilla, María Pilar. "Ciudadanía y autonomía en las organizaciones sociales bolivarianas: Los comités de tierra urbana como movimientos sociales." *Cuadernos del CENDES* 24, no. 66 (2007): 47–73.

———. "Crisis, estado y sociedad civil: Conflictos socio-ambientales en la Venezuela post-Saudita." In *Ambiente, estado y sociedad: Crisis y conflictos socio-ambientales en América Latina y Venezuela*, edited by María Pilar García Guadilla, 25–66. Caracas: Centro de Estudios del Desarrollo, Universidad Simón Bolívar, 1991.

———. "El poder popular y la democracia participativa en Venezuela: Los consejos comunales." Paper presented at the 2007 Meeting of the Latin American Studies Association (LASA), Montreal, 2007.

———. "La praxis de los consejos comunales en Venezuela: ¿Poder popular o instancia clientelar?" *Revista Venezolana de Economía y Ciencias Sociales* 14, no. 1 (2008): 125–51.

Goldstein, Daniel. *The Spectacular City: Violence and Performance in Urban Bolivia*. Durham, N.C.: Duke University Press, 2004.

Goldstein, Donna. *Laughter out of Place: Race, Class, Violence, and Sexuality in a Rio Shantytown*. Berkeley: University of California Press, 2003.

González de la Rocha, Mercedes, Janice Perlman, Helen Safa, Elizabeth Jelin, Bryan R. Roberts, and Peter M. Ward. "From the Marginality of the 1960s to the 'New Poverty' of Today: A LARR Research Forum." *Latin American Research Review* 39, no. 1 (2004): 183–203.

Gosen, Alfredo. *El 23 de Enero*. Caracas: Fundarte, 1990.

Gott, Richard. *In the Shadow of the Liberator: Hugo Chávez and the Transformation of Venezuela*. London: Verso, 2000.

Gould, Jeffrey. *To Lead as Equals: Rural Protest and Political Consciousness in Chinandega, Nicaragua, 1912–1979*. Chapel Hill: University of North Carolina Press, 1990.

Gramsci, Antonio. *Selections from the Prison Notebooks*. New York: International Publishers, 1971.

Grandin, Greg. "Countervailing Powers." *LASA Forum Focus* 28, no. 1 (2007): 14–17.

———. *Empire's Workshop: Latin America and the Roots of U.S. Imperialism*. New York: Metropolitan Books, 2006.

Grimson, Alejandro, and Gabriel Kessler. *On Argentina and the Southern Cone: Neoliberalism and National Imaginations*. New York: Routledge, 2005.

Grohmann, Meter. *Macarao y su gente: Movimiento popular y autogestión en los barrios de Caracas*. Caracas: Nueva Sociedad, 1996.

Guss, David. *The Festive State: Race, Ethnicity, and Nationalism as Cultural Performance*. Berkeley: University of California Press, 2000.

——. "The Selling of San Juan: The Performance of History in an Afro-Venezuelan Community." *American Ethnologist* 20, no. 3 (1993): 451–73.

Gutiérrez Briceño, Thais. "La política social en situaciones de crisis generalizada e incertidumbre en Venezuela." *Revista Venezolana de Gerencia* 7, no. 18 (2002): 220–36.

Gutmann, Matthew. *The Romance of Democracy: Compliant Defiance in Contemporary Mexico.* Berkeley: University of California Press, 2002.

Hale, Charles. "Cultural Politics of Identity in Latin America." *Annual Review of Anthropology* 26 (1997): 567–90.

——. "Neoliberal Multiculturalism: The Remaking of Cultural Rights and Racial Dominance in Central America." *Political and Legal Anthropology Review* 28, no. 1 (2005): 10–28.

Hall, Stuart. "Cultural Identity and Diaspora." *Identity: Community, Culture, Difference,* edited by Jonathan Rutherford, 222–37. London: Lawrence and Wishard, 1990.

Han, Yuhai. "Speech without Words." *positions* 15, no. 2 (2007): 369–401.

Hardt, Michael, and Antonio Negri. *Empire.* Cambridge, Mass.: Harvard University Press, 2000.

Harvey, David. *Cosmopolitanism and the Geographies of Freedom.* New York: Columbia University Press, 2009.

Hayden, Tom. *Street Wars: Gangs and the Future of Violence.* New York: New Press, 2004.

Hernández, Juan Antonio. "Against the Comedy of Civil Society: Posthegemony, Media and the 2002 Coup d'Etat in Venezuela." *Journal of Latin American Cultural Studies* 13, no. 1 (2004): 137–45.

Herrera de Weishaar, María Luisa. *La Vega: Biografía de una parroquia.* Caracas: Presidencia de la República, 1981.

Herrera Salas, Jesús María. *El Negro Miguel y la primera revolución venezolana: La cultura del poder y el poder de la cultura.* Caracas: Vadell Hermanos Editores, 2003.

——. "Racismo y discurso político en Venezuela." *Revista Venezolana de Economía y Ciencias Sociales* 10, no. 2 (2004): 111–28.

Hobsbawm, Eric. *Primitive Rebels: Studies in Archaic Forms of Social Movement in the Nineteenth and Twentieth Centuries.* New York: Norton, 1959.

Hobsbawm, Eric, and Terence Ranger. "Introduction: Inventing Traditions." *The Invention of Tradition,* edited by Eric Hobsbawm and Terence Ranger, 1–14. Cambridge: Cambridge University Press, 1983.

Holston, James. *Insurgent Citizenship: Disjunctions of Democracy and Modernity in Brazil.* Princeton, N.J.: Princeton University Press, 2008.

Huntemann, Nina. "A Promise Diminished: The Politics of Low-Power Radio." *Communities of the Air: Radio Century, Radio Culture,* edited by Susan Merrill Squier, 76–92. Durham, N.C.: Duke University Press, 2003.

Hurtado Salazar, Samuel. "La definición sociopolítica del barrio urbano: Diagnóstico y explicativa de la rehabilitación de los barrios en el caso venezolano." *La cuestión de los barrios, perspectiva actual*, edited by Teolinda Bolívar and Josefina Baldo, 117–26. Caracas: Monte Avila Editores, 1996.

——. *Dinámicas comunales y procesos de articulación social: Las organizaciones populares*. Caracas: Fondo Editorial Tropykos, 1991.

Hylton, Forrest, and Sinclair Thomson. *Revolutionary Horizons: Past and Present in Bolivian Politics*. London: Verso, 2007.

Jaimes Quero, Humberto. *Mentalidades, discurso y espacio en la Caracas de finales del siglo XX: Mentalidades venezolanas vistas a través del graffiti*. Caracas: Fundación Para la Cultura Urbana, 2003.

James, Daniel. *Doña María's Story: Life History, Memory, and Political Identity*. Durham, N.C.: Duke University Press, 2000.

——. *Resistance and Integration: Peronism and the Argentine Working Class, 1946–1976*. New York: Cambridge University Press, 1988.

Jessop, Bob. "Globalization and the National State." *Paradigm Lost: State Theory Reconsidered*, edited by Stanley Aronowitz and Peter Bratsis, 185–220. Minneapolis: University of Minnesota Press, 2002.

——. "Liberalism, Neoliberalism, and Urban Governance: A State-Theoretical Perspective." *Antipode* 34, no. 3 (2002): 452–72.

Karl, Terry Lynn. "Petroleum and Political Pacts: The Transition to Democracy in Venezuela." *Latin American Research Review* 22, no. 1 (1987): 63–94.

Karst, Kenneth, Murray Schwartz, and Audrey Schwartz. *The Evolution of Law in the Barrios of Caracas*. Los Angeles: Latin American Center, University of California, 1973.

Klubock, Thomas. *Contested Communities: Class, Gender, and Politics in Chile's El Teniente Copper Mine, 1904–1951*. Durham, N.C.: Duke University Press, 1998.

Kornblith, Miriam. *Venezuela en los noventa: Las crisis de la democracia*. Caracas: Ediciones IESA, 1998.

Laitin, David. *Identity in Formation: The Russian-Speaking Populations in the Near Abroad*. Ithaca, N.Y.: Cornell University Press, 1998.

Lancaster, Roger. *Thanks to God and the Revolution: Popular Religion and Class Consciousness in the New Nicaragua*. New York: Columbia University Press, 1988.

Lander, Edgardo. *Neoliberalismo, sociedad civil y democracia: Ensayos sobre América Latina y Venezuela*. Caracas: Universidad Central de Venezuela, 1995.

Laurie, Nina, Robert Andolina, and Sarah Radcliffe. "The Excluded 'Indigenous'? The Implications of Multi-Ethnic Policies for Water Reform in Bolivia." *Multiculturalism in Latin America: Indigenous Rights, Diversity, and Democracy*, edited by Rachel Sieder, 252–76. New York: Palgrave Macmillan, 2002.

Leeds, Elizabeth. "Cocaine and Parallel Polities in the Brazilian Urban Periphery:

Constraints on Local-Level Democratization." *Latin American Research Review* 31, no. 3 (1996): 47–83.

Levine, Daniel. "Beyond the Exhaustion of the Model: Survival and Transformation of Democracy in Venezuela." *Reinventing Legitimacy: Democracy and Political Change in Venezuela*, edited by Damarys Canache and Michael R. Kulisheck, 187–214. Westport, Conn.: Greenwood Press, 1998.

———. "The Decline and Fall of Democracy in Venezuela: Ten Theses." *Bulletin of Latin American Research* 21, no. 2 (2002): 248–69.

Lewis, Oscar. *La Vida: A Puerto Rican Family in the Culture of Poverty*. New York: Vintage, 1966.

Li, Tania Murray. "Articulating Indigenous Identity in Indonesia: Resource Politics and the Tribal Slot." *Comparative Studies in Society and History* 42, no. 1 (2000): 149–79.

———. *The Will to Improve*. Durham, N.C.: Duke University Press, 2007.

Lind, Amy Conger. *Gendered Paradoxes: Women's Movements, State Restructuring, and Global Development in Ecuador*. University Park: Penn State University Press, 2005.

Lomnitz, Larissa. *Networks and Marginality: Life in a Mexican Shantytown*. New York: Academic, 1977.

López Maya, Margarita. "Caracas: The State, Popular Participation, and How to Make Things Work." Paper presented at the conference "The Popular Sectors and the State in Chávez's Venezuela," Department of Political Science, Yale University, March 2008.

———. "Hugo Chávez Frías: His Movement and His Presidency." *Venezuelan Politics in the Chávez Era: Class, Polarization and Conflict*, edited by Steve Ellner and Daniel Hellinger, 73–91. Boulder, Colo.: Lynne Riener, 2003.

———. "The Venezuelan Caracazo of 1989: Popular Protest and Institutional Weakness," *Journal of Latin American Studies* 35 (2003): 127–30.

López Maya, Margarita, David Smilde, and Keta Stephany. *Protesta y cultura en Venezuela: Los marcos de acción colectiva en 1999*. Caracas: CENDES, 1999.

López Villa, Manual A. "La arquitectura del 2 de diciembre." *Boletín del Centro de Investigaciones Históricas y Estéticas* 27 (1986): 172.

Marrero, Antonio "Pelón," ed. *San Agustín: Un santo pecador o un pueblo creador*. Caracas: Fundarte, 2004.

Martín-Barbero, Jesús. *Communication, Culture and Hegemony: From the Media to Mediations*. London: Sage Publications, 1993.

Martínez, Santiago. "Comentaristas." *Política social: Exclusión y equidad en Venezuela durante los años noventa*, edited by Lourdes Alvares, Helia Isabel del Rosario, and Jesús Robles, 221–29. Caracas: Nueva Sociedad, 1999.

Martínez, Tomás Eloy, and Susana Rotker. "Oviedo y Baños: La fundación literaria de la nacionalidad venezolana." José de Oviedo y Baños, *Historia de la conquista y población de la provincia de Venezuela*, edited by Tomás Eloy Martínez, ix–lx. Caracas: Biblioteca Ayacucho, 2004.

Mayobre, José Antonio. "Venezuela and the Media: The New Paradigm." *Latin Politics, Global Media*, edited by Elizabeth Fox and Silvio Waisbord, 176–86. Austin: University of Texas Press, 2002.

McCann, Brian. "The Political Evolution of Rio de Janeiro's Favelas: Recent Works." *Latin American Research Review* 41, no. 3 (2006): 149–63.

McChesney, Robert W. *The Problem of the Media: U.S. Communication Politics in the Twenty-First Century*. New York: Monthly Review Press, 2004.

McCoy, Jennifer. "From Representative to Participatory Democracy? Regime Transformation in Venezuela." *The Unraveling of Representative Democracy in Venezuela*, edited by Jennifer McCoy and David Myers, 263–95. Baltimore: Johns Hopkins University Press, 2004.

McCoy, Jennifer, and David Myers, eds. *The Unraveling of Representative Democracy in Venezuela*. Baltimore: Johns Hopkins University Press, 2004.

Medeiros, Carmen. "Civilizing the Popular? The Law of Popular Participation and the Design of a New Civil Society in 1990s Bolivia." *Critique of Anthropology* 21, no. 4 (2001): 401–25.

Meiskin Woods, Ellen. "Unhappy Families: Global Capitalism in a World of Nation-States." *Monthly Review* 51, no. 3 (1999): 1–12.

Mercer, Kobena. "Black Hair/Style Politics." *Marginalization and Contemporary Cultures*, edited by Russell Ferguson, Martha Gever, Trinh T. Minh-ha, and Cornel West, 247–64. Cambridge, Mass.: MIT Press, 1990.

Mintz, Sidney, and Richard Price. *The Birth of African-American Culture*. Boston: Beacon Press, 1976.

Molina, Jennifer. "El Alameda cuenta la historia de San Agustín." *Parroquia Adentro* 3, no. 17 (2004): 3.

Molina, José. "The Presidential and Parliamentary Elections of the Bolivarian Revolution in Venezuela: Change and Continuity (1998–2000)." *Bulletin of Latin American Research* 21, no. 2 (2002): 219–47.

Molina, José, and Carmen Pérez. "Radical Change at the Ballot Box: Causes and Consequences of Electoral Behavior in Venezuela's 2000 Elections." *Latin American Politics and Society* 46, no. 1 (2004): 103–34.

Morgen, Sandra. "'It is the Whole Power of the City against Us': The Development of Political Consciousness in a Women's Health Care Coalition." *Women and the Politics of Empowerment*, edited by Sandra Morgen and Ann Bookman, 97–115. Philadelphia: Temple University Press, 1988.

Mujica Chirinos, Norbis. "Caracterización de la política social y la política económica del actual gobierno venezolano: 1999–2004." *Revista Venezolana de Gerencia* 12, no. 1 (2006): 31–57.

———. "Estado y políticas sociales en Venezuela ¿La quinta república o el regreso al pasado?" *Revista Venezolana de Gerencia* 7, no. 18 (2002): 237–66.

Naím, Moisés. "The Real Story behind Venezuela's Woes." *Journal of Democracy* 12, no. 2 (2001): 17–31.

Newman, Kathy. "The Forgotten Fifteen Million: Black Radio, Radicalism, and the Construction of the 'Negro Market.'" *Communities of the Air: Radio Century, Radio Culture*, edited by Susan Merrill Squier, 109–33. Durham, N.C.: Duke University Press, 2003.

Olivera, Oscar. *¡Cochabamba! Water War in Bolivia*. Cambridge: South End Press, 2004.

Ong, Aihwa. *Neoliberalism as Exception: Mutations in Citizenship and Sovereignty*. Durham, N.C: Duke University Press, 2006.

Oviedo y Baños, José de. *Historia de la conquista y población de la provincia de Venezuela*. Edited by Tomás Eloy Martínez. Caracas: Biblioteca Ayacucho, 2004.

Paley, Julia. *Marketing Democracy: Power and Social Movements in Post-Dictatorship Chile*. Berkeley: University of California Press, 2001.

Panitch, Leo. "Globalization and the State." *Socialist Register 1994*, edited by Ralph Miliband and Leo Panitch, 60–93. London: Merlin Press, 1994.

Parker, Dick. "Chávez and the Search for an Alternative to Neoliberalism." *Latin American Perspectives* 141, no. 2 (2005): 39–50.

Penfold-Becerra, Michael. "Electoral Dynamics and Decentralization in Venezuela." *Decentralization and Democracy in Latin America*, edited by Alfred Montero and David Samuels, 155–79. Notre Dame: University of Notre Dame Press, 2004.

Perlman, Janice. *The Myth of Marginality: Urban Poverty and Politics in Rio de Janeiro*. Berkeley: University of California Press, 1976.

Petras, James, and Henry Veltmeyer. *Social Movements and State Power: Argentina, Brazil, Bolivia, Ecuador*. London: Pluto Press, 2005.

Petzoldt, Fania, and Jacinta Bevilacqua. *Nosotras también nos jugamos la vida: Testimonios de la mujer venezolana en la lucha clandestina: 1948–1958*. Caracas: Editorial Ateneo de Caracas, 1979.

Pollak-Eltz, Angelina. *La negritud en Venezuela*. Caracas: Cuadernos Lagoven, 1992.

Portes, Alejandro, and Kelly Hoffman. "Latin American Class Structures: Their Composition and Change during the Neoliberal Era." *Latin American Research Review* 38, no. 1 (2003): 41–82.

Postero, Nancy Grey. *Now We are Citizens: Indigenous Politics in Postmulticultural Bolivia*. Stanford, Calif.: Stanford University Press, 2007.

Quinn, Eithne. *Nuthin' but a "G" Thang: The Culture and Commerce of Gangsta Rap*. New York: Columbia University Press, 2005.

Ramírez Roa, Rosaly. "La política extraviada en la Venezuela de los años '90: Entre rigidez institucional y neo-populismo." *Revista de Ciencia Política* 23, no. 1 (2003): 137–57.

Ramos, Nelly. "Trabajadora cultural a tiempo completo." *San Agustín: Un santo pecador o un pueblo creador*, edited by Antonio "Pelón" Marrero, 173–82. Caracas: Fundarte, 2004.

Ramos Rollón, María Luisa. *De las protestas a las propuestas: Identidad, acción y relevancia política del movimiento vecinal en Venezuela*. Caracas: Instituto de Estudios de Iberoamérica y Portugal, 1995.

Ray, Talton. *The Politics of the Barrios of Venezuela*. Berkeley: University of California Press, 1969.

Remedi, Gustavo. "The Production of Local Public Spheres: Community Radio Stations." *Latin American Cultural Studies. A Reader*, edited by Ana Del Sarto, Alicia Ríos, and Abril Trigo. Durham, N.C.: Duke University Press, 1997.

Rengifo, Felipe. "Mandingo: Embajador de San Agustín en Alemania." *San Agustín: Un santo pecador o un pueblo creador*, edited by Antonio "Pelón" Marrero, 157–66. Caracas: Fundarte, 2004.

Reyes, Antonio. *Caciques aborígenes venezolanos*. Caracas: Ediciones Perfiles, 1950.

Roberts, Kenneth. "Social Correlates of Party System Demise and Populist Resurgence in Venezuela." *Latin American Politics and Society* 45, no. 3 (2003): 35–57.

———. "Social Polarization and the Populist Resurgence in Venezuela." *Venezuelan Politics in the Chavez Era: Class, Polarization and Conflict*, edited by Steve Ellner and Daniel Hellinger, 55–72. Boulder, Colo.: Lynne Riener, 2003.

Robinson, William. *Transnational Conflicts: Central America, Social Change, and Globalization*. London: Verso, 2003.

Rodríguez, Francisco. "How Not to Defend the Revolution: Mark Weisbrot and the Misinterpretation of Venezuelan Evidence." *Wesleyan Economic Working Papers*. Wesleyan University, Middletown, Conn., 2008.

Rodríguez, Francisco, and Daniel Ortega. "Freed from Illiteracy? A Closer Look at Venezuela's 'Misión Robinson' Literacy Campaign." *Economic Development and Cultural Change* 57, no. 1 (2008): 1–30.

Rojas, Cristina. *Civilization and Violence: Regimes of Representation in Nineteenth-Century Colombia*. Minneapolis: University of Minnesota Press, 2002.

Rosas, Alexis. *Objetivo Chávez: El periodismo como arma*. Caracas: Editorial Texto, 2005.

Rose, Nikolas. *Governing the Soul: Shaping of the Private Self*. London: Free Association Books, 1999.

Rosnick, David, and Mark Weisbrot. "Illiteracy Revisited: What Ortega and Rodríguez Read in the Household Survey." *Working Paper*. Washington: Center for Economic and Policy Research, May 2008.

Salamanca, Luis. "Civil Society: Late Bloomers." *The Unraveling of Representative Democracy in Venezuela*, edited by Jennifer McCoy and David Myers, 93–114. Baltimore: Johns Hopkins University Press, 2004.

Salas, Yolanda. *Bolívar y la historia en la conciencia popular*. Caracas: Universidad Simón Bolívar, 1987.

———. "La dramatización social y política del imaginario popular: El fenómeno del Bolivarismo en Venezuela." *Estudios latinoamericanos sobre cultura y transformaciones sociales en tiempos de globalización*, edited by Daniel Mato, 201–21. Buenos Aires: CLACSO, 2001.

———. "En nombre del pueblo: Nación, patrimonio, identidad y cigarro." *Políticas de identidades y diferencias sociales en tiempos de globalización*, edited by Daniel Mato, 147–72. Caracas: FACES-UCV, 2003.

———. *Manuel Piar: El héroe de múltiples rostros*. Caracas: Fundef, 2004.

———. "Morir para vivir: La (in)certidumbre del espacio (in)civilizado." *Estudios latinoamericanos sobre cultura y transformaciones sociales en tiempos de globalización II*, edited by Daniel Mato, 241–49. Buenos Aires: CLACSO, 2001.

———. " 'La revolución bolivariana' y 'la sociedad civil': La construcción de subjetividades nacionales en situación de conflicto." *Revista Venezolana de Economía y Ciencias Sociales* 10, no. 2 (2004): 91–110.

Saldaña-Portillo, María Josefina. *The Revolutionary Imagination in the Americas and the Age of Development*. Durham, N.C.: Duke University Press, 2003.

Sanjinés, Javier. "Outside In and Inside Out: Visualizing Society in Bolivia." *The Latin American Subaltern Studies Reader*, edited by Ileana Rodríguez, 228–310. Durham, N.C.: Duke University Press, 2001.

Sanjuán, Ana María. "Democracy, Citizenship, and Violence in Venezuela." *Citizens of Fear: Urban Violence in Latin America*, edited by Susana Rotker, 87–101. New Brunswick, N.J.: Rutgers University Press, 2002.

Sassen, Saskia. *Globalization and Its Discontents*. New York: New Press, 1998.

Sawyer, Suzana. *Crude Chronicles: Indigenous Politics, Multinational Oil, and Neoliberalism in Ecuador*. Durham, N.C.: Duke University Press, 2004.

Scheper-Hughes, Nancy. *Saints, Scholars, and Schizophrenics: Mental Illness in Rural Ireland*. Berkeley: University of California Press, 2001.

Schiller, Naomi. "Catia Sees You: Community Television, Clientelism, and the State in the Chávez Era." *Participation, Politics and Culture in Venezuela's Bolivarian Democracy*, edited by David Smilde and Daniel C. Hellinger. Durham, N.C.: Duke University Press, forthcoming.

Scott, James. *Seeing like a State: How Certain Schemes to Improve the Human Condition Have Failed*. New Haven, Conn.: Yale University Press, 1998.

Silva Michelena, Héctor. "La política social en Venezuela durante los años ochenta y noventa." In *Política social: Exclusión y equidad en Venezuela durante los años noventa*, edited by Lourdes Alvares, Helia Isabel del Rosario, and Jesús Robles, 85–114. Caracas: Nueva Sociedad, 1999.

Smilde, David. *Reason to Believe: Cultural Agency in Latin American Evangelicalism*. Berkeley: University of California Press, 2007.

Smith, Neil, and Setha Low. "Introduction: The Imperative of Public Space." *The

Politics of Public Space, edited by Setha Low and Neil Smith, 1–16. New York: Routledge, 2006.

Smulovitz, Calatina, and Enrique Peruzzotti. "Societal Accountability in Latin America." *Journal of Democracy* 11, no. 4 (2000): 147–58.

———, eds. *Enforcing the Rule of Law: Social Accountability in the New Latin American Democracies*. Pittsburgh: University of Pittsburgh Press, 2006.

Stephen, Lynn. *Women and Social Movements in Latin America: Power from Below*. Austin: University of Texas Press, 1997.

———. *¡Zapata Lives! Histories and Cultural Politics in Southern Mexico*. Berkeley: University of California Press, 2002.

Strange, Susan. *The Retreat of the State: The Diffusion of Power in the World Economy*. New York: Cambridge University Press, 1996.

Tanner-Hawkins, Eliza. "Community Media in Venezuela." Paper presented at the 2006 Meeting of the Latin American Studies Association (LASA), San Juan, Puerto Rico, 2006.

Taussig, Michael. *The Magic of the State*. New York: Routledge, 1997.

Urla, Jacqueline. "Outlaw Language: Creating Alternative Public Spheres in Basque Free Radio." *The Politics of Culture in the Shadow of Capital*, edited by Lisa Lowe and David Lloyd, 280–300. Durham, N.C.: Duke University Press, 1997.

Valdivieso, Magdalena. "Confrontación, machismo y femocracia: Representaciones del 'heroísmo' en la polarización política en Venezuela." *Revista Venezolana de Economía y Ciencias Sociales* 10, no. 2 (2004): 137–54.

Velasco, Alejandro. "We Are Still Rebels: The Challenge of Popular History in Bolivarian Venezuela." *Participation, Politics and Culture in Venezuela's Bolivarian Democracy*, edited by David Smilde and Daniel C. Hellinger. Duke University Press, forthcoming.

Walton, John. "Debt, Protest, and the State in Latin America." *Power and Popular Protest: Latin American Social Movements*, edited by Susan Eckstein, 299–328. Berkeley: University of California Press, 2001.

Ward, Peter. "Introduction and Overview: Marginality Then and Now." *Latin American Research Review* 39, no. 1 (2004): 183–7.

Weisbrot, Mark. "How Not to Attack an Economist (and An Economy): Getting the Numbers Right." Washington: Center for Economic and Policy Research, April 2008.

———. "The United States and the World: Where Are We Headed?" *Working paper*. Washington: Center for Economic and Policy Research, September 2008.

Weyland, Kurt. "Economic Voting Reconsidered: Crisis and Charisma in the Election of Hugo Chávez." *Comparative Political Studies* 36, no. 7 (2003): 822–48.

Wilpert, Gregory. *Changing Venezuela by Taking Power: The History and Policies of the Chávez Government*. London: Verso, 2007.

Wisotski, Rubén. *El pueblo es la cultura: Conversación con Farruco Sesto, Ministro de la Cultura*. Caracas: Fundación Editorial el Perro y la Rana, 2006.

Wright, Winthrop. *Café con Leche: Race, Class, and National Image in Venezuela*. Austin: University of Texas Press, 1990.

Yan, Hairong. "Neoliberal Governmentality and Neohumanism: Organizing Suzhi/ Value Flow through Labor Recruitment Networks." *Cultural Anthropology* 18, no. 4 (2003): 493–523.

Yarrington, Doug. *A Coffee Frontier: Land, Society, and Politics in Duaca, Venezuela, 1830–1936*. Pittsburgh: University of Pittsburgh Press, 1997.

Young, Iris Marion. *Justice and the Politics of Difference*. Princeton, N.J.: Princeton University Press, 1990.

Yúdice, George. *The Expediency of Culture: Uses of Culture in the Global Era*. Durham, N.C.: Duke University Press, 2003.

Index

Candelaria parish, 43

Candomblé, 123

CANTV. *See* National Telephone Company of Venezuela (CANTV)

Caracas: haciendas in, 41; parish formation in, 43; urbanization of, 40. *See also* specific barrios and parishes

Caracas Slum Upgrading Project, 81

Caracazo street riots (1989), 13, 21, 39, 68

Caricuao parish, 13–14

Carles, Carlos, 169–70, 173, 233, 266; ANMCLA and, 247, 252; CONATEL and, 204, 210; decision making and, 183–84, 199; knowledge production and, 200; socialism and, 265; "Tomando Perola" and, 184; unauthorized stations and, 201

Carmen, El, barrio, 14–15, 50–51, 134, 140

Carmona, Pedro, 117, 118

Carretera Negra barrio, 15, 105

Casa Cultural Alameda. *See* Alameda Theater/Casa Cultural Alameda

Casas Alimentarias, 82

Cascos Blancos, 51, 77

Casitas, Las, sector, 15

Castro, Fidel, 32, 48

Catedral parish, 43

Catia TVe: autonomy and, 29; Catedral parish and, 171; CONATEL and, 201–3; funding and, 235; media associations, 192–93, 211; political connections, 186–88; programming, 173; signal strength, 181

Causa R, La (political party), 59

Cayapo (newspaper), 5, 169

CBS (Círculos Bolivarianos), 5, 28, 117, 120, 238, 250

CCSB (Coordinadora Cultural Simón Bolívar), 13, 26

CEBS (Christian Base Communities), 60

CEDICE (Center for the Dissemination of Economic Knowledge), 70

Ceiba, La, barrio, 11, 12

Center for the Dissemination of Economic Knowledge (CEDICE), 70

Central Bank of Venezuela, 142

Central Office of Coordination and Planning (CORDIPLAN), 45

Central Office of Information (OCEI), 90

Central University of Venezuela (UCV), 31, 44, 54, 83, 92, 121, 225

Centro Cultural Corp Banca, 138

Centro de Estudios para la Paz, 83

Centro Madre Erika, 76

Centros Comunales, 45

Centro Simón Bolívar (CSB), 53, 54, 217

Cerros, 12, 40–41, 42, 44, 52–53, 69, 134, 216

Chacao (chief), 152, 154

Chacao municipality, 10, 59, 77, 121, 218

Charneca, La, barrio, 11, 12, 41, 44, 53, 212

Chávez, Hugo: administration of, 19; agenda of, 21–25, 196; alternative radio and, 202, 206; Bolivarian programs and, 1; Castro and, 32; civil society and, 114, 115–22; community media and, 165–67; community organizations and, 5; Consejos Comunales and, 249; control of industry, 242; cooperatives and, 7, 189, 201; coups, 21, 25–26, 59, 71, 85, 195, 218, 220; cultural identity and, 136–48; economic policy of, 2–4; election of, 2; media affiliation and, 186–87, 191; media collectives and, 161–62; mining and, 242–47; multicultural reform and, 157–58; neoliberal orthodoxy and, 259; petitions and, 125; procedural democracy and,

Day of Indigenous resistance, 84

Debt crisis (1980s), 3, 20, 34, 60, 258

Decentralization: ANMCLA and, 251–52, 255, 262; Borges on, 144–45; laws on, 258; neoliberal reforms and, 58–59, 258; party system and, 4

De cierta manera (film), 213

Deindustrialization, 218, 259, 282 n. 28

De la Rúa, Fernando, 258

Delinquency, 57–58, 77, 93, 135, 218

Deloria, Philip, 120

Democracy: breakdown of, 4; pacted, 45, 47, 76; participatory, 28; social movements and, 35, 234; substantive, 235, 240, 254

Democratic Coordinator (Coordinadora Democrática), 116

Departamento Libertador, 43

Deregulation: as austerity measure, 68; of media, 26, 27; violence and, 67

Diablos Danzantes (fiesta), 123

Díaz, Nicolas, 160–61

Dirección de Investigación de los Servicios de Inteligencia y Prevención (DISIP), 51–52

Dirlik, Arif, 170–71, 181

DISIP. See Dirección de Investigación de los Servicios de Inteligencia y Prevención (DISIP)

Divorce law, 58

Drug dealing, 64, 65–66, 76, 93

Drums: demonstration of, 213; fiestas and, 123, 132, 141; San Juan Bautista and, 123; as symbol of defiance, 18–19, 145

Dunning, Thad, 81

Duno Gottberg, Luis, 118

Duque, José Roberto, 5

Economics: anti-neoliberal, 2–3, 21–22, 23, 24, 71, 80, 115–16, 162; Chicago boys, 22; global, 22, 23; neo-

liberal reforms, 3, 68–73; oil rents and, 23; survival, 74

Education: free, 55; school conditions, 50; universal, 80, 81

Eekhout, Blanca, 187, 235

EFORDRI (Escuelas de Formación Deportiva Recreativa Integral), 96

El Gordo. See Pérez, Edgar (El Gordo)

El Indio. See Betancourt, Oscar (El Indio)

Ellner, Steve, 3

Emergency Plan, 45

Encuentro de los Santos Negros. See Meeting of Black Saints

Equal rights, 57, 58, 60. See also Inequality

Erasos, Los, barrio, 57–58

Ernesto Guevara de la Serna Brigade, 60

Escobar, Arturo, 18, 19, 181

Escuelas de Formación Deportiva Recreativa Integral (EFORDRI), 96

Esquina Caliente, La, 182

Ethnography and politics, 29–35

Everyday wars of position, 24–29, 115, 253–54, 258

Exclusion: AD and, 47; barrio movements and, 3, 9, 63, 114; Chavismo and, 85, 114, 116, 117; cultural identity and, 158; discourses of, 2, 34; fiestas and, 129; stereotypes and, 117–21

FACUR (Federation of Associations of Urban Communities), 56

Fair trade agreements, 23

Fajardo, Francisco, 151–52

Fedecámaras, 116, 117

Federation of Associations of Urban Communities (FACUR), 56

Feminine Circles. See Círculos Femeninos

Feminist movement, 58

Fernández, Rafael, 184, 185

FEVA (Venezuelan Federation of Female Lawyers), 58

FIDES (Intergubernatorial Fund for Decentralization), 188

Fiesta de San Juan, 123

Fiesta de San Pedro, 123

Fiestas in barrios, 26, 34, 60, 114, 122–30, 157–59; African culture/slavery and, 125, 129; *cofradías* and, 127–28; drums and, 123, 132; exclusion and, 129; main festivals, 123; police and, 130–31, 133–34; staged, 140–41; state sponsorship for, 139–42, 143. *See also* specific fiestas

Flores, Alfred, 248

Flores, Ely, 173, 201, 209, 249–50, 266

Florida, La, 41

Folklore (concept), 141

Folklore Service, 136

Foreign investment, 20, 86, 191, 234, 258

Foreign trade, 42

Foucault, Michel, 22, 197

Foundation for Culture and the Arts. *See* Fundarte

Foundation for the Development of the Community and Municipal Promotion (FUNDACOMUN), 46, 81

Foundation for Urban Culture. *See* Fundación para la Cultura Urbana

Foundation Madera, 228

Foundation of Ethnomusicology and Folklore (FUNDEF), 31, 141, 142

Fox, Elizabeth, 195

Free market: modernization and, 20–21

Free Trade Area of the Americas (FTAA), 241

FREINDECO (Front for Integration of the Community), 57

Freire, Paulo, 50

FRENDAV. *See* Front for the Defense of Water and Life (FRENDAV)

Frente por la Defensa de Agua y la Vida (FRENDAV), 241–42, 254

Friedman, Elizabeth, 58

Front for Integration of the Community (FREINDECO), 57

Front for the Defense of Water and Life (FRENDAV), 241–42, 254

FTAA. *See* Free Trade Area of the Americas (FTAA)

Fujimori, Alberto, 3

Fundabarrios, 236–37

Fundación Bigott, 137, 138, 139, 142

Fundación Pampero, 138

Fundación para la Cultura Urbana, 138

Fundación Polar, 138, 142. *See also* Grupo Polar

FUNDACOMUN. *See* Foundation for the Development of the Community and Municipal Promotion (FUNDACOMUN)

Fundarte, 139, 140, 143, 144, 167, 222

FUNDEF. *See* Foundation of Ethnomusicology and Folklore (FUNDEF)

Gaitera musical tradition, 52

Gallegos, Romulo, 136

Gangs, 64–67, 262

García Canclini, Nestor, 128

García Guadilla, María Pilar, 85

Gas privatization, 28

Gas Wars, 28

Gender inequality, 35, 88, 225–26, 253, 255

General Commission of Organized Groups of the San Agustín Parish, 218

Global economics, 22, 23

Globovisión, 118, 195

Goldstein, Daniel, 128–29

Goldstein, Donna, 108, 110

Hurtado Salazar, Samuel, 46
Hylton, Forrest, 28

IBC Group, 26, 195
ICAS (Interim Country Assistance Strategy), 81
Iconography in barrios, 148–57
IESA (Institute of Higher Management Studies), 22, 23, 70
IMF. *See* International Monetary Fund (IMF)
Immigrant rights movement, 33–34, 261
Import Substitution Industrialization (ISI), 3, 68, 74, 136, 260
Improve, will to, 28
Improvement Councils. *See* Juntas Pro-Mejoras
Inacio da Silva, Lula, 259
Indigeneity: authority over, 149; censuring of practices, 123; community media and, 177–78, 179; cultural identity and, 2, 122, 149–50; decision making and, 246, 254, 264; murals of chiefs, 13, 26, 114, 120, 148–57, 262; racism and, 118–20, 121, 180
Individualism and responsibility, 75
Industrialization, 22, 41, 54, 74, 136
Inequality: gender, 35; in popular sectors, 57, 60, 63; regional, 35; state and, 47, 67. *See also* Equal rights
Information access, 26
INOS (National Institute of Sanitation Works), 46
Institute of Higher Management Studies (IESA), 22, 23, 70
Intergubernatorial Fund for Decentralization (FIDES), 188
Interim Country Assistance Strategy (ICAS), 81
International Monetary Fund (IMF), 20, 23, 68, 72; conditions of, 23; Pérez on, 20

Iron industry, 137
ISI. *See* Import Substitution Industrialization (ISI)
Istúriz, Aristóbulo, 118, 119, 120
Italian immigrants, 41
Iturrieta, Elias, 118
Izarra, Andres, 188

James, Daniel, 6, 101, 103, 214, 215
Jara, Victor, 53, 55
Jewish immigrants, 41
John the Baptist, Saint. *See* San Juan Bautista
John XXIII, Pope, 50
Joint Programming Operative Plan of Diagnostic Revision, 143
Journalists, use of term, 169
Junta Patriótica, 45
Juntas de Vecinos, 46
Juntas Parroquiales, 249
Juntas Pro-Mejoras, 45, 46, 57
Juvenile delinquency. *See* Delinquency

Karl, Terry, 45
Kessler, Gabriel, 24
Kirchner, Néstor, 259
Klubock, Thomas, 260
Kyoto Agreement, 243

Labor Law reforms, 58
Labor market, 66, 73, 74
Laitin, David, 113
Lancaster, Roger, 125, 236
Lander, Edgardo, 46, 57
Land redistribution, 23
Lands Law, 81
Larrazábal, Wolfgang, 44, 45
Laughter therapy, 108–10
Laurie, Nina, 222
Law and order, 58
Law of Mecenazgo, 142
Law of Telecommunications, 166, 194, 196, 198, 239

Music: black, 262; traditional, 129, 135.
See also Drums; *specific music groups*
MVR. *See* Movimiento Quinta Republica (MVR)

Nacional, El (newspaper), 117, 118, 119
National Association of Alternative and Community Media (ANMCLA): assemblies and, 247–53; collective structures and, 210; CONATEL occupation and, 204; decentralization and, 251–52, 255, 262; decision making and, 248, 262–63; formation of, 237–41; gender and, 253; mobilizations and, 243, 246–47; political culture and, 255; Radio Alternativa and, 203; as revolutionary, 247, 252; as sectarian, 192, 193, 202; as social movement, 240; unity and, 249
National Cement Factory, 41
National Commission of Telecommunications (CONATEL): competing visions, 263; grants and, 188–89; occupation of, 203–10, 211; as regulatory authority, 194–98; technical training and, 193; unauthorized stations and, 201–2, 211
National Congress, 51, 58, 194
National Council of Culture. *See* Consejo Nacional de la Cultura (CONAC)
National Council of the Community, 45
National Film Library. *See* Cinematica Nacional
National Folklore Village, 137
National Institute of Sanitation Works (INOS), 46
National Publicity Corporation (CORPA), 49
National Telephone Company of Venezuela (CANTV), 23, 194, 195
Natural gas, nationalization of, 258–59
Negra Lorenza, La (song), 109, 214

Negro Felipe, 156
Negro Miguel, 156
Negro Primero, 1, 148, 156, 157, 164, 175
Neighborhood associations, 56–58
Neoliberalism: anti-neoliberalism, 21, 22, 80; community-based movements and, 62–63; cultural institutions and, 145–46; global economics and, 22; governmentality and, 24; hybridization and, 24; making of neoliberal state, 67–74; market integration and, 80; multiculturalism, 122; rationalities of, 24, 27; reforms, 34, 58; as repressive, 76–77, 79; state and, 34, 40, 67–79; violence and, 66. *See also* Post-neoliberalism
Netuno, 196
Newman, Kathy, 179
New National Idea, 43
Newspapers. *See under* Media
New Turn, 49
NGOS (Non-Governmental Organizations), 71, 72, 116, 262
Nonviolent mass action, 34
Núcleos Endógenos de Desarrollo, 248, 250
Nuevo Día, Un (radio station), 164–65, 191
Nuevo Viraje, El. *See* New Turn

OCEI (Central Office of Information), 90
Ochoa, Williams, 51, 54, 124, 127, 129, 130, 134–35, 140, 173
Oikos, 260
Oil industry: cultural sponsorship and, 139; expansion of, 42, 43; increased prices, 21–22, 81; reforms and, 40; restructuring, 3, 242; social programs and, 4, 42, 46, 85–86; state control of, 20–21, 22, 137; wealth from, 20, 21, 23, 68

Plan de Recuperación y Estabilización Económica (PERE), 72
Plan de Solidaridad Social, 72
Plan Estratégico Social 2001–2007 (PES), 81
Plan for Confronting Poverty (PEP), 71, 72
Plan for Recuperation and Economic Stabilization (PERE), 72
Plan of Cultural Funding, 143, 146
Plan of Extraordinary Works, 45
Plan of Social Solidarity, 72
Plaza Bolívar, 182
Plaza O'Leary, 140–41
PLOC. See Proyecto de Ley Orgánica de la Cultura (PLOC)
PM. See Metropolitana (PM)
Poder Popular (radio program), 174, 176
Police: in barrio stations, 77–78; corruption in, 66, 78–79; fiestas and, 130–31, 133–34; harassment by, 26; lack of, 17; militarization and, 180, 261; violence and, 61, 97–98
Politics: cultural, 19; ethnography and, 29–35; everyday, 209, 264; identity, 122, 157–59; micro politics, 17; middle-class involvement in, 56; oil wealth and, 20; parties, 18, 20; party system, 4; society and, 5, 20, 24, 25. See also specific parties
Populism, 46–47
Porter, Doug, 80
Portes, Alejandro, 72
Postero, Nancy, 24, 122, 244
Post-neoliberalism: accountability and, 234; anti-neoliberalism and, 22; defined, 23, 24; imaginary of, 24; state and, 19–24, 234, 259–60. See also Neoliberalism
Poverty: in barrios, 2, 15, 17, 74–79, 125; gangs and, 67; neoliberalism and, 69, 73–79; pro-poor agenda, 23; reduction programs, 80, 82–83

Power, social/political, 20, 24, 25, 59, 250
Presidential Commission for Reform of the State (COPRE), 59
Primera, Ali, 39
Privatization, 23; of gas, 28; of media, 27, 117, 167, 194, 210; of public services, 58, 66–67; of public space, 261; of water, 28, 242
Privatization Law (1992), 69
Program of Associated Cinema Halls, 144
Project of the Organic Law of Culture (PLOC), 139, 141, 143, 144, 145, 146
Property and citizenship, 57
Protest music, 55
Proyecto de Ley Orgánica de la Cultura (PLOC), 139, 141, 143, 144, 145, 146
PSUV (United Socialist Party of Venezuela), 266
Public housing: demographics, 12. See under Housing
Public services, 58–59
Public space: in barrios, 65, 218; militarized, 180, 261; privatized, 261; resignification of, 35, 134, 157–58, 233
Public works programs, 45

Quinn, Eithne, 75
Quintana, Marcelo, 206
Quintero, Rafael, 42, 53

Race-class dynamics, 25, 33, 88
Racism, 87–88, 118–20, 157
Radcliffe, Sarah, 222
Radio Activa la Vega, 165, 189
Radio Ali Primera, 191, 205
Radio Al Son del 23, 171, 174, 181, 182, 186–87, 193
Radio Alternativa de Caracas, 203–6, 209
Radio Antimano, 179
Radio Caracas Televisión, 195

Social policy: under Caldera, 71–72; under Chávez, 79–86; under Pérez, 67, 70–71

Society: civil, 25; politics and, 4, 20, 24, 25; society-state dynamics, 45–49, 85, 115, 118, 237–41

Society of Friends of the Neighborhoods (SABS), 60

Sojo, Juan Pablo, 150

Solo Pueblo, Un (music group), 129

Sosa Plan, 71

Soup kitchens. See Casas Alimentarias

Spirituality and blackness, 1

State: collaboration with social movements, 27, 28; cultural producers and, 136–48, 158; hierarchy in, 28, 85; hybrid formation of, 23, 24, 136; nationalization of industries by, 23–24, 137; neoliberal, 34, 40, 67–79; patronage and clientists in, 137; in post-neoliberal era, 19–24, 259–60; redistributive role of, 46; as repressive, 76–77, 79; state-society dynamics, 45–49, 85, 115, 118, 237–41; violence and, 69

Stephen, Lynn, 30, 105

Strategic ambiguity, 28

Strategic social plan (PES), 81

Street vending, 73

Sucre en Comunidad (newspaper), 165, 173, 182, 191, 192

Sucre parish, 43

Syncretism, 124

Tambores. See Drums

Taussig, Michael, 150

Teatro Alameda. See Alameda Theater/Casa Cultural Alameda

Teatro Municipal, 216

Teatro Nacional, 216

Technocracy, 23, 70, 263–64

Telcel, 195

Telecommunications. See Media

Televen, 195

Television stations. See specific stations

Terapia de la risa. See Laughter therapy

Terepaima (chief), 151–53

Thomson, Sinclair, 28

Tiempo de Caricuao, El (newspaper), 165, 179, 186

Tiuna (chief), 153, 175

Totoño. See Blanco, Jesús (Totoño)

Trade unions, 18, 46, 59–60, 114, 116–17, 159, 182, 261

Transnational elites, 25, 73

Tupamaros movement, 226

Turner, Tina, 109

TVC, 195

23 de Enero parish, 10, 12–13, 15; advertising for, 192; barrio-based movement in, 60; bullet marks in, 39; La Cañada sector, 12, 220; community-based organizations, 52; cybercafes in, 163; fiestas in, 60; guerrilla insurgency in, 48–49; migrants in, 126; murals in, 60–61, 148, 150, 153–54, 165; occupation of, 220; La Piedrita barrio, 163, 165, 173; radio and, 171, 172, 181, 187; Tupamaros movement and, 226; Zona Central, 13, 39

UBES (Unidades de Batalla Electoral), 29, 238, 250

UBSS (Unidades de Batalla Social), 29, 238

UBV (Universidad Bolivariana de Venezuela), 239

UCV (Universidad Central de Venezuela), 31, 44, 54, 83, 92, 121, 225

UNDP (United Nations Development Program), 80

Unemployment: benefits for, 50; cooperatives and, 236; following debt cri-

Sujatha Fernandes is an assistant professor in the
Department of Sociology at Queens College and the
Graduate Center of the City University of New York.

Library of Congress Cataloging-in-Publication Data
Fernandes, Sujatha.
Who can stop the drums? Urban social movements
in Chávez's Venezuela / Sujatha Fernandes.
p. cm.
Includes bibliographical references and index.
ISBN 978-0-8223-4665-4 (cloth : alk. paper)
ISBN 978-0-8223-4677-7 (pbk. : alk. paper)
1. Chávez Frías, Hugo.
2. Social movements—Venezuela—History—20th century.
3. Sociology, Urban—Venezuela.
4. Venezuela—Politics and government—1999– I. Title.
HN363.5.F47 2010
305.5'6209877090511—dc22   2009042053

Who Can Stop
the Drums?